Dedicated to
Michael and Grace

who light the candle
and eat the food
with me.

Acknowledgments

I am especially grateful to:

Jeff Basom, for his incredible creativity with whole foods and for sharing his skills with me. His recipes or adaptations of his recipes for Lemon Basil Potato Salad, Creamy Mushroom-Basil Soup, Creamy Broccoli Soup, Greens in Cashew Curry Sauce, Roasted Potatoes & Carrots, Homemade Whole Grain Bread, Banana Blueberry Poppyseed Muffins, and Homemade Curry Paste are proudly featured in this book.

Annemarie Colbin, who remains my most influential teacher on the subject of food and healing.

Nina Petrulis, for her help on the section on breastfeeding and her undying support of this project.

And Nancy Rankin, for her inspiration and work on the beginnings of this book. Parts of the book came from our work together in Two Moms Cooking School.

I would also like to thank the following people and organizations for their various contributions of recipe ideas and expertise:

Lea Aemissegger, Rachel Albert-Matesz, Aunt Cathy, Minx Boren, Mary Bowman, Karen Brown, Rita Carey, Lea Carrillo, Goldie Caughlin, Mim Collins, Abby Dylan, Connie Feutz, Dr. Bruce Gardner, Terry Kady and Essential Sandwiches, Jack Kelly, Monique and Miko Keranen, Holly Koteen, Chris Lair, Buck Levin, Theresa Lewis, Judy Loebl, Meredith McCarty, the Nutrition Faculty at Bastyr University, Puget Consumers Co-op, Karen D. Seibert and her master's thesis, Silence-Heart-Nest Restaurant, Paige Tyley, Jackie Williams, Susan Wickett Ford, Sherry Willis, and Susan Wilson.

My heartfelt thanks to LuraMedia, especially Lura Geiger, Marcia Broucek, and Pam Greer, who worked to give this book its first start. This edition was made possible with the talent of my friends, Michael Boer and Joy Taylor. And, finally, I would never have started this journey without Michael and Grace and their perpetual support of who I am.

Table of Contents

Foreword

Few of us can look at the state of the world and not feel despair. The breakdown of the family unit sets up the breakdown of a firm system of values, including caretaking. And when families no longer take care of their own, other social structures must fill the gap. Joseph Chilton Pearce, in *Evolution's End*, says that the breakdown of society begins with the breaking of the mother–child bond through medicated birth and the hospital practice of separating the newborn from its mother — and, it should be noted, by the replacement of the home cook with the factory.

Many of us no longer live in the place where we were born, or in the same town as our parents. The extended family and the stable networks of longtime friends and acquaintances are not always there to help us along, or to show us the tried and true, well-established traditions. Therefore, we must recreate ourselves anew wherever we live. We must establish our own traditions, and create new connections and relationships with kindred communities, by choice and not automatically by physical proximity. We need to examine our "customs" to see if they have been around for a few hundred years, or whether they're just recently established. The more recent the custom, the closer we might wish to scrutinize it for efficacy, usefulness, its effect on our health.

In the past 50 or 60 years, we have established many new customs in our way of eating. Canned, frozen, chemically preserved, irradiated, and microwaved foods are new in the history of humanity; so are refined foods such as sugar and white flour, artificial sweeteners, preservatives, colorings, emulsifiers, and other unnatural ingredients. Is it coincidental or significant that the breakdown of our society is occurring simultaneously with the widespread consumption of refined and artificial foods? Could it be that by our dietary customs — consumption of unnatural foods and large amounts of meat and milk from animals raised on antibiotics and hormones — we are building a new kind of human being, one that has little connection with the healthier ways of the past?

It often seems that there is little that we can do to help the wrongs of our society. However, we can always help ourselves, our families and friends, and our surroundings. We can, each of us, make an effort to light the darkness around us. As our numbers multiply, so will our little lights. And our first areas of concern can be how we raise our families and what we feed them. We have considerable power over our health by our choices in food. If we are in charge of feeding others, we have a great influence over their health as well — not only in the amount and kinds of nutrients in the food, but also its quality and the energy and love put into preparing and serving it.

The importance of homemade food cannot be overestimated. To have a real person cook and prepare our meals is a crucial element in our well-being. As many of us have been raised on commercial or processed foods, we need to relearn the skill of nurturing through nourishment. That's why books such as this one are so needed, and so helpful.

You will find here a sensible, workable, effective approach to healthful eating. It relies on well-tested principles, it's fad-proof, and the foods taste great. I brought up my own children on such a regime; now that they are in their 20s, I can say with certainty that the system works. Cynthia Lair has put her intelligence, her commitment, and her love into this book just as surely as she puts those ingredients in her family's meals. You will find here a connection with a community of parents serious about their familys' health and a connection with a tradition older than freeze-dried foods with artificial colors and flavors. You'll find tips and ideas that can help you every day, and recipes that are delicious and easy to make.

As concerned parents, as concerned human beings, let us always remember that the best place to start improving the world is at home.

Annemarie Colbin, CHES
The Natural Gourmet Cookery School
New York, NY

Preface

One of the things that excites me the most about food and diet is being open to change. I feel that as long I stay on the path of whole, fresh, organic foods, I can ramble where my instincts and tastebuds guide me. The seasons change, families move to new climates, children have growing spurts — all of the changes we experience in our lives affect our food choices.

I studied and practiced macrobiotics, a Japanese dietary philosophy based on the principles of yin and yang, in the early '80s. The diet was miraculous for me after years of stringent dieting where my criteria for what to eat had been based on how many calories the food contained. Diet pop, coffee, canned tuna, cottage cheese, and iceberg lettuce made the cut. Not only did I rarely lose any weight, but I was often irritable and faced constant health problems due to being malnourished. So the big heaping bowls of brown rice and cooked vegetables and beans immediately improved body and mood. And the Eastern philosophies that surrounded macrobiotics nourished my spirit.

In 1987 I became pregnant. My criteria for choosing food shifted again. This time I was educated enough to stay within the realm of whole, fresh, organic foods, but I no longer craved typical macrobiotic fare. I wanted food I had eaten as a child. That craving marked the beginnings of this book as I began to update old family favorites. Why not make tacos with black beans? Wouldn't tempeh work in spaghetti as well as ground beef? Can you make gingerbread cookies with barley malt?

What would happen if you fed a baby homemade, whole, fresh, organic, cereal instead of that stuff out of boxes? As a busy mom I found it labor-intensive to prepare separate, pureed meals for my baby. I thought, "Hey! Why not feed my baby some of this great food my husband and I are eating? Wouldn't that be a lot easier?" Indeed it was. Now I felt I had something to share with other parents and began creating this book.

The scope of what I learned from practicing and teaching this way of eating went beyond good nutrition. I discovered that the act of sitting down together and eating the same food has enormous power. This ritual is part of the spiritual glue that holds us together as a family.

My hope is that by encouraging families to share wholesome, homecooked meals together, through my classes and this book, seeds for a better future will be planted. Learning to prepare and eat simple, whole foods that the Earth naturally provides can transform lives. When you feed your family whole foods, your family becomes more whole.

Feeding
Your Family
Whole Foods

have recently read several books that were set in the late 1800s in this country. Only 100 years ago, our great grandparents created a dinner plate very different from what is typical today. Food on the table was, for the most part, grown, raised, caught or shot. The only fresh fruits and vegetables available were what grew in season in one's climate. Often, folks ate the same foods day after day. Corn mush and rabbit stew was a regular hit on the prairie. Day after day, Laura and Mary, in **Little House on the Prairie**, ate corn mush. I felt so relieved when summer came and they got to go blackberry picking.

Each summer I visit Wichita, Kansas, to see my family. My sister's house is near a big suburban supermarket. This place has everything! There is every imaginable kind of food available. People push giant grocery carts piled high with packages of every color, shape and size. Besides a vast array of food, there's a post office, a paperback book section, video rentals, a banking facility, dry cleaners, a prescription drug counter, and free colon cancer screening tests — all in the same store! The number of choices and amount of stimuli are overwhelming. The question, "What should we eat for dinner?" had 10,000 answers. And there were several thousand more choices of what to do after dinner.

If I don't have my priorities in place, a trip to the grocery store can be like getting lost in the woods. Not only do I function better with a list in hand, but I need a clear concept of what is healthy and wholesome and what isn't. I want our hard-earned family dollars to buy food that will vitalize our bodies, minds, and spirits.

In this book I have carved out my own interpretation of the more-than-ample information available about nutrition. I have used research and data from today as well as some of the simple common sense of yesteryear. The information isn't meant to be the final word for you or for me. I encourage you to start your own journey with food and health. Once you truly understand the power you hold as you stroll down a grocery store aisle, your dinner plate may never look the same.

Why Share a Common Meal?

In a time when families are dealing with two careers, longer working hours and children with numerous extracurricular activities, the fate of the shared, homecooked, family meal seems in jeopardy. But the fact is that many families juggle commitments in order to eat together as often as possible.[1] We know that eating meals together increases the enjoyment of the meal, solidifies family bonds and encourages communication about the day's activities among family members. If we are willing to make the extra effort required to share a common meals, then our lives are richer as we break bread together; family solidarity is built.

Children love the predictability of positive family events that occur daily and shared family meals are very beneficial to them. Family dinner conversation helps expand children's vocabulary skills and increases success in learning to read.[2] Mealtime is also where children learn many of their social skills including table manners and the art of conversation. Much of family history relating to culture and race is passed on to children by parents at the dinner table. Food rituals may illuminate a family's ethnic heritage when traditional meals are served. These things help stabilize the child's identity as a member of a particular group. Studies show that children who participate in regular family meals and other rituals have more emotional resilience to help them handle stress and chaos in other areas of life.[3] Marooning babies in high chairs or plopping children in front of the tube while they are being fed robs them of what could be an otherwise enriching experience.

There are also nutritional advantages to eating meals together. Children who dine without parents or siblings eat fewer servings from the necessary food groups.[4] This is partly true because when parents are present they can monitor a child's food intake, ensuring nutritional adequacy. Eating together also gives parents the opportunity to model good eating habits such as choosing healthy foods, chewing food well, and stopping when full.

1 McLaughlin, A. T. Family Dinners Provide Food for Thought as Well. The Christian Science Monitor (March 14)1, 10, 1996.

2 Mealtime Conversations Help Kids Communicate. USA Today (December 19):3, 1995.

3 Goleman, D. Family Rituals May Promote Better Emotional Adjustment. The New York Times. (March 11):B6-B7, 1992.

4 The Breakdown of the Family Meal. Tufts University Nutrition Newsletter Special Report 9(5): 3-5, July 1991.

The quality of the food used in the daily ritual holds great importance too. Until the last century humans have survived on foods grown in nature. As industrialization and agribusiness made headway, refined, lifeless food full of chemicals became not only available, but popular. Our attraction to these fractionated foods may be out of habit and convenience rather than true appetite. Deep in our cells we know that whole, fresh, natural foods are the best nourishment for body and soul. Eating whole foods can help feed the desire for wholeness within ourselves. This spiritual benefit is magnified when the entire family partakes of nature's bounty together. Not only are the individuals of the family enriched and nourished, the family is strengthened as well.

In one of my recent classes a student asked me if a chicken leg was a whole food? "Don't you have to eat all of the chicken for it to be a whole food???" she asked. I posed the question to my friend and mentor Annemarie Colbin, who wisely told me that yes, you would have to eat the whole chicken … over time. She reminded me that when tribal people killed a buffalo, the whole buffalo was used, much of it as food, the rest for other practical needs. The sharing of this whole animal by a group of people was part of what held them together. Not only the ritual of a shared meal is important here. Each member of the tribe had consumed a part of something that had recently been a powerful whole. On some level this helps hold the tribe together. It is a unifying force.

The intention of this book is to encourage families to share meals of whole foods. That is why it is recommended that babies and children eat the same foods that their parents are eating. There is ample support in our world for developing individualism. What is sometimes missing, what we often long for in the depths of our soul is that connectedness to the whole. We have an opportunity to help satisfy this yearning every day at the dining table by choosing whole foods and by sharing the meal as a family.

What is a Whole Food?

For more than 10 years, I have taught whole foods cooking classes. Early in the class, I always ask my students, "What is a whole food?" My favorite response was from a young woman who said, "A food that hasn't been cut." If you want to know whether a food is whole or not, ask yourself these questions:

Can I imagine it growing?

It is easy to picture a wheatfield or an apple on a tree. Tough to picture a field of marshmallows.

How many ingredients does it have?

A whole food has only one ingredient — itself.

What's been done to the food since it was harvested?

The less, the better. Many foods we eat no longer resemble anything found in nature. Stripped, refined, bleached, injected, hydrogenated, chemically treated, irradiated, and gassed; modern foods literally have had the life taken out of them. Read the list of ingredients on the labels; if you can't pronounce it, don't eat it.

Is this product "part" of a food or the "whole" entity?

Juice is only a part of a fruit. Oil is only part of the olive. When you eat a lot of partial foods, your body in its natural wisdom will crave the parts it didn't get.

Well-Balanced Family Meals

Tradition

To find a sound method for balancing meals we must not only look at nutritional data and government recommendations. The dietary history of our species as well as our family history should be considered. Many traditional meals are based on the culture's staple grain, a bean/legume dish and a variety of vegetables — some cooked and some raw. Meat, dairy and nuts, the more expensive food items, are used as flavorings or toppings. They can be costly to our pocketbook and to our health if overused. Here are some examples of how this simple way of balancing meals can be seen in a variety of ethnic cuisine:

- Rice, miso soup, pickled vegetables and sea vegetables, small pieces of fish (*Japanese*)

- Tabouli, pita bread (wheat), hummus, cucumbers and tomatoes, small amount of feta cheese (*Middle Eastern*)

- Cornbread, black-eyed peas cooked with ham hocks, sweet potatoes, collard greens (*American South*)

Season

Choosing produce that is in season is important. Also choosing foods that are lighter and cooler for warm weather and foods that are denser and more warming for cold weather is helpful. Pastas, salads, steamed vegetables, and raw fruit are examples of warm weather food. Stews, baked casseroles, roasted vegetables and dried fruit are examples of cold weather food.

Color

Make sure each meal has a wide variety of color. There is nothing more unappealing than an all–brown meal. When your meals contain green, orange, red, and yellow, you not only create a meal that is visually appealing but one that contains a wide variety of vitamins and minerals.

Cooking Techniques

Use a variety of cooking techniques when planning a well-balanced meal. A meal where all of the dishes are baked, for example, can sit very heavy in the stomach. If you are serving a simmered lentil-vegetable stew, you might choose pasta which is boiled, greens served raw in a salad and baked apples to go with it.

Daily Meal Planning

My method of meal planning is simple. Breakfast is usually a whole grain cereal and fresh fruit. An easy way to remember how to plan dinner is: grain, bean, two vegetables (one cooked and one raw or one green and one other color). Lunches evolve from dinner leftovers and include fresh vegetables and fruits. This simple, healthful, economical way of balancing a meal keeps everyone healthy and energetic.

Consider balance for the whole day, not just one meal. It doesn't matter so much that each meal is perfectly balanced as long as throughout the day a wide variety of whole foods are eaten.

Using the sound nutritional concepts of the USDA's Eating Right Pyramid and combining them with all I know about healthy, whole foods eating, I have created a chart to help families with meal planning. Quality is stressed more than quantities.

Let's look at the different categories of whole foods used in the chart on page 12. By arranging them according to "Main Dishes" and "Side Dishes and Toppings," it is easy to see which foods to emphasize and which to keep in smaller portions when planning meals.

MAIN DISHES

Whole Grains

The whole grains include the familiar whole wheat, brown rice, barley, oats, corn, buckwheat, and rye as well as the less familiar millet, quinoa, spelt, amaranth, and teff. For daily consumption whole grains are superior to refined grains because the whole product contains protein, fiber, B vitamins, calcium, iron, vitamin E, and LIFE (the germ of the grain is the live part). Eating grains in their whole, natural form is satisfying and beneficial. Whole grains can also be ground into flours or cereals, made into pasta, noodles, and spaghetti. Brown rice has even been made into a milk-like beverage and a frozen dessert.

As you discover the benefits of whole grains, remember to rotate grains in your diet. When you eat the same grain every day, you are more likely to develop an allergy to it. If you have brown rice on Monday, try quinoa on Tuesday. Each grain has something unique to offer the body.

Well-Balanced Family Meals

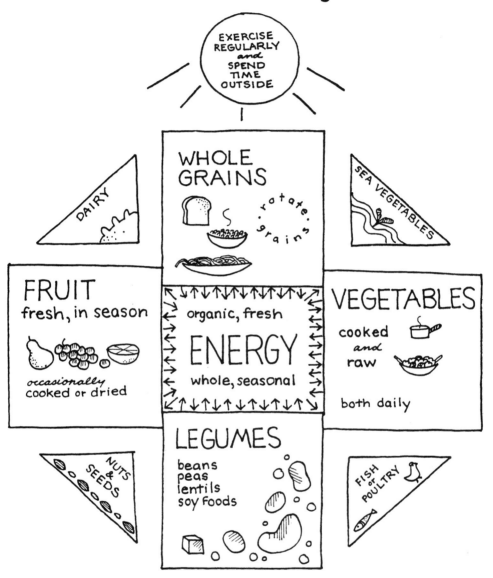

MAIN DISHES (squares)
Whole Grains, Vegetables, Legumes, Fruits

SIDE DISHES AND TOPPINGS (triangles)
Dairy, Sea Vegetables, Fish or Poultry, Nuts and Seeds

Vegetables

Eat both cooked vegetables and raw vegetables every day. Cooking vegetables lessens some of their nutritional value yet makes the food more digestible and easier to assimilate. Raw vegetables are rich in nutrients and some enzymes that can't be found in cooked vegetables; however, some vegetables, such as broccoli and cauliflower, are harder to digest eaten raw. You need to eat both cooked and raw vegetable dishes.

Eat all colors. Don't form prejudices. Try dark green, light green, white, purple, red, yellow, orange, gold, black, brown; eat vegetables you've never had before. Lean toward nutrient-dense vegetables: dark leafy greens (collards, kale, watercress, spinach, chard) and orange (winter squash, sweet potato, carrot). These are super-nutritious vegetables which contain vitamins and minerals you can't get too much of. Give dark green and orange a daily appearance on your plate. Buy organic and/or locally-produced produce whenever possible.

Legumes

For centuries, many cultures have combined legumes (beans, peas, lentils, and soy products) with whole grains to create delicious daily fare. Current research buries the notion that special food combining is necessary to get adequate protein from vegetable foods. Only 20 percent of your protein intake needs to contain a complete protein, that is, a complete set of amino acids. You carry an amino acid pool of some 80 to 90 grams of complete protein in your body that can be called upon to fill any gaps. Nevertheless, grain and bean combinations are the base of some of the most exciting and delicious cuisine in the world.

Beans are rich in protein and complex carbohydrates, high in fiber, low in calories and they contain appreciable amounts of calcium, iron, and other nutrients. Beans accept herbs and spices graciously to create hearty, mouth-watering dishes. And beans are inexpensive and available everywhere — what more could you ask from a food?

You can choose from traditional beans such as navy, kidney, lima, pinto, garbanzo, and black beans; the familiar peas and lentils or offbeat varieties of legumes such as azuki beans, Christmas limas, Swedish brown beans, and calypso beans. Tips for reducing the properties in beans which can cause gas are on page 72. Soybeans are used to make a variety of versatile products including tofu, tempeh and soy sauce. The various soy products are discussed in greater detail in the "Identifying, Shopping, and Storing Whole Foods" on page 252 in the Appendix.

Fruit

In-season fruit is least expensive and most delicious. It's sometimes hard to decipher what is in season since we import fruit from many parts of the world. Local and/or organic produce reflects what is in season. Buying produce seasonally helps remind you of the rhythm of the passing seasons and keeps us in tune with nature: strawberries every June, plums in September. Eat fruit in its whole, fresh state. Include some cooked fruits and dried fruits in your diet, especially in winter.

Drinking juice is not the same as eating a piece of whole fruit. Juice lacks fiber, which slows the rate of sugar absorption and juice is not a whole food. Children can get the equivalent of a sugar "high" on straight fruit juice. They may crave juice for quick energy and fill up on it instead of eating more nutritious food. Avoid serving juice with meals. I recommend diluting juice for children, one-half juice, one-half filtered water.

Include vitamin C-rich fruits regularly, such as oranges, strawberries, grapefruit, melons, or kiwi. Buy organic fruit, especially for babies, children, and pregnant moms.

SIDE DISHES AND TOPPINGS

Sea Vegetables

These jewels from the ocean are unknown to most American palates. The sea vegetables used in this book include arame, dulse, dulse flakes, hijiki, kombu, nori, and wakame. These are only a sampling of the variety of sea vegetables to be found. Each kind is unique, and offers the cook an array of varied tastes and textures.

Sea vegetables have a rich and diverse nutritional profile. Ounce for ounce sea vegetables are higher in vitamins and minerals than any other class of food because they are grown in sea water where minerals are constantly being renewed. They are a rich source of vitamins A, B, C, and E, as well as calcium and iron. Many trace elements and some key minerals such as zinc and iodine are difficult to obtain in vegetables today because modern farming methods have badly depleted our soil. Including sea vegetables in your diet is the best way I know to provide ample vitamins and minerals in the diet and avoid costly supplements.

The taste may seem strong or unfamiliar at first, so use a good recipe when first incorporating sea vegetables in the diet. Not even my relatives from Kansas shy away from Mim's Hiziki Pate (page 100). Many sea vegetables (such as nori) can be toasted and crushed or ground into a powder that can be put in a salt shaker and used as a condiment.

You may wonder about the pollution factor in these vegetables. Harvesters of sea vegetables conscientiously seek out chaste waters to grow and forage their crops. As with other ocean vegetation, sea vegetables won't flourish in polluted areas.

Fish and Poultry

You may choose to eat fish or poultry occasionally as a side dish with grains and vegetables. Fish and poultry are included in this book for B12 value and because you may not want or need to be a vegetarian. I believe that including small portions of concentrated animal protein in the diet can be beneficial to nursing mothers and growing children. Three to 4 ounces of fish or poultry is an ample daily portion. Flesh foods are denser and more filling giving our bodies a heavier feeling, a slower energy. Including some fish in the diet can be a nice balance to the lighter, quicker energy that results from eating fruits and vegetables. Fish or poultry can be a useful balancing food for children who have consumed too many fruits, juices, and sweets.

By using animal products in small portions, we help preserve natural resources. Raising livestock uses enormous amounts of land and water. More than half of the whole grains produced in this country, particularly corn, millet, and barley, are used for animal feed. By using fish and poultry as a side dish, we reduce the amount of pesticides and other pollutants that we consume. Purchase fresh (not previously frozen) fish and free-range, organically fed poultry.

I have not included red meat in this book mostly because of the high fat and cholesterol content and because raising beef for consumption is a poor use of our natural resources. If you choose to eat red meat, look for organically fed animals that have not been given hormones or antibiotics. As with fish and poultry, 3-4 ounces is an ample daily portion.

Nuts and Seeds

Nuts and seeds are delicious, whole foods that contain many beneficial nutrients. Almonds are rich in calcium; pumpkin seeds are high in iron. Nuts and seeds contain high-quality fats. The added calories can be useful for pregnant or nursing moms and active children. To keep nuts and seeds in proper perspective in the diet, think of them as condiments, using only a tablespoon or so at a time.

Dairy

The choice to include or exclude dairy products can be confusing, especially when it comes to children. I have been schooled in the ill-effects of dairy as well as the importance of including it. For me, the evidence seems to lean toward keeping dairy intake moderate to minimal.

Perhaps the most compelling reason is the quality of most commercial dairy products. Pollution of livestock is a problem, not only because pesticides and industrial wastes are found in the food cattle consume, but also because antibiotics and hormones are regularly administered to the animals. Many farms are producing organic dairy products that are antibiotic- and hormone-free. I would encourage you to seek out those products and purchase them regularly. Some children tolerate dairy products from smaller animals, such as goat milk or sheep cheese, better than products coming from cows.

I prefer not to use non-fat or reduced-fat dairy products. These products are no longer whole, natural foods. Their nutritional composition has been altered leaving a disproportionately high protein content. Parents should be aware that using low-fat or nonfat milk is inappropriate for children under two years of age. These products are too high in protein and minerals, which can stress young kidneys.

Dairy has been traditionally used as a condiment or garnish. Thinking of it as such will keep this concentrated food in proper perspective in your diet. I have suggested using dairy in small amounts in a few of the recipes in this book for added calcium, a source of high-quality fat and for the familiar taste.

The Sun

The sun links all life on our planet. Without the energy from the sun, human life could not be sustained. We depend on the sun for our food, we depend on our food for life. By choosing food that is organic, fresh, whole, and seasonal, we provide a higher quality energy for our bodies and stay more in tune with the planet we live on.

I used the image of the sun to remind you of one of the uses of our energy. Regularly exercising improves the body, mind and mood. Calcium absorption is vastly improved by regular walking, running or other weight-bearing exercise. The human body was designed to move. When children are encouraged to play outdoors, they experience the joy of movement, develop strong bodies, and exercise their imaginations.

Well-Balanced Menus

- Mexican Bean and Corn Casserole, p. 152
  Spinach Salad with Balsamic Vinaigrette, p. 185
  Raspberry Pudding Gel, p. 228

- Quinoa, p. 64
  Szechwan Tempeh, p. 164
  Baked Winter Squash, p. 194
  Sesame Greens, p. 174

- Peasant Kasha, Potatoes, and Mushrooms, p. 150
  Rosemary Red Soup, p. 128
  Greens in Cashew Curry Sauce, p. 175
  Pear Plum Crisp, p. 232

- Bok Choy and Buckwheat Noodles in Seasoned Broth, p. 160
  Sweet Squash Corn Muffins, p. 200
  Winter Fruit Compote with Nut Cream, p. 230

- Nut Burgers, p. 158
  Split Pea Soup with Fresh Peas and Potatoes, p. 129
  Romaine Radicchio Salad with Lemon-Olive Oil Dressing, p. 178

- Basmati Brown Rice, p. 58
  Rainbow Trout Poached in Herbs, p. 169
  Luscious Beet Salad, p. 180
  Gracie's Yellow Birthday Cake with Strawberry Sauce, p. 240, 244

Spending time outside improves a parent's energy, too. Go outside at least 15 minutes a day unless you are ill. Throw on a sweater, slicker, or snowsuit, soak up some vitamin D, and breathe some fresh air. Problems that seem big in small rooms diminish outdoors.

Why Buy Organic?

Buying organic products is a form of voting. Your organic purchase says that you support the growers and manufacturers who are producing food without the use of the synthetic fertilizers, insecticides, fungicides, herbicides or pesticides that pollute your bodies and your world. Buying organic produce, especially locally grown produce, also helps keep you in tune with the seasons. Soils rich in organic material and nutrients are needed to create healthy, insect-resistant plants. Many believe that organic produce tastes better and contains more nutrients.

The term "certified organic" means the product has been grown according to strict uniform standards which are verified by independent state or private organizations. The independent organization inspects the farm, interviews the grower, takes soil samples, and certifies that the product is grown according to standards they have set. An example of one of these organizations is the non-profit Organic Growers and Buyers Association (OGBA). A symbol on the front label identifies the independent organization that has certified an organic product. Unless that symbol appears on the front label or you know the farmer, it is difficult to know if a product is really organic. When in doubt, check with the produce manager or the buyer at your supermarket.

The federal government has set standards for the production, processing, and certification of organic food in the Organic Food Production Act of 1990. If this Act is implemented, all foods labeled organic will require third-party certification. The U.S. Department of Agriculture will oversee the program.

Organic food often costs more because production costs, as well as transportation and marketing costs, are higher. Organic farming is more labor intensive, with more hand weeding and thinning than commercial farming. Yield per acre can be less because of losses to pests. Organic fertility programs demand tons of natural fertilizers to be worked into the soil. By contrast, mere pounds of synthetic fertilizer are needed in conventional fertilizer programs. However, there is mounting evidence that if all indirect costs of conventional food production (clean-up of polluted water, replacement of eroded soils, health care for farmers and workers) were factored into the price of food, organic foods would most likely be cheaper.

You might be surprised at the variety of organic products available, including whole grains, beans, nuts, seeds, bread, pasta, flour, oil, dried fruit, jam, frozen vegetables, butter, milk, breakfast cereals, catsup, pickles and pickle relish, tomato sauce, fruit juices, and soy beverages. As consumers demand high-quality organic products, more will be created.

Make a special effort to use organic products when preparing food for pregnant or nursing moms, infants, and children. Toxins found in the mother's food can cross the placenta to the growing fetus or wind up in breast milk. What may be tolerated by a mature adult may prove harsh to the immature system of fetus or infant. In *Pesticides in the Diets of Infants and Children*, a report published by the National Research Council in the 1988, concern was raised about the protection of our infants and children. Current regulatory practices used to control pesticides in foods are based on studies of pesticide exposure to the general population, without regard to the special needs of infants. Some of the most pesticide-saturated foods are ones that we routinely give children to snack on, including peanut butter, peanuts, raisins, and potato chips. Non-organic apples, peaches, strawberries, and celery can contain as many as 80 pesticide residues. To learn more about the pollution of our food read David Steinman's *Diet for a Poisoned Planet: How to Choose Safe Foods for You & Your Family* (Ballantine Books, NY, 1990). Use your power as a consumer to demand the best for our children, our planet, and the future of both. Don't panic, buy organic.

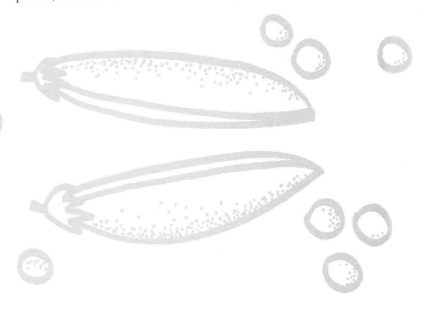

Good Reasons to Buy Organic

Protect Future Generations

Organic foods reduce health risks to ourselves, our children and our children's children.

Keep Chemicals Off Your Plate

Organic foods carry a guarantee. They contain no synthetic pesticides, fertilizers or growth hormones. No prohibited substances may be applied to land on which organic food is grown for at least three years.

Support Small Farms

By purchasing organic foods, you support the growing number of family farms dedicated to protecting our natural resources while producing high-quality, healthful food.

Prevent Soil Erosion

Organic agriculture also helps promote biological diversity through a system of crop rotation, natural fertilizers, and soil conservation and renewal.

Protect Water Quality

Organic agriculture protects our water resources from polluting chemicals. The Environmental Protection Agency estimates that pesticides contaminate groundwater in 38 states.

Promote Biodiversity and Protect Wildlife

Organic farmers respect the balance of a healthy ecosystem and work in harmony with nature. Birds and beneficial insects control pests. Wildlife is an essential part of a total farm and is encouraged by including forage crops in rotation and by retaining fence rows, wetlands and other natural areas. When you buy organic, you help farmers build a healthy environment for wildlife.

Better Taste and Flavor

Organic food tastes great. Many chefs across the country are demanding organic produce because they think it tastes better.

How to Make Changes

The first step in changing the way you eat is to become conscious of what goes in your mouth. Think about what you are buying at the store. Does this product deserve your hard-earned money? What's in it? Are you buying it out of habit or because the label looks attractive? Think about your food as you prepare it, as you eat it. Where did this food originate? Will it add to your vitality? For a while observe what you eat without changing anything. You might keep a food diary, but don't judge yourself during this process.

Take baby steps. Pick one thing to change, such as switching from white bread to whole grain bread or learning to eat the fast-cooking grain, quinoa. Make small changes over weeks and months, and create the time and space needed to give your family deeply nourishing food a little at a time.

In order to modify old habits, you must feel an intrinsic desire to change. Many people change their diets for health reasons, often the result of a live-or-die situation. But there are reasons to make changes before a crisis occurs. In my classes, I have heard many stories of children who are influencing their parents to eat better. In one class, I had three pairs of mothers and daughters; all three daughters instigated their enrollment. It is inspiring to see the family align with each other about food and health.

Sometimes people tell me they can't change their family's food because one family member simply won't have it. If you're in this situation, talk to the person who objects. Let them know that your motivation comes from love. Perhaps the reluctant family member will agree to one small change — for instance, making one vegetarian meal a week or having a fresh green salad every evening or maybe brown rice instead of white rice once in a while. Go slowly, slowly. Make changing what you eat a gentle, healing process. There is no rush. Lasting changes take a lot of thought and a lot of patience.

Starting
Your Baby
on Whole Foods

The beginning of my journey into motherhood was a challenge. I had a two-week-old infant that liked to curl her fists up in tight balls and scream for several hours straight every evening. Her condition was relegated to the catchall term "colic." I worried about my breast milk being okay. I worried about her tiny digestive system. I was exhausted. I felt lost.

I chose to stay right with Grace during her long tirades. I held her, walked with her, bounced her and hung in there with her. When I could get past my own frustration, I would think about how difficult her transition must have been… from spirit to water baby in my womb to infant out in the world. It must be so hard to suddenly find your soul in a helpless, tiny body; a body that requires ingesting food and eliminating waste and wearing clothes and seeing lights and hearing noise. My heart would go out to this tiny child who seemed to be quite angry about making this transition. Often silent tears would slide down my cheek, not only for her discomfort, but for mine.

Most of us are searching for a sense of belonging and being loved all our lives. Giving food is one of our primary means of expressing love. There is nothing that can duplicate the reassurance that is conveyed when a baby's food is accompanied by the face, hands, voice, breast or chest of a loving parent.

Start With the Best, the Breast

There is no better food you can give your newborn child than breast milk. Every year a new study appears discovering some nutrient or immunological factor found in breast milk that cannot be duplicated in the laboratory. Breast milk is designed by nature to help our species thrive. We have only begun to discover the myriad ways in which breast milk nourishes and protects both mother and child.

The first substance from the mother's breast after birth is a thick liquid called colostrum. Colostrum does just what is needed immediately after birth: It helps the baby pass meconium, a substance in the baby's bowels that needs to come out before ordinary digestion can begin. Colostrum contains half of the immunological properties the newborn needs, ensuring immediate protection. Colostrum also decreases the absorption of bilirubin, reducing the chance of jaundice. Colostrum decreases as the mother's milk matures in the 10 to 14 days following birth.

Breast milk is the only food your baby will need for six months. No extra water, juice, tea, or anything else is needed. Giving your baby a bottle of anything during the first few weeks of breastfeeding can cause nipple confusion. The breast and bottle require different sucking styles. Going from one to the other can result in frustration for mother and baby. In our society where the need for variety verges on obsessive, it is hard to believe that babies can thrive on the simplicity of breast milk alone. When well-meaning relatives and friends encourage you to feed the baby something else, thank them for their advice. They may be unaware of the bonuses Mother Nature included in breast milk (see "Breastfeeding Bonuses," page 27).

In researching breastfeeding and breast milk, I was awed by one discovery. A biological communication is established between mother and baby during nursing: the milk responds to the needs of the baby. Formula is static, but breast milk is not. It is a living, constantly changing food.

For example, the milk produced for a premature baby is different than the milk that comes in for a full-term infant. Breast milk even changes within a single feeding. The milk that comes out of the breast at the beginning of the feeding is more watery and satisfies thirst quickly. Toward the end of the feeding, the milk (called the hind milk) becomes richer in fat. Both are vital for baby.

In addition, the interaction between the baby's mouth and the mother's nipple signals the mother's body to increase certain nutrients in the milk if needed or restrict substances that appear dangerous. No human-made substance can duplicate the sensitive response of human breast milk. It's truly a miracle of nature.

Cultural influences have led women to believe breastfeeding is a hardship. Even when women choose to nurse, their husbands, relatives, and friends may pressure them into early weaning because they are socially uncomfortable seeing the child and the mother's breast together. Social conditioning from advertisements by formula manufacturers and guidance by health-care practitioners unfamiliar with the advantages of breastfeeding perpetuate this message. To raise children strengthened by breastfeeding requires the courage to ignore such outdated social stigmas.

If you are pregnant, contact your local La Leche League before the birth for additional support. This amazing international organization has a network of meetings, counselors and literature that promote and support breastfeeding. The Childbirth Education Association (CEA) provides breastfeeding classes and early mothering support classes. Breast-feeding is not simply a matter of doing what you've seen many women in your family do before. We are isolated; no longer privy to the shared wisdom of the greater family. Natural ways often need to be explained and justified. Nevertheless, the resources for natural wisdom remain within our reach and within ourselves.

In instances where breastfeeding may not be possible, such as adoption, formula is the preferred second choice. No single brand of formula appears to be any better than another. Most commercial formulas contain sugar, salt, and cheap fats such as beef tallow or coconut oil, which are susceptible to rancidity.[1] Some creative nutritionists, naturopaths or other health-care practitioners have attempted to invent better homemade formulas that usually combine soy milk or goat milk and high-quality vitamin and mineral supplements. You might explore your community and see if there is a reasonable alternative that you and your health-care practitioner can agree upon.

Parents have an instinctual need to nourish their children. The premise of this book is based on that drive. I encourage you to make whatever changes you require, in your lifestyle or in your

---

1 Palmer, Gabrielle, "The Politics of Breastfeeding" (Pandora Press, 1988) pp. 42-48.

Breastfeeding Bonuses

Bonuses for baby

- Colostrum, the first substance from the mother's breast, helps baby pass meconium and reduces the chance of jaundice. It supplies your baby with immunilogical properties.

- Breast milk contains antibodies to illnesses the mother has had, protecting baby against infections and reducing the risk of allergies.

- Your baby can easily absorb the iron in breast milk thanks to the presence of specialized proteins and vitamin C.

- Sucking at the breast enhances good hand–eye coordination and promotes proper jaw and teeth alignment.

Bonuses for mother

- After birth, immediate breastfeeding helps contract the uterus and reduce the risk of hemorrhaging.

- The hormone prolactin, which appears in the mother as a result of breastfeeding, is a relaxant. It is the hormone thought to help new moms feel "motherly."

- Breastfeeding aids in natural weight loss by using up an extra 500 calories a day.

- Studies show that breastfeeding for at least 25 months total during a mother's life reduces the risk of breast cancer (which now strikes one out of nine women in this country).

Bonuses for everyone

- Breastfeeding gives mother and child a deep sense of security and love, and encourages physical closeness.

- Breastfeeding saves time and money. Formula feeding is very expensive!

- Outings with baby are easier using naturally hygienic breast milk: no bottles, no sterilizing, no heating things up, no formula, no fuss.

head, in order to experience the power of breastfeeding in your family. It is a part of womanhood we need to reclaim and pass on to the next generation.

Foods for Breastfeeding Moms

Sometimes women who have been very careful about their eating habits during pregnancy may forget, during nursing, that their bodies are still the source of nutrition for their child. Continuing good eating habits is important during breastfeeding, though sometimes harder to remember with a wee one in tow. The substances taken in by the nursing mother have a strong effect on the milk she produces.

For instance, the alcohol from a single drink consumed by a nursing mother appears in the breast milk in the same concentration as the mother's blood within 30 minutes. Nicotine ingested by a nursing mother who smokes cigarettes passes into the breast milk as well. Foods eaten by mom sometimes disagree with the breast-fed child, especially high-dosage vitamins, supplements high in iron, artificial sweeteners, caffeine, heavily spiced foods, and occasionally dairy products. Colicky or fussy babies may improve if the nursing mother's diet is changed. Consult with your health practitioner or lactation counselor.

Many women feel rushed to get rid of weight gained during pregnancy. The nursing period is not an appropriate time to diet. Dieting can compromise the mother's stamina and her milk supply. Environmental contaminants stored in the mother's body fat can be released into the milk if she loses more than four pounds a month. Overindulging in caffeine found in coffee, diet soft drinks, or over-the-counter drugs can result in an over-stimulated baby. Breastfeeding as long as is comfortable, regular nutritious meals and exercise are the most important factors in finding your way back into your old jeans.

A common misconception in the United States is that nursing moms need to drink milk in order to make milk. Not true. Cows do not drink milk in order to make milk, they eat grass. Acknowledging the wisdom of women in all parts of the world and throughout several centuries can give us helpful clues today.

The post-natal diet of tribal women throughout the world reveals a consistency of custom. Tribal diets focus on grain-vegetable soups, soft-cooked grains and vegetables, greens, and fish soups. Women drink large quantities of warm water and tea to encourage the flow of milk. Fats, sweets, cold liquids and, in some cases, meat are specifically avoided.[1]

At one time African women used a grain called "linga-linga" when nursing. The same grain used in Peru was called "quinoa." This grain has an especially high mineral content. Quinoa has been rediscovered and is now grown and sold in this country. I use this delicious grain in several recipes throughout the book. Another grain purported to aid in producing a good milk supply is sweet brown rice, a cousin of brown rice that has a higher fat content. This grain is often eaten in the form of mochi or amasake. Foods that are known to produce rich breast milk, then and now, include whole grains, vegetables (especially dark green and orange ones), legumes, fish, and warm herbal teas — whole foods prepared in simple, satisfying ways.

Departing from cultural wisdom, it is interesting to note modern scientific recommendations. The Recommended Dietary Allowances (RDA) from the National Academy of Sciences proposes that lactating women need an extra 500 calories a day. Their recommendation includes an extra 15 grams of protein each day as well as additional calcium, folic acid, vitamin C, and zinc. Meeting the additional requirements of nursing a child can be simple and satisfying. Eat meals made from nutrient-dense whole foods, such as the ones listed in the chart on page 30 and used in the recipes in this book. Consuming foods that contain only empty calories, such as soft drinks, candy, pastries, and salty snack foods, will not add necessary nutrients to your milk, but will add inches to your hips!

High-quality breast milk doesn't require you to eat perfectly balanced, homecooked meals each and every day. Nature provides plenty of leeway. Do your best to eat well and sensibly throughout the day; drink plenty of liquids; sleep when you can and love yourself and your baby. Your milk will be blessed food.

1   Goldsmith, Judith, "Childbirth Wisdom", (East West Books, 1990).

Great Foods for Breastfeeding Moms

These are foods that have above average levels of one or more of the following nutrients: protein, calcium, iron, folic acid, Vitamin A and Vitamin C. The RDA recommendations for these nutrients are elevated during lactation.

Grains	quinoa, millet, sweet brown rice (mochi)
Beans	chickpeas, pinto and navy beans, lentils, split peas, soyfoods
Vegetables	anything dark green or orange
Fruits	oranges, lemons, berries, grapes, grapefruit, apricots, peaches, melon
Nuts and Seeds	almonds, pine nuts, sesame and pumpkin seeds
Sea Vegetables	dulse, hiziki, arame, wakame
Dairy	organic yogurts and cheeses, fresh goat milks and cheeses
Fish and Poultry	fresh fish; free-range, organically fed poultry and eggs from them

Starting Solids

When to start baby on solids

There is no hurry. Look at your baby, not the calendar. Your baby will let you know when it's time to start. When your baby is around six or seven months old, he or she will give visible signs of readiness for solid foods. Here's what to watch for:

•**Can your baby sit up unattended?** Sitting upright is necessary for swallowing thicker substances.

•**Is your baby able to pick up small objects?** This indicates that baby could put a small bit of food in their mouth.

•**Does your baby show interest in what you're eating?** Mimicking your chewing, watching food go in your mouth or even grabbing for your food are all signs of interest.

•**If you offer baby a little taste of food, are they able to swallow it, or is it pushed back out with the tongue?** There is some practice involved here; the tongue-thrusting reflex is a physiological protection device that begins to diminish around six months of age.

•**Has your baby begun teething?** Some cultures regard the appearance of teeth as a sign of readiness for solid food.

Your baby's digestive enzymes are not fully developed for several years; however, at six months of age they are developed enough for experimental feedings. Starting solids too early can result in allergies brought on by exposing the immature digestive system to foods it can't handle. Don't be fooled into thinking your baby will sleep through the night if you start giving solid foods. This is a myth in our "hurry up" society. Trust your observations. Wait until your child is physically prepared for solids before introducing them.

How to start baby on solids

Again, there is no hurry. The initial step is to introduce new tastes and textures. Your baby is still getting all the nutrition needed from breast milk or formula. The transition to solid food as the primary source of nutrition should be long and slow. Once you feel baby may be ready to experiment with solids, here's how to start:

•**Use one, simple, whole food.** A soft fruit or a cooked sweet vegetable is a good choice.

• **Puree the food in a blender or processor, or mash with a fork.**

• **Mix the food with a little breast milk or formula.** This will give your baby a familiar taste.

• **Begin with only a teaspoon of food.**

• **Choose a quiet time of the day that isn't a regular nursing or bottle time.**

• **Talk to your baby about the food and the eating procedure.** Later they will be able to respond to cues such as "Open your mouth!" or "Bananas, Henry?"

• **Taste a little of the food yourself.** You can model eating for your baby. Homemade baby food will be appreciated here.

• **Offer the food from your finger or from a spoon, or allow baby to grab** (messier for you, fascinating for baby).

• **Stay with one feeding a day of one simple food.** Wait about 5 days before introducing another new food. With each new food tried, be aware of allergic reactions such as rashes around the mouth or anus, diarrhea, skin reactions, lethargy or unusual fussiness. Eliminate, for the time being, any food that causes a reaction and try it again when baby is several months older. Common allergens and other potentially disruptive foods that should be avoided are listed on page 36.

• **After several weeks of one small meal a day, you can increase to two small meals a day.** If your baby doesn't seem to enjoy eating solid foods, stop the feedings for a few weeks.

What foods to offer

Whether your baby's first solid food should be a cereal, a fruit or a vegetable can be left up to you. If your child is labeled underweight, a health-care practitioner or a relative may encourage you to start with cereals, but babies digest fruits and vegetables more easily and quickly than whole grains. Also be sure the underweight label is a fair assessment. Current growth charts are owned and distributed by Ross Laboratories, one of the largest formula manufacturers. The charts reflect the growth rate of mostly formula-fed babies, who tend to be larger than breast-fed babies.

Stay with simple fruits, vegetables, and whole grains for the first few months of solids. My favorite beginning fruits and vegetables are applesauce, avocado, bananas, carrots, sweet potato, peas, and winter squash. The least allergenic grains, the ones I recommend starting with, are brown rice, sweet brown rice, quinoa and millet. For instructions on how to make your own whole grain baby cereal see page 74.

Babies will let you know what their favorite foods are. My daughter hated tried and true mashed banana, but adored sweet potatoes and applesauce. Each child is unique. Remember to rotate the grains used for cereal to reduce the chance of allergies. Rotation provides your baby with a wider variety of nutrients since each grain is unique.

Be aware that many some commercial baby food manufacturers replace real food with water and thickening agents in their products. Commercial baby foods are very high-priced compared to similar regular foods, especially foods such as baby food juices and applesauce. Baby food manufacturers encourage a mystique about their products making parents believe that commercial baby food has special properties that can't be duplicated in your own kitchen. This is clearly untrue. Why pay high prices for nutritionally inferior food for your baby? Parents can easily prepare safe, nutritious, and economical foods for their infants at home.[1]

Hints for making simple adaptations for babies are given at the end of most of the recipes in the recipe section. Any time you see **FOR BABIES 6 MONTHS & OLDER** at the bottom of a recipe, an idea for taking part of the dish and making food for a baby just starting solids follows.

Should I give my baby supplements?

My first response is, "How could we have survived as a species so long if babies don't thrive without artificial supplements?" Many parents are encouraged to give their baby iron supplements starting at around six months. I never blindly accepted that I needed to supplement my baby's diet with iron or other nutrients. Ferrous sulfate, the most common iron supplement, is poorly absorbed and can cause indigestion and constipation. I looked into the matter and this is what I found:

Your baby was born with a good store of iron which has come from the mother during pregnancy. This is one reason why hematocrit levels are monitored in pregnant women and why women are encouraged to increase their iron intake during

---

1 Stallone, D., Ph.D., M.P.H. and Jacobson, M., Ph.D. "Cheating Babies: Nutritional Quality and Cost of Commercial Baby Food." Center for Science in the Public Interest. Washington, DC, April 1995.

pregnancy. Part of a baby's iron supply comes through the umbilical cord shortly after birth, so it is important that the cord not be clamped or cut for at least five to ten minutes after the birth. Premature cutting of the cord is unnecessary and diminishes baby's iron stores.

Breast milk contains a small amount of absorbable iron to meet baby's needs. Babies can absorb up to 50 percent of the iron in breast milk, but only 4 percent of the iron in fortified formula. Vitamin C in breast milk increases the absorption of the iron. Lactoferrin and transferrin, two specialized proteins in mother's milk, regulate the iron supply to baby. As long as the mother was not anemic during pregnancy, the breast-fed baby should have adequate iron for the first year of life.

Around six months, when solid foods are introduced, your baby begins to get iron and other nutrients from sources other than breast milk or formula, or stores accumulated in utero. With the transition into a simple, whole foods diet, your baby should not need supplements. It is advisable to be in sync with your health-care practitioner regarding supplementation.

Why start your baby on a refined grain cereal that has had most of it's vitamins, minerals, protein and fiber removed and some iron added back in? Serve whole grain cereals and freshly prepared fruits and vegetables, giving your baby naturally occurring vitamins and minerals in the proportions his or her body needs. For extra minerals, such as iron, add sea vegetables to baby's diet and use cast-iron cookware.

Safety Tips for Homemade Baby Food

- Before using any equipment to prepare baby food, wash it with hot water and soap.

- Never serve your baby food hot off the stove. Room temperature or slightly warm is fine. Hungry baby, but cereal's too hot? Stir it with an ice cube for quick cooling.

- Microwaving sometimes heats food unevenly. This can create "hot spots" in baby's food or bottle that can burn your baby's mouth. Use caution if microwaving or avoid it.

- If you've made a large batch of food, remove a small portion to a separate dish to serve your baby.

- Discard leftover food that has had spoon-to-mouth contact.

- Store leftovers that have not had spoon-to-mouth contact in the refrigerator and use within two or three days.

- Freeze extra pureed food in ice-cube trays. Frozen cubes can then be stored in the freezer in plastic bags. For a quick meal, place a cube or two of frozen food in a small dish and heat in a covered pan of boiling water. Use frozen baby food within four weeks.

- Store ground grains for cereals in sterile jars in the refrigerator or freezer (canning jars or jelly jars work fine).

- Label all stored food.

"Not-So-Good" Food for Babies

Caffeine

Caffeine is a stimulant, not a food. Soft drinks and cocoa not only contain sugar; they have as much caffeine as coffee. Caffeine can cause elevated blood sugar and stimulate the heart and lungs. This kind of stimulation can be detrimental for babies.

Chemical Additives

Avoid aspartame, saccharin, fructose, other chemical sweeteners, BHT, artificial flavors and colors, MSG, nitrates and other additives. The effect of chemical additives on adults is not entirely known. There certainly can be no benefit to introducing chemicals to your baby's immature system. Read labels.

Chocolate

Chocolate products almost always contain sugar and caffeine. Chocolate can also be a severe allergen. Chocolate is an inappropriate food for children under two years old and should be used sparingly thereafter.

Common Allergens

Wheat, citrus, cow's milk products, corn and egg whites are common allergens. Many health-care practitioners agree on foregoing these foods in baby's diet. Foods that are common allergens do not need to be avoided forever. Hold off for the first year and then experiment. With common food allergens it is always best to use them on a rotational basis, once every 3-5 days.

Cow's Milk

Cow's milk is not appropriate for babies under one year old. It can cause occult bleeding of the intestines, resulting in iron-deficiency anemia.

Raw Honey

Uncooked honey sometimes contains botulism toxins in amounts that are detrimental to infants. Barley malt or brown rice syrup can be substituted for honey.

Salt

Heavily salted foods can stress baby's immature kidneys. Salted food can also interfere with your baby's natural appetite. Sufficient salt (sodium) is readily available in many foods in their natural state. Adding a bit of salt to cooking grains that will later be served to baby is fine. This is a very negligible amount. Avoid processed foods, which often contain large amounts of sodium, and salty snack foods such as pretzels or potato chips.

Sugar

A prime source of empty calories, sugar has almost no nutritive value. Eating large amounts of sugary foods can displace more nutritional foods, resulting in vitamin and mineral deficiencies. Refined sugar consumption has been linked with tooth decay, heart disease, atherosclerosis, diabetes, obesity, learning difficulties, and behavior problems. Why let your baby develop a taste for it?

Foods Babies Often Choke On

To prevent accidents, never give the following foods to babies under one year old. When trying any new snack, be sure that your baby is within eyesight and earshot so that you can be quick to help if a problem develops. Have children sit down when eating as choking most often occurs when children are walking or running.

Apple chunks or slices
Dry cereal
Grapes
Hard candy
Hard cookies
Hot dogs (even tofu dogs)
Meat chunks
Peanut butter or other nut butter sandwiches
Popcorn
Potato chips
Raw carrot sticks or slices
Rice cakes
Whole nuts and seeds
Whole or unseeded berries

Expanding the Diet
of the Older Baby

Babies who have been eating simple cereals, vegetables, and fruits for about three or four months are ready for more food choices. Ground nuts and seeds, the smaller beans (lentils and peas), and new food combinations can be added to your baby's diet. Hold off on larger beans, fish, and animal foods until baby has some side incisors and molars (usually after they are walking). As your baby begins to take less breast or bottle milk, these new foods fill in the nutritional spaces. Occasional small quantities of sea vegetables can provide additional vitamins and minerals for your baby.

The proper time to introduce dairy products (made from cow's milk) is highly disputed. Many practitioners feel dairy is such a common allergen that all dairy products should be avoided until a child is at least 2 years of age. This can be difficult if you have chosen to wean your child from formula or breast milk before age 2. Others feel that cow's milk should be avoided, but cultured dairy products, such as yogurt (plain, no sugar) or cheese, are okay after 9 months. I advocate waiting to introduce dairy. I have seen fewer problems associated with respiratory illnesses, ear infections, and digestive disorders in dairy-free babies. The key is to be aware of your baby's reaction when you choose to introduce dairy. If you use dairy foods, don't overemphasize them so they don't crowd out other important foods.

With the addition of a few new foods to baby's diet, moms, dads and other caretakers will have no problem finding items from their wholesome meals to offer baby. My child became less interested in pureed foods around 11 months old and wanted food she could pick up and feed herself. This is where the list of finger foods on page 39 can come in handy.

Your baby deserves food that is delicious as well as nutritious. I often do a taste test with my students when I teach baby food classes. Freshly made whole grain cereal wins hands down over powdered commercial baby cereal mixed with water. The homemade version looks better, smells better and TASTES better! Making baby food does not need to be a laborious task. Food for your baby can easily evolve from wholesome food the rest of the family is eating. This simple method is economical, ecological, highly nutritious and supportive of sound health for everyone.

Ideas for Finger Foods

Around the time babies start walking, they become interested in picking up food with their own hands and feeding themselves. Use your judgment about what your baby can handle. Stay within earshot when experimenting with finger foods. These snacks are generally okay for babies 1 year old and up.

- Pieces of ripe peach, nectarine, banana, plum or melon
- Pieces of steamed apple or pear
- Dried fruit (soaked in water to make it softer)
- Whole grain bread, whole wheat pita
- Crispy cakes (brand name of a rice cracker that melts in the mouth)
- Whole grain noodles or pasta
- Oatios, brown rice crispies, whole grain flakes or other high-quality dry cereals
- Cooked whole grains
- Pieces of baked or boiled potato (white or sweet)
- Pieces of baked or steamed squash
- Chopped vegetables steamed until soft (carrots, peas, zucchini...)
- Nori (tear into small pieces; melts in the mouth)
- Well-cooked beans
- Tofu (cooked in cubes or mashed with a fork)

Attracting
Your Children
to Healthy Eating

When I picked my daughter up from Kindergarten, she usually wanted to stay and play until all the other children were gone, so I often watched the children in her class.

One year, there was a mischievous elflike boy named Jonathan in her class. He would run and hide when the teachers wanted him to come in. He would dart outside without putting his shoes on. Once he sat down in the mud. He delighted in testing boundaries. I formed opinions about him. I thought of him as a "handful." One time I thought that they probably needed an extra teacher just for Jonathan.

I was invited to school to make lunch with the children one Friday. I brought pinto beans, whole wheat tortillas, brown rice, avocados, salsa, cheese, and lettuce and proceeded to make the fixings for a burrito lunch. The kitchen is near the classroom and the children were welcome to help. Some would stop by and assist for 10 or 15 minutes and then drift on to play.

One child stayed right by my side all morning — Jonathan. He mashed beans, peeled avocados and squeezed lemons. He followed instructions and was not only helpful, but gleeful about making guacamole. I was humbled. This little elf reminded me about "respect," a word that means "to look again."

Children are remarkably malleable. As soon as we label them, thinking that we can predict their behavior in some way, they surprise us by doing the opposite. Children invite us to experience the world with awe. They remind us that we do not know what will happen next. Don't presume that Fred will never eat lima beans and Judy will always want her apple peeled. Stay open to the little bits of magic lurking in every corner.

Maybe you'll discover an elf in your kitchen.

Parents as Role Models

What are your eating habits? Children model themselves after their parents. The tiniest baby notices every move you make, every forkful that goes into your mouth. I once had a well-intentioned friend who carefully prepared homemade, whole grain baby cereals and organic purees for her baby while she and her husband dined on fast-food take-out and doughnuts. As soon as the child could walk and grab, the baby wanted what mommy and daddy were eating. As much of a cliché as it may sound, the primary job parents have in the food and nutrition department is to set a good example. This gravitation toward the parent's eating habits will wax and wane. Children hit many rebellious stages where rejecting whatever parents do is the course of the day, but the underlying patterns they were shown about food remain. Here are four suggestions to help you become models of healthful eating habits for your children.

Become aware of how you feel about food.

What are some of your favorite foods? What kind of feelings would surface if you could never have them again? What are some foods you hate? Do you know why you hate them? Many hated foods have their roots in our childhood. How closely have you modeled your parent's eating habits? Are vegetables something you're supposed to eat or do you really like them? Is sugar something you deserve if you've been good, had a bad day, or finished your plate?

These unspoken attitudes are clearly transmitted to children. We may not be able to change our feelings about food just because we become parents, but we can become aware of how we think, feel, and act about various food choices. Take stock. Figure out which ones you may be unconsciously acting out, and decide if they are beneficial to pass on to your children.

Set boundaries about food choices and mealtime.

Many child-rearing books encourage parents to set gentle but firm boundaries with children to help them feel safe and protected. This concept applies to eating as well. Be sure to set boundaries that you can follow, too. It's not fair to have a strict no-sugar policy and then stay up late for some adults-only Godiva chocolates. Helpful boundaries for feeding children which offer ways to instill nutritious eating habits in your children with minimum stress are outlined in Setting Boundaries on page 45.

Take time to educate.

As soon as your child can talk, you can begin to communicate information about nutrition. Offer specific reasons for each food choice rather than saying, "You can't have this. It's bad for you." With young children you can reflect back to them how it seems that they act or look when they've eaten foods with a poor nutritional profile (whiny, grumpy, tired, "speedy").

Take your children shopping with you. Talk to them about what you're buying and why, such as why you might choose organic produce. As your children get older, let them play detective in the store: Present them with a challenge, such as finding a jar of tomato sauce that's organic or a loaf of bread without sweeteners. Encourage your children to help you cook by slowing down and allowing for the longer preparation time necessary to include a willing participant. Check the section called Involving Young Children in the Kitchen on page 49 for ideas. As children get older, talk to them about how the more nutritious foods can help them attain some of their desires (clearer skin, faster times on the 100-yard dash, better concentration). They may not accept everything you tell them, but occasionally they will see and feel results and that can be powerful!

Let go.

Learning to bend the rules, being flexible, and letting go are perhaps the most important lessons of parenting. Relaxing around birthday parties and other social gatherings where junk foods are offered is a lot easier if you know what's served at home is nutritionally sound. A woman in one of my classes proudly announced that she bakes no-sugar, whole wheat birthday cakes for her child to take to parties instead of allowing the child to share the cake being served. Rules that cause a child to feel uncomfortable in social situations are unnecessary and can be just as unhealthy as sugary cake. Watch out for setting up too many "forbidden fruits." Highly restricted foods may become irresistible and take on more power than they warrant.

We need to respect and think about our child's food choices. Children have a lot to teach us. Have you ever had the experience of offering food to your child all day only to be repeatedly refused, then realized later they were coming down with a cold? The child's intuition not to eat at that time was right on the nose. My child, Grace, used to regularly come home from a birthday party and ask for several sheets of nori to eat. How did she know that one of the consequences of too much sugar is that it creates a mineral debt in the body and that seaweed contains more minerals than any other food? Many children intuitively select what their bodies need.

Children have a lot to teach us about simplicity, too. You may notice young children tend to dislike casseroles or salad dishes containing many different ingredients. They'd rather have a plain food. A child's preferences can set a good example for parents to follow.

I have a sign on my refrigerator that says "Be a model, not a critic." It would be so much easier to glibly express platitudes and warnings to our children as we merrily indulge in our addictions and whims. Let's let our children see us respect, be grateful for, and eat nourishing food with the knowledge that whole foods make us healthier on many levels.

Setting Boundaries

All children need and want boundaries. When we set boundaries, we are saying we care about them. When they're infants, we keep our children very close to our bodies. With each year we give them a little more space to roam and a few more choices to make, even as we continue to provide a circle of boundaries to protect them. This concept also applies to food. An infant is given the simple security of breast or bottle. Preschoolers may be able to clearly tell you if they would prefer an apple or a rice cake. A 10-year-old can help plan the dinner menu. Keep the choices simple and limited for the younger ones while allowing older children more input. Apply that range to each boundary outlined below. The following suggestions apply to children between the ages of 3 and 10.

Provide excellent choices.

Stock your cupboards and your refrigerator with fresh, healthful, whole foods products. When all of the food in your home is food you feel good about serving your children, you can eliminate many problems around eating. It won't matter what your child chooses or asks for. You can't expect to keep junk foods and sugary items around the house and not be badgered, especially if your child sees you eating those items. If it's not there, it's harder to fight about.

If you pack a lunchbox for your child, make sure the choices inside are good ones. When there are candies and soft drinks and such in the lunchbox, children often eat or drink the sweets and skip the rest; however, if each item is substantial and nutritious, you don't need to worry about what your child eats or doesn't eat.

Honor mealtimes.

Share at least one common meal with your whole family each day. A family meal is not only a time for nourishment, but an opportunity for children to experience some social education (see "Why Share a Common Meal?" on page 7). Emphasize social patterns with ritual: lighting candles, saying a verse, setting the table a special way, serving food a certain way. Consider keeping a regular time for the evening meal.

What's served is served.

Do not make the mistake of preparing a separate meal for your child. Let each person receive some portion of each dish that has been prepared. If your child refuses to eat one of the foods, encourage them to sample one or two bites, then say no more. This exposure to many foods will expand your child's repertoire. A child sometimes refuses food because of appearance, then appreciates it when tasted.

Children who refuse to eat anything on the plate should be asked to excuse themselves and told that no other food will be served until breakfast or until 8 o'clock that night or whatever seems reasonable according to your child's age. If they come whining for food later, consider offering the leftover dinner. One way to avoid the "untouched meal" syndrome is to make sure that each meal has a sure winner: a simple side dish you know your child will like (see "Keep it simple" below).

Incorporate a "no-critics-at-the-table" rule. Teach your children that it is inappropriate for any participant at the table to offer harsh and cruel reviews such as, "I hate everything! or "This looks awful!" Remind such reviewers that their words are unkind and ask them to excuse themselves from the dinner table. Suggest alternative ways for expressing dislike of the dinner menu. Let them know they will be welcome at dinner the next night, where they can practice being more considerate. I find that children who help prepare the food for a meal are less critical at the dinner table.

Keep it simple.

Children usually like simple food, and will sometimes refuse foods that have several ingredients. Let your child learn to appreciate simple foods by regularly offering them. There is nothing wrong with plain carrots, plain baked squash, plain noodles or plain brown rice. Sometimes it takes an elaborate salad to please me when my five-year-old is happy with plain sliced cucumbers or lettuce without dressing. When planning meals, include something plain and simple that you're certain your child will like, even if it's just a side dish of sliced bread or carrot sticks or applesauce.

Don't bribe, reward, or punish with food.

Offering or withholding sweets or any other "forbidden" food in exchange for good behavior is not a good idea. It forms all kinds of hard-to-reverse psychological attachments to food. Food is something you eat in order to get energy to play and to grow.

Avoid tension and save money by not serving desserts with weekly dinners. Reserve home-baked goodies occasionally as snacks and mealtimes won't become a constant negotiation about dessert. Save desserts for special occasions or weekend meals.

Be firmer during stressful times.

When your child is ill or has an infection, remove foods known to be stressful to the system. Enforce your greater knowledge and forbid sweets, dairy products, animal proteins, and fried foods. Bodies recover from illnesses much quicker when they are given simple foods, such as soups and grains. Explain what you're doing in a way your child will understand.

Holidays can be stressful, too. Most holidays we celebrate seem to center around sugar. Provide some reasonable rules to curb the heavy intake of sugary foods at these times. When my child is given a bag of candy at a birthday party, we usually let her choose one piece a day to eat. This works, as she sometimes loses interest after a few days. If your child is over age 5, let them help create the rules.

Listen to your child.

Children have good instincts. If they are being offered excellent foods, they will eat exactly what their body needs. That may mean only fruit for several days (especially when it's warm outside), then they may request something heartier, like fish. Children create a balanced diet over many days rather than within one day. Watch. Often they will hit all the food groups over a week or two. To eliminate worry about sufficient nutrients, offer excellent choices from a variety of whole foods steadily and consistently.

Children's wonderful intuition can go awry. Refined sugar and flour, foods with chemical additives and highly salted foods can be addictive, and excessive amounts of any can mar your child's natural good judgment. When heavy doses of unnatural foods have been consumed and children begin expressing cravings for more, parents need to intervene and restore balance.

When setting boundaries, remember to respect your child's individuality. Children who are very sensitive to certain foods may benefit from firmer boundaries. Others may show so little interest in food that you may not need to set many limits. Some children are natural vegetarians, while other may want or need some animal protein. Listen to your child's requests and guide them toward the healthier, whole foods way of fulfilling them. Young children appreciate the boundaries we set for them. It helps them feel guided, protected, and safe.

For Parents of Picky Eaters

1. Have your child help plan, shop for and prepare meals. See "Involving Young Children in the Kitchen" (page 49).

2. Don't be tempted to make separate meals for your picky eater. What's served for the meal is what's served. Include a small "no thank-you" helping of each dish that has been prepared for the meal.

3. Include one healthful dish at each meal that you know your child will enjoy. Something as simple as applesauce or bread is fine.

4. Try new ways of presenting the food. Examples abound in "Presenting Food so it Appeals to Young Children" (page 51), "My Child Won't Eat Vegetables" (page 53) and at the bottom of many of the recipes in the recipe section.

Involving Your Children in the Kitchen

Children need to feel a sense of belonging. It is one of their primary drives. In the days of farms and big families, children were a natural part of daily activities. Every child was needed to do chores in order for food to get to the table. Today, children often lose the opportunity to be needed, to contribute to the daily work routine of house and family. Meals are something prepared for the children, not by the children.

Even children who have just begun to walk can help out in the kitchen. They can learn all sorts of things about food, cooking, nutrition, math, science and recycling by helping prepare food. Kitchen participation helps teach self-reliance and the importance of contributing to the functioning of the household.

Most 3- to 6-year-olds can handle the following tasks. Match the task to your child's skill level. If the task seems too difficult at first, let it go and try again in several months. Remember to use simple, short sentences to describe how the work is done and do the task slowly as you show and tell your child how it is done. Be patient, and pretty soon you'll have an ace helper in the kitchen.

Helping your helper:

• Clear out a low cupboard for your child. Keep pots and pans there so your toddler can play near you, copying you.

• For your pre-schooler, use the space to store unbreakable dishes that they can serve with or use for imaginary house-play. Older children may enjoy having their own kitchen tools or ingredients to make simple snacks on a reachable shelf.

• Get a sturdy stool or small chair that your child can move to be able to reach the counter and sink.

Things your child can do to help with meals:

Shopping

Help with menu selection
Carry groceries into house
Unload grocery bags and put things away

Preparing Foods

Retrieve items from the refrigerator

Pick herbs, fruits, or vegetables from the garden

Wash fruits and vegetables

Peel carrots, cucumbers, potatoes

Grate carrots, cheese

Cut vegetables or fruit (your child should be at least 4 or 5 years old)

Spin the salad spinner

Tear lettuce or greens into small pieces

Toss a salad

Crack nuts

Grind grains or nuts in a grinder or processor

Tell you when something is boiling

Put spreads on breads, crackers, rice cakes, or tortillas

Pour pancake batter with cup

Flip pancakes

Helping with Baking

Measure and pour liquid ingredients

Measure and add dry ingredients

Sift flour

Stir wet or dry ingredients

Knead dough

Roll out dough with rolling pin

Turn blenders and food processors on and off

Use mixer with supervision

Form cookies with hands

Cut out cookies with cutters

Oil pans and cookie sheets

Put muffin cups in muffin tins

Tell you when the timer goes off

Serving

Set the table with mats, silverware, cups or glasses, and napkins

Put candles on table and light candles with assistance

Pick flowers and put them in a vase of water

Make placemats out of construction paper, crayons, and pens

Roll napkins into napkin rings

Make place cards for guests

Call the family to dinner

Cleaning

Carry dishes from table to sink

Wash dishes

Dry dishes

Load dishes in dishwasher

Unload dishes from dishwasher

Sweep the floor (a child-size broom is helpful)

Wipe table or placemats with a sponge

Put recyclable items in bins

Take food scraps to worm bin or compost pile

Sort clean silverware into compartments

Presenting Food So it Appeals to Young Children

Beauty is in the eye of the beholder. Presentation is very important for young children. Your child may refuse a sandwich unless it's cut a certain way or has the bread crusts removed. You may be able to delight a child into eating something new by putting a face on it or cutting it into a heart shape. Dust off your imagination and expand on the following ideas for creative food preparation for youngsters.

Decorate food.

Here are some starter suggestions. I'm sure you'll think of more.

• Stock a variety of cookie cutters and use them to cut sandwiches and pancakes. Find cutters in the shapes of your child's favorite animals. Asian markets sometimes have small, strong cutters for making vegetables into beautiful shapes. These can be fun for turning zucchini or carrot slices into flowers.

• Serving brown rice, potatoes or other foods with a large ice cream scoop makes miniature mountains on your child's plate.

• Make food friendlier by using raisins, small pieces of vegetables, small crackers or whatever you can dream up to put a face on the food. Bowls of soup, mashed potatoes, or plates of rice suddenly become funny personalities for your child to devour. Apple slices make sweeping smiles, olives make 3-D eyeballs.

I once cut a sheet of nori into paper dolls for my three-year-old. Decorating food will bring humor and light to you and your child's day.

Use delightful dinnerware and playful packaging.

• You might try buying a special plate, cup or even silverware for your child. This can be as extravagant as a complete Winnie-the-Pooh set or simply "Jack's yellow plate." Having personal dinnerware can enhance your child's enjoyment of meals. Children also derive security from being able to count on the same bowl or spoon every day. Serving red zinger tea in a special cup or plopping a crazy straw into a smoothie can make all the difference.

• Lunchbox packaging can have charm too. Your child may love having lunch packed in a recyclable paper bag with a silly face drawn on the outside. Another child may prefer a basket with a lid and ribbons tied on the handle. Asian markets sell interesting merchandise designed for packing food to go. Sometimes you can find beautiful container boxes in pretty colors that have little compartments inside.

• Fun surprises hidden inside a lunchbox need not be sweets. How about a marble, a seashell, an envelope with a note or stickers inside, a little pad of paper and a tiny pencil? There are many ways to convey a loving message.

Tell a story.

• Can you turn a plate of spaghetti into a pail of hay for a pretend lamb in your kitchen?

• Can a bowl of yellow split pea soup be a bowl of melted gold for your pirate?

Pretend play is very important to young folks. Why not use it to everyone's advantage in the nutrition department? Make up a wild story about what you're serving that will make it impossible not to devour (or at least taste).

"My Child Won't Eat Vegetables"

One of the most common worries expressed in my cooking classes is that kids won't eat vegetables. With children who eat their fair share of whole grains, fruits, and beans, you can relax some; these foods contain a wide variety of vitamins and minerals are present in these foods. However, parents are right to be concerned if their children subsist mainly on sugar, milk, and white flour products. Vegetables are rich in vitamins not found in refined foods or animal products.

Remember that some children's favorite foods ARE vegetables, such as corn, sweet potatoes, carrots, and winter squash. One excellent way to improve your child's interest in vegetables is to let them help you plant and harvest a small vegetable garden.

Don't make a big fuss if your child refuses vegetables. Instead, eat them yourself and regularly offer them to your child. Remembering that beauty is in the eye of the beholder, here are some ways to prepare and serve vegetables that may appeal to your child.

Juices

Students who take my classes report great success in getting children to drink various vegetable juices. Carrot juice is a favorite, especially mixed with a little apple juice. But remember, juice is not a whole food; the fiber is gone and the sugars become highly concentrated. Dilute vegetable and fruit juices; one half juice, one half water.

Dippers

You can use raw vegetables as dippers for your child's favorite dip. Bean dips, guacamole, and tofu dips can be scooped up on a carrot stick, celery stick or a slice of zucchini. To make vegetables easier to chew and digest, boil or steam them for two to three minutes. Remove and immediately plunge into ice water to stop the cooking process. Drain and chill in refrigerator and serve with dip. This process enhances the flavor of cauliflower, carrots, and broccoli.

Soups

Children who refuse a serving of vegetables will often eat the same vegetable in a soup. If vegetables in their whole form are a turn-off, puree the soup (see Rosemary Red Soup on page 128 or Golden Mushroom Basil Soup on page 130).

Muffins

You can add vegetables to muffins and other baked goods (as in Sweet Squash Corn Muffins on page 200 or Halloween Cookies, page 223). Zucchini, corn, squash, carrots, and sweet potatoes taste great in a muffin mix.

Sandwich spreads

When you're pureeing beans or tofu or avocado into a tasty sandwich spread, add vegetables. Parsley, cilantro, fresh basil, red pepper, or scallions work well to enhance flavor and nutritive value. Sometimes I add corn, grated zucchini, or chopped green peppers to burritos. Amidst the beans, salsa, tortillas and all, they are hardly noticed.

Salads

Sometimes it's just the sight of combined ingredients that turn kids off to salads. Experiment by offering a single raw vegetable or raw vegetables in separate piles, not mixed together. Try different shapes and sizes. Grated beets or radishes, finely sliced cabbage, zucchini, summer squash or daikon (white radish), or even plain lettuce bites can be fun to pick up with small fingers.

Basic Grain and Bean Cookery

Basic Grain and Bean Cookery

This recipe chapter is included for those not familiar with the basic cooking techniques needed to successfully cook whole grains and beans. It is with the knowledge of how to cook the basics that one can begin to dive into various ethnic cuisine, experiment with fresh herbs and spices, and understand how to vary texture as well as flavor.

Water, **salt**, and **heat** are the elements that vary in basic grain and bean cooking. If a dish turns out poorly, usually one of these elements is out of whack. Don't give up if you don't get perfect rice the first time. As with any skill, practice is necessary.

General Notes on Cooking Whole Grains

For tips on shopping and storage, see "Identifying, Shopping, and Storing Whole Foods" beginning on page 252 in the Appendix.

Washing

Brown rice, millet, and quinoa are the grains in this section that need to be washed prior to cooking to remove chaff, dust, or other debris. Grains that have been partially milled, steamed or toasted, such as polenta, steel-cut oats, bulger, or kasha, do not require rinsing. The best way to wash grains is to place the grains in the pan with a generous amount of water. Swirl the grains in the water with your hand. As you touch the grain, remember your gratefulness to the earth for providing this food. Pour off the water through a fine strainer. Repeat this process again until the water you pour off is clear.

Cooking

It is usually necessary to bring the water and grain up to a boil first. Be sure to lower the heat immediately once the water has reached the boiling stage. Using a "flame-tamer" or heat diffuser, a perforated metal plate with a handle, can be very helpful. This kitchen gadget is placed between the pan and the heat source. It brings the heat down quickly and then keeps the heat at a low, even temperature — perfect for cooking grains properly. If your grains turn out too stiff and separate, you may have let the grain cook for too long at a high temperature. If the grain turns out mushy or clumped together, the heat may not have been high enough or you may have used too much water.

DON'T STIR COOKING GRAINS. Whole grains create their own steam holes so that they cook thoroughly. Stirring them disturbs the steam holes. Whole grains that have been ground, or cereals, are another matter. They can be stirred occasionally.

A pinch of sea salt brings out the sweetness in grains and helps the grain to open up. Grains cooked without salt will taste very flat. The only time you don't use salt is when preparing grains to be deep-fried. In this case the grains are usually served with a salty dipping sauce or gravy.

Brown Rice

Rice is the principal food for half of the world's people. Rice with the hull, bran and germ removed is white rice. Rice with just the hull removed is brown rice. Brown rice comes in a variety of types. Short grain, long grain, and basmati are three. All of these varieties can be prepared according to the directions below.

To boil

> 1 cup brown rice
> Pinch of sea salt
> 1¾-2 cups water

Rinse and drain rice. Place rice in a pot with salt and water. Bring to a boil. Turn heat to low. If you have a gas stove, a "flame-tamer" or "heat diffuser" is handy for keeping a low, even heat. Cover the pan and let the rice simmer for 45-50 minutes or until all the water is absorbed. Don't stir the rice while it is cooking.

Preparation time: 55 minutes
Makes 2½ - 3 cups

To pressure-cook

> 1 cup brown rice
> Pinch of sea salt
> 1½ cups water

Pressure-cooking makes a chewier rice which many people find satisfying. Rinse and drain rice. Place rice, salt and water in the pressure cooker. Close cooker. Place on medium heat and bring up to pressure. When pot is up to pressure, you will hear a gentle, steady hissing sound. Lower heat and time for 35-40 minutes. Remove from heat and allow pressure to come down naturally or by running cold water over the top.

Preparation time: 45 minutes
Makes 2½-3 cups

FOR BABIES 6 MONTHS & OLDER
Make rice cereal by taking a small amount of cooked brown rice and blending it with a little breast milk or water until smooth.

Leftover cooked brown rice? Use it to make:

Cereal for baby (puree in blender with water)
Confetti Rice Salad (page 95)
Dilled Brown Rice and Kidney Beans (page 97)
Tempeh Avocado Sushi Rolls (page 101)
Mad Dog Rice Salad (page 103)
Rice Balls Rolled in Sesame Salt (page 106)
Filling for Savory Sandwiches to Go (page 116)
Filling for Grain and Bean Roll-Ups (page 119)
Nut Burgers (page 158)
Rice Bread (page 198)

Bulgur

Bulger is par-boiled, dried, and cracked whole wheat. Wheat was grown as a crop as far back as 7000 BC. Bulger can be used as a base grain for a variety of bean and vegetable dishes, including tabouli, a traditional Mid-Eastern dish (page 102).

> **1 cup water**
> **Pinch of sea salt**
> **1 cup bulgur**

Bring water and salt to a boil in a small pan. Add bulgur. Cover pan and remove from heat. Let stand 10 minutes. Fluff grain with a fork before serving. Add a few drops of oil to the cooked bulgur to keep it loose.

Preparation time: 15 minutes
Makes 2½-3 cups

Couscous

Couscous is actually a tiny pasta made from coarsely ground and steamed wheat. It is usually made from refined grain although whole wheat couscous is becoming more widely available. Couscous can be used as a base grain for beans and stews and it also makes a nice salad when fresh vegetables and a dressing are added to the cooked grain.

> **1 cup water**
> **Pinch of sea salt**
> **1 cup whole wheat couscous**

Bring water and salt to a boil. Add couscous. Cover pan and remove from heat. Let stand 5-10 minutes. Fluff grain with a fork before serving. Stir in a few drops of oil to keep the couscous from clumping.

Preparation time: 15 minutes
Makes 2½ - 3 cups

Kasha

Kasha is roasted buckwheat groats. Buckwheat originally grew wild in Asia and was carried by migrating tribes to eastern Europe, where it is still a significant food for humans. Look for a brown, angular-looking grain. Kasha has a strong and hearty flavor; an excellent grain to eat during cold weather.

> **2 cups water**
> **Pinch of sea salt**
> **1 cup kasha**

Bring water and salt to a boil. Add kasha. Cover the pan, reduce heat and let simmer 15-20 minutes.

Preparation time: 25 minutes
Makes 2½ - 3 cups

FOR BABIES 6 MONTHS & OLDER
Blend cooked kasha and water to make a cereal for baby. Kasha is one of the least allergenic grains for babies.

Millet

Millet is a small, round, yellow grain that is one of the oldest foods known to humans; it is also one of the least allergenic grains. It is still a staple food in parts of Africa. Millet has a sweet, earthy taste that is enriched by dry-toasting the grain before cooking.

1 cup millet
2-3 cups water
Pinch of sea salt

Wash millet and drain. Repeat the rinsing 2 or 3 times. Place millet in a pan and dry-toast it for a richer flavor (this is optional). Heat the washed grain in a pot or skillet, stirring constantly until it is toasted dry and gives off a nutty aroma, about 5-7 minutes. Add water to toasted millet. Use 2 cups water for a fluffy grain. Use 3 cups of water for a creamier grain. Bring water, millet and a pinch of salt to boil, lower heat, cover, and simmer 30-40 minutes, until all the water is absorbed.

Preparation time: 45-50 minutes
Makes 2½ - 3 cups

FOR BABIES 6 MONTHS & OLDER
Blend cooked millet with a little water or breast milk to make an excellent baby cereal.

Leftover cooked millet? Use it to make:
Cereal for baby (puree in blender with water)
Deep-Fried Millet Croquettes (page 146)
Orange Millet Raisin Bread (page 198)
Gracie's Yellow Birthday Cake (page 240)

Rolled or Steel-Cut Oats

In North America oats are chiefly used for animal feed, only 5% for human consumption. Oat groats that have been thinly sliced are called steel-cut oats. Oat groats that have been heated until soft and pressed flat are called rolled oats.

> **1 cup rolled or steel-cut oats**
> **Pinch of sea salt**
> **3 cups water**
> **¼ cup raisins (optional)**
> **½ teaspoon cinnamon (optional)**

Place oats in a pot with salt and water. Bring to a boil, reduce heat, cover and let simmer on low for 20-25 minutes (steel-cut oats will take 25-30 minutes). Add raisins and cinnamon during the last 10 minutes of cooking if desired.

Preparation time: 25 minutes
Makes 2½ - 3 cups

FOR BABIES 10 MONTHS & OLDER

Oatmeal is a fine food for babies. I have suggested 10 months and older because it is not my first choice for a beginner grain; however many babies do fine with it. If using steel-cut oats, blend the cooked grain before serving it to baby as it can have a rather coarse texture.

Polenta

Corn was used as a dietary staple for tribes in North and South America. Today in the U.S., three-quarters of our corn produced is used for feeding livestock. Polenta is coarsely ground corn meal that is cooked and served as a kind of mush or cooked, allowed to set and then sliced. You can use broth instead of water as a cooking liquid or add cheese, vegetables or chilies to the cooked polenta to enliven the taste of plain polenta.

> 5 cups water or stock
> ½ teaspoon salt
> 1 cup polenta or corn grits
> 2 teaspoons extra-virgin olive oil or butter
> 2-3 tablespoons parmesan cheese (optional)

Traditional method

Bring water to rapid boil. Add salt and oil or butter. Slowly add polenta, stirring continuously with a whisk. Lower heat and continue stirring in a clockwise motion with a wooden spoon for 20-30 minutes until mixture can hold the spoon upright on its own. (If using cheese, add it now.) Lightly oil a pie plate or 8-by-8 pan. Pour polenta into pan and smooth the top. Let cool. Slice and serve.

Double-boiler option

Put 3-4 cups boiling water in the top of a double-boiler with salt and butter or olive oil. Slowly add polenta, stirring continuously with a whisk. When mixture begins to heave or sputter, reduce heat to low, cover and let cook 30-40 minutes. (If using cheese, add it now.) Lightly oil a pie plate or 8-by-8 pan. Pour polenta into pan and smooth the top. Let cool. Slice and serve.

Preparation time: 50 minutes
Makes 8 slices

FOR BABIES 10 MONTHS & OLDER
Corn is one of the top food allergies in our country, mostly because of its over-use in processed food products. That is why I have suggested using it for the older baby. Reserve a portion before placing in pan to cool and serve as a mush or let cool and set and slice into small chunks as a finger food for your toddler.

Leftover Polenta? Use it to make:
Pan-fried polenta with maple syrup as a breakfast treat
Brushed with olive oil and grilled
Three Sisters Stew (page 142) over polenta slices
Polenta Pizza (page 148)

Quinoa

(keen-wah)

This grain comes from the Andes Mountains in South America where it was once a staple food for the Incas. It has a delicious light, nutty flavor. When it cooks, the grain opens up to make tiny spirals. Quinoa contains all 8 amino acids and therefore has better protein value than most grains. A nutrient-dense grain; perfect for those who have elevated needs, such as pregnant or nursing mothers.

> **1 cup quinoa**
> **Pinch of sea salt**
> **1¾ cups water**

Rinse quinoa well with warm water and drain. Quinoa has a natural coating called saponin that repels insects and birds and can create a bitter taste. Rinsing with warm water removes the saponin. Place rinsed quinoa, salt, and water in a pot. Bring to a boil, reduce heat to low, cover, and let simmer 15-20 minutes, until all the water is absorbed. Fluff with a fork before serving.

Preparation time: 20-25 minutes
Makes 2½-3 cups

FOR BABIES 6 MONTHS & OLDER
Quinoa is an excellent beginner grain. Simply blend a small amount of cooked grain with some breast milk or water.

Leftover cooked quinoa? Use it to make:

Quick Lemon & Garlic Quinoa Salad (page 105)
Red Bean and Quinoa Chili (page 145)
Quinoa Garlic Herb Bread (page 199)
As a base grain under Curried Lentils and Cauliflower (page 154), Black-Eyed Peas and Arame with Cilantro (page 157), Szechwan Tempeh (page 164), Tempeh and Red Pepper Stroganoff (page 159).

Selecting Whole Grain Noodles & Pasta

Many cooks count on pastas and noodles for quick dinners, but not all noodles are created equal. The usual refined, white-flour noodles have at least two drawbacks: they offer little nutritional value because the nutrient-packed inner germ and fiber-rich outer bran have been removed. Also, we tend to overeat the fiberless product in an attempt to feel full. Some pastas and noodles that are 100% whole grain can be tough, grainy or chewy. A blend of whole grain and refined flour can make a more palatable compromise. Many whole grain noodles and pastas are on the market; here are examples and general directions on preparation.

Amaranth
Flour is ground out of tiny amaranth seeds to make a variety of pastas including spaghetti.

Artichoke
Artichoke noodles are usually made from a blend of refined or whole wheat flour and Jerusalem artichoke flour, which is ground from the roots of the Jerusalem artichoke. Look for artichoke noodles that are made with whole wheat flour. Artichoke noodles come in the standard shapes — angel hair, shells, elbows and fettucine.

Brown rice
Many types of pastas and noodles are made from nutritious brown rice flour. One trade name for a variety of brown rice pastas is Pastarico. Udon, a popular Japanese noodle, and a favorite of mine, is made from a combination of brown rice flour and either whole wheat or refined flour.

Buckwheat
Soba, another traditional Japanese noodle, is made from hearty buckwheat flour. Soba can be made from 100% buckwheat flour (which has a strong taste) or a combination of wheat and buckwheat flour. Some soba noodle products contain herbs, such as mugwort or wild yam which provide additional flavor and nourishment.

Corn
A wide variety of noodles and pastas are made from corn flour, including elbows, shells, and spaghetti.

Quinoa
This recently rediscovered, very nutritious grain is used to make a wide gamut of pastas and noodles including flats, elbows, and pagodas.

Sesame rice
Sesame rice noodles are usually made from 80% whole wheat flour and 10% each rice flour and sesame flour, creating a nutty-tasting noodle.

Soy
Soy noodles contain mostly whole wheat flour with about 10-20% soy flour added. This makes for a high-protein pasta.

Spelt
Another recently revived ancient grain, spelt, proves to be excellent for making noodles and pasta.

Vegetable
Vegetable pastas are made from a combination of whole or refined wheat and vegetable flours. Shop for the whole wheat variety. Spinach is the most common; beet, carrot and tomato paste are also used. Vegetable pastas come in a variety of popular shapes.

Whole wheat
Spaghetti, lasagna, fettucine, alphabets, and elbows can all be found made from hearty whole wheat. Brands vary, find one that cooks up light, not tough.

Cooking Whole Grain Noodles & Pasta

Choose 8 ounces of any whole grain pasta
½-1 teaspoon sea salt
Drop of extra-virgin olive oil

Choose a pot large enough to give the noodles plenty of room to dance, an 8-quart pot works well. Fill pot with water and bring to a boil. Add salt and oil. Drop the noodles in slowly. To prevent sticking, stir the noodles gently with a wooden spoon for the first few minutes. Follow package directions for cooking time. Udon noodles take about 7-8 minutes, while whole wheat noodles can take as long as 12-15 minutes to cook. Whole grain noodles generally take a bit longer than white noodles. Test noodles for doneness by eating one. You are aiming for a tender, yet firm noodle that is chewy. Put cooked noodles in a colander and rinse well. Let them drain well, as excess moisture can lead to mushiness. Toss with a little oil if not serving right away to prevent stickiness.

Eight ounces of uncooked noodles will usually serve four people.

FOR BABIES 10 MONTHS & OLDER
Try one of the non-wheat pastas. Use small, well-cooked pasta as a finger food for babies who have some teeth. Cut long noodles into bite-size pieces.

General Notes on Cooking Beans

Selecting which beans to cook

Buy beans at a store that has a rapid turnover of dried beans and use them within a few months. Sort through beans bought in bulk and pick out any stones or foreign bits before soaking. Smaller beans, such as peas and lentils, do not require soaking. Bigger beans benefit from being soaked. Soaking reduces cooking time and aids digestibility. Since bigger beans require a little extra thought and time, make a double recipe and freeze half for a busy day. Below are lists of favorite small and big beans.

Small Beans/No-Soak Beans

green or brown lentils
red lentils
green or yellow split peas
black-eyed peas
mung beans
azuki beans

Big Beans/Soaking Required

chick-peas (garbanzos)
pinto beans
black beans
lima beans
navy beans
kidney beans
great northern beans
Swedish brown beans
cannelloni beans
Christmas limas

Helpful hints

If your beans are older than six months, they will take much longer to cook until tender. A tender bean is one that you can mash on the roof of your mouth with your tongue. Pressure cooking is my favorite way to cook beans. It gives the beans a creamy texture, deep flavor, and the cooking time is reduced.

Always salt beans at the **end** of cooking time. Salting toughens the outer layer and if you salt the beans early you will have tough beans. Beans need a lot of salt to bring up the flavor. For 1 cup dry beans, add at least 1 teaspoon of salt after they are cooked.

If you want beans for salads, cook by simmering rather than pressure-cooking and salt them when they reach the stage you want. Salting them keeps the outer layer from becoming soft and mushy.

Buying canned, cooked beans is fine when you're in a hurry. Be sure to read labels carefully. Choose organic products and products that don't contain unwanted ingredients such as preservatives, MSG, or high amounts of sodium. Cooking your own beans is much less expensive than buying canned beans and the taste is fresher. Flavorings such as garlic, chilies, and onion are more deeply absorbed if added during cooking. Remember that you can cook a big batch of beans and freeze part for another day, another recipe.

Basic Small Beans

(no soaking)

Green or brown lentils, red lentils, green or yellow split peas, black-eyed peas, mung beans, azuki beans can all be considered small beans. I have suggested that beans be cooked with kombu. Kombu is a sea vegetable or seaweed that is purchased dried. It comes in thick, wrinkly, dark green strips. This sea vegetable has a property that tenderizes beans and helps prevent flatulence. The kombu also adds minerals to the beans.

> 2 cups small dried beans
> 4-5 cups water
> 2- to 3-inch strip of kombu, soaked in water 5 minutes
> 2 teaspoons sea salt

Rinse and drain the beans. Place beans, water and kombu in a 3- or 4-quart pot; bring to a boil. Reduce heat, cover, and simmer. Most of these smaller beans take 45-50 minutes to cook, with the exception of azuki beans (which take an hour) and red lentils (which cook in 20-25 minutes). Don't salt the beans until the end of cooking time.

Preparation time: 30-50 minutes
6 cups of cooked beans

FOR BABIES 10 MONTHS & OLDER
Puree a small amount of cooked beans with water and serve as a thick soup.

Basic Big Beans

(soaking required)

Chick-peas (garbanzos), pinto, black, lima, navy, kidney, great northern, Swedish brown, cannelloni, Christmas limas are some favorite varieties of big beans. See Basic Small Beans (page 69) for an explanation of why kombu is added. Kombu can be found in natural foods stores in the macrobiotic section.

How to soak beans

Place beans in a large bowl. Cover with twice as much water as beans (i.e., for 2 cups beans use 4 cups water) and let stand 8 hours or overnight. Rinse off the soaking water and cook beans according to recipe.

You can also quick-soak beans by bringing the same proportion of beans and water to a boil, turning heat off and letting beans soak for 2 hours. Drain off the soaking water and cook beans according to recipe.

Simmered Beans

> 2 cups dried beans, soaked
> 6 cups water
> 3-inch piece of kombu, soaked 5 minutes in cold water
> 1 teaspoon sea salt

Drain off soaking water. Put soaked beans, fresh water and kombu in a pot; bring to a boil. Lower hear and let simmer, covered, until beans are quite tender (55-60 minutes). A well-cooked bean can be easily mashed on the roof of the mouth with the tongue. Add water during cooking if needed. Salt beans at the end of the cooking time.

Preparation time: 60 minutes
6 cups cooked beans

Pressure-Cooked Beans
  2 cups dried beans, soaked
  4 cups water
  3-inch piece of kombu, soaked 5 minutes in cold water
  1 teaspoon sea salt

Drain off soaking water. Put soaked beans, fresh water and kombu in pressure cooker. Attach lid. Bring up to pressure on medium heat. You should hear a soft hissing sound. Lower heat and let beans cook 40-45 minutes. Remove from heat and allow pressure to come down naturally or run cold water over the top of the cooker. Add salt after cooking.

Preparation time: 45-50 minutes
6 cups cooked beans

Slow-cooked beans

Using an electric slow-cooker allows you to sleep or work while your beans cook. Soak beans overnight or by quick-soak method. Drain off soaking water, then follow directions that apply to your slow-cooker. This typically requires 8 hours on "high." A thick folded towel placed on the lid of your slow-cooker helps conserve heat.

Preparation time: 8 hours
Two cups dried beans makes about 6 cups cooked beans

FOR BABIES 10 MONTHS & OLDER
Use a few well-cooked beans as a finger food.

Leftover Beans? Use them to make:
Santa Fe Black Bean Salad (page 96)
Dilled Brown Rice and Kidney Beans (page 97)
Filling for Savory Sandwiches to Go (page 116)
Grain and Bean Roll-Ups (page 119)
White Beans and Fresh Herbs Soup (page 136)
Dark Beans and Sensuous Spices Soup (page 137)
Three Sisters Stew (page 142)
Mexican Bean and Corn Casserole (page 152)
Black Bean Tostados (page 156)
Garnish for salad
Bean Apple Rye Bread (page 199)

Reducing Flatulence Caused by Eating Beans

Oligosaccharides (sugar molecules) in beans are responsible for producing gases. Sometimes human digestive enzymes do not easily handle oligosaccharides which can leave the small intestines unchanged and move to the lower intestines. In the process, various gases, primarily carbon dioxide, are produced as waste products. Both cooking in water and sprouting decrease the amount of oligosaccharides. Here are tips on reducing the likelihood of flatulence.

1. Soak beans overnight and replace the soaking water with fresh water for cooking.

2. Cook beans with a piece of kombu seaweed. Kombu contains glutamic acid which acts as a natural bean tenderizer. The kombu also adds vitamins and minerals, especially trace minerals, to any dish it is cooked with.

3. Two tablespoons of the herb winter savory or four tablespoons of the Mexican herb epazote added to beans as they cook will reduce the effects of raffinose sugars. Other seasonings that help are cumin, fennel, and ginger.

4. Let beans cook slowly for a long period of time so they are very tender. Can you easily mash the bean on the roof of your mouth?

5. Don't add baking soda to soaking water. It destroys nutrients and affects the flavor and texture.

6. Par-boil beans as a pretreatment. Bring to boil, scoop off and discard foam which accumulates on top before continuing cooking.

7. Use a salt seasoning — sea salt, miso, soy sauce — at the end of cooking time.

8. Eat more beans. You can expect a digestive adjustment when beans are new to the diet. Eat small amounts frequently to allow the body to get used to digesting them.

9. Improve your overall digestion. Chew foods slowly and thoroughly. Avoid washing foods down with liquids. Eat fewer kinds of foods at the same meal. Drink plenty of water between meals.

10. For persistent gas — try pouring a little apple cider vinegar or brown rice vinegar into the cooking liquid during the last stages of cooking. Vinegar softens legumes and breaks down the protein chains and other indigestible compounds. Another option is to marinate the cooked beans in a solution of $^2/_3$ vinegar and $^1/_3$ olive oil, creating a salad-type dish. Marinate while still warm.

Bustling Breakfasts

Whole Grain Baby Cereal

*Making your own baby cereal is nutritious, economical and quite delicious. The grains listed below were chosen because they are the least allergenic and the easiest to digest. Toasting the grains enhances the digestibility and flavor. To make your baby's cereal "iron-fortified" add ¼ teaspoon of dulse flakes to the cooked cereal. Dulse is a sea vegetable that is very high in iron. I don't like calling this "baby cereal" because this cereal is for **everyone**!*

Choose one:
> 1 cup short-grain brown rice
> 1 cup millet
> 1 cup quinoa
> 1 cup sweet brown rice

Toast grain

Place grains in a fine strainer; rinse and drain.

Oven toasting Preheat oven to 350° F. Spread grains on cookie sheet and toast in oven until they give off a nutty aroma (12-15 minutes).

Skillet toasting Place washed grains in large skillet on burner and toast on medium heat, stirring constantly, until grains give off nutty aroma (about 5-8 minutes).

Let toasted grains cool and then store in sealed container. You can toast a big batch of several different grains at one time and store them in separate jars. This will keep baby and all full of wholesome cereal for many moons.

Grind grain

For optimum nutrition, grind the grains in a small electric grinder or food processor just prior to using. Once a grain is ground it begins to lose nutritional value within 24-48 hours. Store the whole toasted grains in labeled, sealed containers and grind the amount you need before cooking.

Cook ground grains into cereal

Baby-size portion of cereal: Mix together 2-3 tablespoons of ground cereal and ½-¾ cups water and a pinch of salt in a small pot; bring it to a boil. Reduce heat to low and simmer, covered, for 5 minutes.

Family-size portion of cereal: For four adult/child-size servings, use 1 cup ground grains, 3-4 cups water and 1 teaspoon salt. Combine cereal, water and salt in a pot; bring to a boil. Reduce heat to low and simmer, covered, for 10-12 minutes. A flame-tamer or heat deflector used while simmering will help prevent scorching or sticking.

Preparation time: 8-15 minutes for toasting, 5-12 minutes to cook cereal
Makes 1 cup toasted grains cook into 4 adult-size portions of cereal

Ancient Grain Raisin Cereal

I like this recipe because there is no wheat, a grain we tend to overdo. There are several interesting whole grains used here. Amaranth, which was grown by the Aztecs, has a very good nutritional profile — high in protein and calcium. The flavor is similar to graham crackers without the sweetness. The grain looks like tiny yellow, brown and black seeds. To find out more about the other grains used in this cereal, see "Identifying, Shopping, and Storing Whole Foods" (page 252).

To make toasted cereal mix
> 1 cup hulled barley
> 1 cup millet
> ½ cup sesame seeds
> 1 cup whole oats
> 1 cup polenta
> 1 cup amaranth

Place barley, millet, sesame seeds, and oats in fine strainer; rinse with water and drain. Combine with polenta and amaranth and toast cereal in one of two ways.

Oven toasting: Preheat oven to 350° F. Spread grains on cookie sheet and toast in oven until they give off a nutty aroma (12-15 minutes).

Skillet toasting: Place washed grains in large skillet on burner and toast on medium heat, stirring constantly, until grains give off nutty aroma (about 5-8 minutes). Let toasted grains cool. Store in a sealed container.

To make cooked cereal
> 1 cup toasted cereal mix
> ¹/₃ cup raisins
> 3 cups water
> Pinch of sea salt

Grind toasted grains in a small electric grinder or food processor. Combine ground cereal, water, raisins and salt in a small pan. Stir constantly as you bring to boil. Turn heat to low, cover and simmer (10-15 minutes). Stir frequently to prevent sticking.

Preparation time: 15-20 minutes for toasting, 15 minutes to cook cereal
Makes 5½ cups dry cereal mix. 1 cup dry mix makes 4 servings cooked cereal

FOR BABIES 6 MONTHS & OLDER
Toast a cup of millet separately and use the toasted millet to make Whole Grain Baby Cereal (see page 74).

5-Grain Morning Cereal

I keep a canister of these toasted grains and in the morning, I grind a cup of dry grains and cook the freshly ground grains into this nutritious cereal. To find out more about the grains used in this cereal, see "Identifying, Shopping, and Storing Whole Foods" (page 252).

To make toasted cereal mix
> 1 cup wheat berries
> 1 cup millet
> 1 cup spelt
> 1 cup brown rice
> 1 cup quinoa

Place all grains in a fine strainer; rinse and drain. Toast grains in one of two ways.

Oven toasting: Preheat oven to 350° F. Spread grains on cookie sheet and toast in oven until they give off a nutty aroma (12-15 minutes).

Skillet toasting: Place washed grains in large skillet on burner and toast on medium heat, stirring constantly, until grains give off nutty aroma (about 5-8 minutes). Let toasted grains cool and store in sealed container.

To make cooked cereal
> 1 cup toasted cereal mix
> 3 cups water
> Pinch of sea salt

Grind toasted cereal mix in small electric grinder. Combine ground cereal, water, and salt in a small pan. Stir constantly and bring to boil. Turn heat to low, cover, and simmer 10-15 minutes. Stir occasionally to prevent sticking.

Preparation time: 15 minutes for toasting, 15-20 minutes to cook cereal
Makes 5 cups dry cereal mix; 1 cup dry mix makes 4 servings cooked cereal

FOR BABIES 6 MONTHS & OLDER
Toast a cup of brown rice or quinoa separately and use the toasted grain to make Whole Grain Baby Cereal (see page 74).

Steel-Cut Oats
with Dates and Cinnamon

Steel-Cut oats are whole oats that have been thinly sliced into pieces. They are different than rolled oats which are oats that have been heated until soft and pressed flat. Steel-cut oats, sometimes called Irish oatmeal, have a heartier flavor and a chewier texture than rolled oats. I like to eat oat cereal with sliced apples, Tamari-Roasted Almonds (page 114) and a dollop of maple yogurt on top.

> 1 cup steel-cut oats
> 3 cups water
> 4 pitted dates, cut in small pieces
> ½ teaspoon cinnamon
> ⅛ teaspoon sea salt

Place ingredients in medium-size pan and stir briefly; bring to boil. Reduce heat to low, cover, and simmer for 20-25 minutes.

Preparation time: 25 minutes
Makes 4-6 servings

FOR BABIES 10 MONTHS & OLDER
Puree cooked cereal briefly before serving.

Sunny Millet with Peaches

One summer day for breakfast, we added ripe peaches to millet and the combination became a favorite. As the season of fresh fruit unfolds, try apricots, pears, or plums. Yum!

¾ cup millet
1 peach, sliced (or other seasonal fruit)
2 cups water
Pinch of sea salt

Topping
Unsweetened apple butter

Place millet in fine strainer; rinse and drain. Combine millet, fruit, water, and salt in a two-quart saucepan; bring to boil. Cover and simmer on low for 20-25 minutes (until all water is absorbed). Serve in bowls with dollops of apple butter on top.

Preparation time: 30 minutes
Makes 4 servings

FOR BABIES 6 MONTHS & OLDER
Remove some cooked millet, puree and serve.

Orange-Millet with Currants
Substitute 1 cup orange juice for 1 cup water and use ¼ cup currants instead of peach.

Orange Hazelnut Muesli

Muesli is handy for camping trips and hurried breakfasts. Preparing rolled oats this way gives them a slightly different texture you'll enjoy.

> 2 cups boiling water
> 2 cups rolled oats or rolled barley (or some of both)
> $^1/_3$ cup hazelnuts, chopped
> $^1/_3$ cup raisins
> $^1/_2$ teaspoon cinnamon
> Juice of 2 oranges

Optional toppings
> Grated apple
> Sliced pears
> Dollop of plain yogurt

Place grain, nuts, raisins, and cinnamon in mixing bowl. Pour boiling water over mixture and stir. Juice oranges; add juice to mixture and stir again. Cover bowl with plate or cloth and allow moisture to soften grains overnight. Serve topped with apple, pear, and/or yogurt.

Preparation time: 10 minutes (excluding overnight)
Makes 4 servings

FOR BABIES 6 MONTHS & OLDER
Steam some apple or pear slices until soft. Puree and serve.

VARIATION FOR CHILDREN
Some may prefer a plainer muesli. Omit nuts and raisins, and let others who enjoy them add them as toppings in the morning.

Nut and Seed Granola

To keep granola within the realm of a "low-fat" diet, use it as a topping on hot cereal, fresh fruit, or puddings. Homemade granola makes a quick snack for children on the move.

3 cups rolled oats
½ cup sesame seeds
½ cup sunflower seeds
½ cup pumpkin seeds
½ cup almonds, chopped
1 cup whole wheat pastry flour
½ teaspoon cinnamon
Pinch sea salt
⅓ cup cold-pressed vegetable oil
⅓ cup brown rice syrup or maple syrup
¼ cup apple or orange juice
1 teaspoon vanilla
¼ teaspoon almond extract

Preheat oven to 300° F. In a large mixing bowl, combine oats, seeds, almonds, flour, cinnamon and salt; mix well. In a separate bowl, combine oil, syrup, juice, and extracts. Slowly pour wet ingredients over dry ingredients, using a spatula to fold and evenly coat the dry mixture with the wet. Spread on cookie sheet or in a shallow pan and bake. Turn granola every 15 or 20 minutes so that it toasts evenly. Bake until granola is dry and golden (45-60 minutes). Store in airtight jar.

Preparation time: 70 minutes
Makes 8 cups

FOR BABIES 10 MONTHS & OLDER
Use some of the rolled oats to make your baby a bowl of warm oatmeal. See page 62 for directions.

Kasha Breakfast Pilaf

The versatile kasha (roasted buckwheat) need not be reserved for dinner. A Ukrainian restaurant I went to on New York's Lower East Side serves kasha and eggs to large breakfast crowds. This hearty breakfast is a favorite of mine during the chilly winter months. To learn more about kasha, ghee, or tahini, see "Identifying, Shopping, and Storing Whole Foods" (page 252).

2 teaspoons unrefined sesame oil or ghee
1 small onion, chopped
1 clove garlic, minced
Pinch of sea salt
2 cups boiling water
1 cup kasha
¼ cup chopped parsley

Optional toppings
Tamari or shoyu
Tahini

Heat oil in a 2-quart pan or a 10-inch skillet. Add onions, garlic, and salt; sauté until onion is soft. Add kasha to onion mixture and stir well. Add boiling water, reduce heat to low, cover, and allow to set for 15 minutes. Remove lid, add parsley, and fluff before serving. Top each serving with a small bit of tamari and/or tahini if desired.

Preparation time: 20 minutes
Makes 4-6 servings

FOR BABIES 10 MONTHS & OLDER

Puree some of the cooked kasha with a little water and serve.

Jam-Filled Mochi

Mochi is made from sweet brown rice that has been cooked, pounded into a paste, and then compressed into dense bars. When broken into squares and baked, it puffs up like a cream puff and gets gooey inside. Mochi comes plain or in several flavors; cinnamon-raisin mochi is the breakfast favorite at our home. Look for mochi in the refrigerated or freezer section of your natural foods store. Sweet brown rice is an excellent food for nursing moms. Children love this warm chewy breakfast treat.

1 block mochi
All-fruit jam or preserves (your favorite flavor)

Preheat oven to 400° F. Break mochi into squares. The block is usually scored so that it can be broken easily into 2-by-2-inch squares. Place squares on a lightly oiled cookie sheet and put in oven. Bake until mochi puffs up (10-12 minutes). Remove from oven. Open each square and slip a teaspoon or two of jam inside. Serve immediately.

Preparation time: 15 minutes
Makes 6 mochi squares

FOR BABIES 6 MONTHS & OLDER
Mochi is a little too sticky and chewy for a mouth with few teeth. Make some baby cereal out of sweet brown rice (See Whole Grain Baby Cereal, page 74) so you can both benefit from this unique type of rice.

Essene Bread and Fresh Fruit

The Essenes were a sect of monks from early Biblical times who prepared a sweet, moist, flourless bread by slow-baking sprouted wheat. Look for Essene bread in the refrigerated or frozen food section at your natural foods store. One of my favorite warm-weather breakfasts is a thick slice of Essene bread warmed in the oven and served with a bowl of fresh fruit.

> **4 one-inch slices of Essene bread**
> **4-6 cups fresh, seasonal fruit (blueberries, strawberries, peaches...)**

Heat oven to 300° F. Place bread slices on cookie sheet and warm oven for 5-10 minutes. Serve warm bread with bowl of fresh fruit.

Preparation time: 12-15 minutes
Makes 4 servings

FOR BABIES 6 MONTHS & OLDER
Puree some fresh peaches or blueberries with a little water and serve.

FOR BABIES 10 MONTHS & OLDER
Serve as is.

Warming Miso Soup
with Gingerroot

People often don't think of having soup for breakfast, but this soup is nutritious, energizing, and a great way to "break fast." Miso is a salty paste made from cooked and aged soybeans. The soybeans are mixed with various grains and other ingredients to produce different flavors. Fresh gingerroot helps stimulate the digestive system and has a warming effect on the body.

> 4-inch piece of wakame
> 6 cups water
> 1 tablespoon grated gingerroot
> ¼ pound firm tofu, cut in cubes
> 4 tablespoons light or mellow unpastuerized miso

Garnish
> 2 scallions, thinly sliced

Place wakame in small bowl of water and soak for 5 minutes. Put 6 cups water in 3-quart pot and bring to a simmer. Remove wakame from water and chop into small pieces removing the spine. Add chopped wakame to water. Simmer 10 minutes, adding gingerroot and tofu cubes in the last minute or two of cooking time. Pour a bit of broth into each serving bowl and dissolve 1 tablespoon of miso into each bowl. Fill bowl with soup, and stir gently. Garnish each bowl with scallions.

Preparation time: 15 minutes
Makes 4 servings

FOR BABIES 10 MONTHS & OLDER
Remove a little of the cooked wakame from the soup. Chop very fine and add to pureed cereal or vegetables you are serving to baby. Adds extra calcium and other minerals.

Goldie's Whole Grain Pancake Mix

This basic pancake mix comes from Goldie Caughlan, Nutrition Educator at Puget Consumers Co-op in Seattle. There are many types of whole grain flours besides wheat that can be used to make baked goods. This recipe utilizes a combination of several. One perk of this mix is that it works equally well for waffles.

Dry pancake mix

> 2 cups barley flour or kamut flour
> 2 cups whole wheat pastry flour
> 1 cup buckwheat flour
> 1 cup blue cornmeal
> 3 tablespoons baking powder
> 1 teaspoon cinnamon

Combine all ingredients and store in an airtight container.

Makes 6 cups dry mix

Buttermilk Banana Pancakes

Buttermilk is a cultured dairy product that is easy to digest and actually quite low in fat! It adds a rich flavor to pancakes. For a dairy-free version substitute soy milk with 1 tablespoon lemon juice added to it.

1 egg
1½ cup dry whole-grain pancake mix
1 cup buttermilk
½ cup water
1 ripe banana
oil for griddle

Separate egg; pour egg white in one bowl and yolk in another. Beat egg white until stiff peaks form. Set aside. In a large bowl, combine egg yolk, dry mix, buttermilk, and water. Mix thoroughly with a whisk. Cut banana into thin slices. Add egg white and bananas to batter and gently fold in.

Heat griddle to medium-high and coat surface with small amount of oil. Pour enough batter onto griddle to form a 5-inch diameter pancake. When pancake has cooked on the bottom, flip with a spatula and cook the other side. Keep cooked pancakes in a warm oven until ready to serve.

Preparation time: 25-30 minutes
Makes 10 five-inch pancakes

FOR BABIES 6 MONTHS AND OLDER
Reserve some ripe banana. Mash and serve.

VARIATION FOR CHILDREN
Put batter in a squeeze bottle and squeeze batter onto griddle in shapes of initials, age of child, animals...

Blueberry Sauce

This topping tastes great on pancakes, waffles, or hot cereal and also makes a beautiful finishing touch to Tofu Cheesecake (page 234). I have used kudzu as a thickener. Kudzu comes from the dried root of the kudzu plant. It gives thickened liquids a glossy sheen and is thought to be soothing to the digestive track. You can substitute 2 tablespoons of arrowroot for one table-spoon of kudzu.

> 2 tablespoons kudzu
> 1 cup fruit juice (apple or berry)
> 1 cup blueberries (fresh or frozen)
> 2 tablespoons concentrated fruit sweetener
> 1 teaspoon freshly squeezed lemon juice

Dissolve kudzu in fruit juice. Combine kudzu-juice mixture with blueberries and sweetener in small saucepan. Bring mixture to a simmer, stirring constantly. Cook for about 3 minutes, until mixture turns clear and purple. Remove from heat, stir in lemon juice and serve immediately.

Preparation time: 10 minutes
Makes 2 cups

FOR BABIES 6 MONTHS & OLDER
Reserve some fresh blueberries, puree with a little water and serve.

Tofu Vegetable Breakfast Burrito

This colorful dish makes a hearty Sunday breakfast. Any vegetables can be substituted for the ones listed; this combination is scrumptious. Serve with a fresh fruit salad for brunch. Also works as a yummy, well-balanced dinner served with a fresh green salad.

2-3 teaspoons extra-virgin olive oil
½ medium onion, chopped
2 cloves garlic, minced
½ red pepper, chopped
½ green pepper, chopped
1 teaspoon cumin
½ teaspoon coriander
1 pound firm tofu, crumbled
1 teaspoon turmeric
2-3 small potatoes, baked and chopped into chunks
1 tablespoon tamari or shoyu
¼ cup chopped cilantro
6 whole wheat tortillas
salsa

Heat oil in a 10-inch skillet on medium heat. Add onions and garlic and sauté. Add peppers, cumin, and coriander and continue to sauté until vegetables are soft. Crumble tofu into skillet with vegetables and stir. Sprinkle in turmeric and mix. Add chopped potatoes, tamari and cilantro and stir. Place about ⅓ cup of the filling mixture in a whole wheat tortilla, roll it up and top with salsa. Serve warm.

Preparation time: 15-20 minutes
Makes 6 servings

FOR BABIES 6 MONTHS & OLDER
Reserve a few pieces of the baked potato. Puree with a little water, warm and serve.

FOR BABIES 10 MONTHS & OLDER
Reserve extra tofu, cut fresh tofu into cubes and serve.

Healthy Home Fries

Just about everybody loves fried spuds. By steaming the potatoes first, you minimize the amount of oil needed. I like to serve these alongside pancakes for a stick-with-you breakfast to begin an active day. I also pack these in my child's lunchbox!

6 small red potatoes
2-3 teaspoons extra-virgin olive oil
1 onion, chopped
¼ teaspoon sea salt
Fresh-ground pepper

Scrub potatoes and slice into ¼-inch rounds. Place in steamer basket and steam 7-10 minutes, until tender. Heat oil in a large skillet. Add onion and sauté until soft. Add steamed potatoes. Flip potatoes occasionally until browned on all sides. Season with salt and pepper and serve immediately.

Preparation time: 25-30 minutes
Makes 4 servings

FOR BABIES 6 MONTHS & OLDER

Reserve plain boiled or baked potatoes and blend or mash with breast milk or water.

Tempeh Bacon

Tempeh, originally an Indonesian food, is made from soybeans that have been cooked and split to remove the hull. A culture is added to the cooked beans, which age for several days before forming into a solid piece which can be cut and sliced. This high-protein food can be baked, boiled, fried, or steamed. When fried and seasoned, this tasty meat-like substance can be used to accompany pancakes or turned into a vegetarian "TLT" sandwich.

> ¼ cup high-oleic safflower oil
> 1 8-ounce package tempeh, cut into ¼" strips
> ½ teaspoon each: oregano, thyme, and basil
> 1 tablespoon tamari or shoyu

Heat 10-inch skillet, add 2 tablespoons oil and then ½ of the tempeh strips. Let them quick-fry, about 30 seconds on each side. Sprinkle half of herbs over tempeh as it fries. Remove tempeh and place on a paper towel. Repeat process with remaining oil, tempeh and herbs. When finished, sprinkle fried tempeh with tamari and serve.

Preparation time: 7-10 minutes
Makes 4-6 servings

FOR BABIES 6 MONTHS & OLDER
Include some fresh melon with this breakfast. For baby simply give a few chunks of melon a quick whir in the blender. If the melon is quite ripe, babies with teeth can eat chunks as finger food.

Commercial Breakfast Cereals

Quite a variety of organic, whole-grain, fruit-sweetened cereals are available today. Many resemble the familiar sugary, refined cereals of the '50s. Read the list of ingredients on cereal boxes. Find products that match your criteria for a wholesome breakfast. Ask your local grocer to stock cereals you wish to buy regularly.

Various milks to put on cereal

Many people use cow's milk, but there are alternatives that most natural foods stores and some traditional grocery stores carry. Soy milks, amasake, White Almond beverage, and Rice Dream beverage can be found on the shelf in aseptic packages which are to be refrigerated after opening. Goat milk is usually kept with dairy products in the refrigerated section. Nut milk can be made at home.

• Amasake, a creamy drink made from sweet brown rice

• Goat's milk

• Nut milk (page 248)

• Oat milk

• Rice Dream, a non-dairy beverage made from brown rice and water

• Soy milk or Soy beverage (Edensoy and Westsoy are popular commercial names); soy milks come plain, flavored, "lite" (low fat) and "plus" or "extra" (added nutrients)

• White Almond Beverage, a non-dairy beverage made from water, almonds, and brown rice syrup

over the river and through the woods

Lively
Lunchboxes

Karen's Sesame Noodles

My daughter's godmother, Karen Brown, always made these for our potlucks in New York, and they were the first entree to disappear. Udon or soba noodles work well in this dish. Tahini is a creamy paste made of crushed, hulled sesame seeds. Different nut and seed butters can be interchanged in this recipe to vary the flavor.

Noodles
> 8 ounces whole grain noodles

Sauce
> 3 tablespoons tahini
>
> 1 tablespoon almond or cashew butter
>
> 1 teaspoon maple syrup
>
> 2 tablespoons brown rice vinegar
>
> 2 tablespoons tamari or shoyu
>
> 1 teaspoon toasted sesame oil
>
> 1 tablespoon water, or to desired consistency

Cook noodles in plenty of boiling water according to directions on package. While noodles cook, put ingredients for sauce in small bowl and blend until creamy. Rinse and drain cooked noodles. Pour sauce over noodles and toss well.

Preparation time: 15 minutes
Makes 4 servings

FOR BABIES 10 MONTHS & OLDER
Omit sauce. Cut plain noodles into bite-size pieces and serve.

VARIATION FOR CHILDREN
Try serving the sauce on the side and letting children dip the noodles in the sauce.

Confetti Rice Salad

This whole grain salad looks beautiful. Brightly colored vegetables lend eye appeal and the vinaigrette integrates the fresh flavors. Serve with a bean soup, such as Dark Bean Soup with Sensuous Spices (page 137), for a well-balanced meal.

Salad

4 cups cooked brown rice
1 cup red pepper, chopped
1 carrot, grated or chopped
2 tablespoons fresh chives or 1 scallion, finely chopped
1 cup chopped red cabbage
1 cup chopped parsley or ½ parsley/½ cilantro
⅓ cup sunflower seeds

Dressing

6 tablespoons unrefined sesame oil
4 tablespoons brown rice vinegar
2 teaspoons toasted sesame oil
1 teaspoon tamari

Toss brown rice with chopped vegetables and sunflower seeds until evenly mixed. Pour vinaigrette ingredients in a bottle or jar; shake vigorously. Drizzle dressing on rice and vegetables; toss gently.

Preparation time: 10 minutes if rice already cooked
Makes 8 servings

FOR BABIES 6 MONTHS & OLDER

Reserve some of the cooked brown rice and a few tablespoons of water. Blend all ingredients in a blender for a fine cereal. Steaming an extra carrot and pureeing it with a little water and parsley is another option.

VARIATION FOR CHILDREN

Reserve some cooked rice and cut-up vegetables; serve separately omitting the vinaigrette.

Santa Fe Black Bean Salad

A delicious combination of Southwestern flavors, perfect for a potluck, lunchbox entree or a summer meal. Serve with corn tortillas or Polenta (page 63) and Mustard Green Salad (page 182) for a lively, well-balanced meal.

Salad

> 1 red pepper, roasted, peeled, and cut into small strips
> 2 cups cooked black beans
> ½ cup cooked corn
> ⅓ cup chopped cilantro

Dressing

> 2-3 cloves garlic minced with ½ teaspoon sea salt
> 2 tablespoons extra-virgin olive oil
> 2 tablespoons lime juice
> ¼ teaspoon cayenne

To roast red peppers

For gas stove: Place pepper directly on the low flame of a gas burner, letting skin char. Keep turning pepper until skin is charred on all sides. Let cool, remove black char under cool running water. Cut pepper open and remove seeds and stem.

For an electric range: Place red pepper in shallow pan and put in oven under the broiler. Let the skin char. Turn pepper every few minutes until skin is completely charred. Remove pepper from oven and place in brown paper bag. Close bag and let pepper sweat for 15-30 minutes. Remove pepper and peel off charred skin under cool, running water. Cut pepper open and remove seeds and stem.

To make salad

Combine strips of roasted red pepper, beans, corn, and cilantro in medium-size mixing bowl; set aside. Place garlic and salt on a cutting board; chop to a paste-like consistency. In a separate small bowl, mix together garlic paste, oil, lime juice, and cayenne. Pour dressing over beans and vegetables; toss gently.

Preparation time: 20 minutes
Makes 3 cups or 6 servings

FOR BABIES 10 MONTHS & OLDER
Reserve some plain cooked black beans and corn and puree together.

Dilled Brown Rice and Kidney Beans

A wonderful summer salad that can be used for picnics, potlucks or a cold supper. Dill and red onion give the grain-and-bean combination a genuine zip. Umeboshi plum vinegar, the leftover juice from the umeboshi plum-pickling process, gives a unique salty-sour taste to food. This recipe is incentive for keeping already-cooked brown rice and beans on hand.

Salad
>   2 cups cooked brown rice
>   1½ cups cooked kidney beans
>   ½ cup red onion, chopped

Dressing
>   3 tablespoons extra-virgin olive oil
>   3 tablespoons brown rice vinegar
>   1 tablespoon umeboshi plum vinegar
>   2 tablespoons fresh dill (or 2 teaspoons dried)

Mix oil, vinegars, and dill with whisk or shake in small jar. Pour dressing over rice, onion, and beans; toss gently. If possible, let set an hour or two as flavors mellow with time.

Preparation time: 10 minutes if rice already cooked
Makes 4 servings

FOR BABIES 6 MONTHS & OLDER
Reserve some of the cooked brown rice and blend with water or breast milk.

FOR BABIES 10 MONTHS & OLDER
Reserve some plain cooked kidney beans and plain rice and blend to desired consistency; add water if necessary.

Lemon Basil Potato Salad

Fresh basil makes an impressive contribution to the flavor of soups, vegetables, noodles, beans, and fish. Try growing basil in your yard or in your kitchen window. This is a not-just-for-lunch kind of salad. Try serving it with Dr. Bruce's Awesome Grilled Salmon (page 167) for your next summer dinner party.

Salad
>   6-8 cups cubed red potatoes

Dressing
>   3-4 cloves garlic
>   1/3 cup tightly packed fresh basil
>   ½ teaspoon sea salt
>   1 teaspoon lemon zest
>   3-4 tablespoons extra-virgin olive oil
>   3-4 tablespoons freshly squeezed lemon juice

Wash, scrub, and cut potatoes. Place potatoes in large pot of boiling water. Cook 10-12 minutes or until tender. While potatoes are cooking, place garlic, basil, salt, and lemon zest on cutting board. Chop together to a paste-like consistency. Combine paste with oil and lemon juice; set aside. Drain potatoes and let cool. Pour dressing over slightly warm potatoes; toss gently. Serve immediately or chill to serve later.

Preparation time: 20 minutes
Makes 6 servings

FOR BABIES 6 MONTHS & OLDER
Reserve some boiled potatoes and mash with water or breast milk.

Aunt Cathy's Crunchy Ramen Cole Slaw

Ramen is a small block of curly noodles that can be prepared in just min-utes. It is made from a variety of flours and usually comes packaged with a packet of dry seasonings to be used in cooking. Look for ramen made from whole grain flours. This cole slaw uses the noodles dry to create a wonder-ful texture and taste.

Salad

> 3-4 tablespoons toasted sunflower seeds
> 3 cups shredded cabbage
> 3 scallions, finely sliced
> ½ cup grated carrot
> ½ package (single serving size) brown rice ramen

Dressing

> 4 tablespoons extra-virgin olive oil
> 3 tablespoons balsamic vinegar
> Sea salt
> Freshly ground pepper

Toast sunflower seeds by placing in dry skillet on medium heat. Stir or shake constantly until seeds begin to emit a nutty aroma (about 5 minutes). Combine cabbage, scallions, sunflower seeds, and carrot in large mixing bowl. Break block of ramen noodles in half. Using a rolling pin, roll over uncooked noodles to break into small pieces; add to salad. Toss salad with oil and vinegar, add salt and pepper to taste.

Preparation time: 10-15 minutes
Makes 6 servings

FOR BABIES 10 MONTHS & OLDER
Cook unused half of ramen noodles according to package directions. Cut into small pieces and serve plain.

Hiziki Pate

Hiziki, of all the sea vegetables, is the richest in calcium. Its thick, black strands have a firm texture and look striking with other colors. The strong "sea" taste can be moderated by cooking hiziki in apple juice and by combining it with other vegetables. A very creative friend, Mim Collins, and her teacher, Roberta Lewis, came up with this scrumptious way to use hiziki. I have seen 2-year-olds, as well adults, gobble it up with glee.

1 cup hiziki, dry
1-1½ cups water or apple juice
1 tablespoon tamari or shoyu
½ pound firm tofu, crumbled with a fork
¼ cup sesame seeds, toasted, then ground
2 tablespoons white or mellow miso
½ bunch parsley, chopped fine
2 scallions, thinly sliced

Soak hiziki in water for 5 minutes and chop fine. Put hiziki in a medium-size pan and add water or apple juice to cover; bring to simmer. Cover pan and cook until juice is absorbed, about 20 minutes. Toward the end of the cooking time, season hiziki with tamari.

While hiziki is cooking, prepare other ingredients. Sesame seeds can be toasted in a skillet on the stove for 5-8 minutes, then ground. Gently mix tofu, sesame seeds, miso, parsley, and scallions together in a bowl. Let the hiziki cool and then add to the mixture. For a more pureed texture put mixture in food processor and pulse a few times. Serve with whole grain crackers, bread or as a side dish. Will keep 3 days in the refrigerator.

Preparation time: 30-40 minutes
Makes 2½-3 cups

FOR BABIES 10 MONTHS & OLDER
Serve cubes of plain tofu and finely chopped strands of cooked hiziki.

Tempeh Avocado Sushi Rolls

These rolls are beautiful and nutritious for parties, picnics, and lunchboxes. Nori and other seaweed products are available at natural foods stores and Asian markets. Mirin is a versatile cooking wine made from sweet brown rice with a taste similar to sherry, used to give the rice a slightly sweet taste.

  3 cups cooked short-grain rice
  2 tablespoons brown rice vinegar
  2 tablespoons mirin or dry sherry
  4 sheets toasted nori
  2 tablespoons high-oleic safflower oil
  4 ounces tempeh
  1 ripe avocado
  1 carrot

Dipping sauce
  ¼ cup tamari
  1 tablespoon wasabi paste
  1 tablespoon grated daikon (Japanese white radish)
  ¼ cup water

Place cooked rice in a large bowl. Add vinegar and mirin and toss together. It is best to season the rice while it is still warm. Cut tempeh into long thin strips. Heat oil in a skillet. Add tempeh, turning strips until brown on all sides. Remove and place on a paper towel. Cut the avocado into thin slices (you may use only half the avocado). Cut the carrot lengthwise into long thin strips.

Lay nori shiny side down on a bamboo sushi mat. Spread rice mixture onto the nori leaving ½" open on the top and bottom. Place strips of filling lengthwise in the middle of the rice. Lift bamboo rolling mat from edge nearest you and begin to roll, tucking firmly into the center while bending the mat up, taking care not to catch it in the roll. Gently squeeze the roll to make it even. Set the roll aside and repeat the procedure with the remaining nori.

Using a wet, sharp knife, cut the roll into equal pieces using a back and forth sawing motion. Put all ingredients for dipping sauce together in a small attractive bowl. Best if served immediately, but will hold well for several hours.

Preparation time: 30 minutes, if rice pre-cooked
Makes 24 pieces

FOR BABIES 6 MONTHS & OLDER
Reserve some rice before dressing it. Puree rice and a few bits of nori together with water or breast milk and serve. Mashed avocado is also an option.

Tabouli

Traditional tabouli salad makes good lunchbox fare or a quick summer meal and packs well for a picnic or potluck. Serve tabouli with Hummus (page 110) and a fresh green salad. I have used shoyu or tamari for the salty flavor in the dressing. These are naturally brewed soy sauces that contain no chemicals, preservatives, sugar, or MSG. Try making tabouli with quinoa (page 64) instead of bulgar for a new twist.

Salad
>   1 cup whole wheat bulgur
>   1 cup boiling water
>   ⅓ cup finely chopped parsley
>   2 scallions, finely chopped
>   ½ cup cucumber, chopped in small pieces
>   ½ cup tomato, chopped in small bites
>   ¼ cup chopped mint

Dressing
>   ¼ cup freshly squeezed lemon juice
>   3 tablespoons extra-virgin olive oil
>   1 tablespoon tamari or shoyu

Place bulgur in a mixing bowl. Pour boiling water over bulgur, cover, and let stand 15 minutes. Fluff grain with fork. While grain is cooling to room temperature, chop vegetables. Add parsley, scallions, cucumber, tomato and mint to cooled bulgur; toss gently. Blend lemon juice, oil, and tamari with whisk. Pour over bulgur and vegetables; toss again. Serve immediately or store in refrigerator in covered container.

Preparation time: 30 minutes
Makes 4 servings

FOR BABIES 10 MONTHS & OLDER
Reserve some plain bulgur and serve as finger food with chopped cucumber and mint on the side.

VARIATION FOR CHILDREN
Keeping chopped vegetables separate from grain and serving small piles of each may work for those who refuse salads or combinations of foods.

Mad Dog Rice Salad

This incredible dish, created by novelist Jack Kelly, is a nutritionally complete meal in itself because it contains whole grains, beans (tofu), and many vegetables.

Salad

>   3 cups cooked brown rice
>   1 cup fresh or frozen green peas
>   1 cup fresh or frozen baby lima beans
>   2 teaspoons extra-virgin olive oil
>   1 onion, chopped
>   ½ pound tofu, cut in cubes
>   1 carrot, cut in small pieces
>   1 stalk celery, chopped

Dressing

>   2 tablespoons extra-virgin olive oil
>   Juice of ½ lemon
>   1 teaspoon tamari or shoyu
>   1 teaspoon toasted sesame oil
>   1½ teaspoons balsamic vinegar

This salad works best if freshly cooked rice is used. Warm rice absorbs the dressing better, creating a more flavorful dish. If using leftover rice, be sure it is at room temperature before dressing. Mix ingredients for dressing in small bowl or jar; pour over rice. Toss thoroughly; set aside. Bring water to boil in small pan and blanch peas and limas; drain and set aside. Heat oil in skillet and sauté onion until soft but not limp. Prepare tofu. To impart better texture to tofu, drop cubes in pan of boiling water until they rise to the top, then drain. Add peas, limas, onion, tofu, carrot, and celery to dressed rice; toss thoroughly. Serve immediately or cover and refrigerate. Return to room temperature before serving.

Preparation time: 65-75 minutes
Makes 6 cups

FOR BABIES 6 MONTHS & OLDER
Cook extra peas and baby limas and puree in blender.
VARIATION FOR CHILDREN
Serve individual portions of peas, brown rice or tofu cubes.

Asian Noodle Salad
with Toasted Sesame Dressing

I have taught a class called "Whole Foods Salads" many times and Asian Noodle Salad is often the favorite dish. You can create a most impressive summer meal by serving this with Hiziki Pate (page 100) and Luscious Beet Salad (page 180). Nutritionally impressive too!

Salad

> 1 8-ounce package soba noodles
> ¼ cup chopped cilantro leaves
> ¼ cup toasted sesame seeds

Dressing

> 2 tablespoons toasted sesame oil
> 3 tablespoons tamari or shoyu
> 3 tablespoons balsamic vinegar
> 1 tablespoon maple syrup
> 1 tablespoon hot pepper oil

Optional Additions

> Chopped red cabbage
> Cubed tofu
> Finely sliced radishes
> Sliced scallions

Cook soba noodles according to package directions. Drain and rinse in colander. Combine toasted sesame oil, tamari, vinegar, maple syrup, and hot pepper oil in small bowl; whisk together. Place drained noodles in a large bowl. Add dressing, cilantro and sesame seeds; toss gently. Add optional chopped vegetables and toss again.

Preparation time: 20-25 minutes
Makes 4-6 servings

FOR BABIES 10 MONTHS & OLDER

Reserve some plain noodles and cut up into small pieces.

VARIATION FOR CHILDREN

Omit hot pepper oil in dressing. Some children may prefer plain noodles without any dressing and cut-up vegetables on the side.

Quick Lemon & Garlic Quinoa Salad

Quinoa has an excellent nutritional profile (10.5 grams of protein per cup). This unique whole grain, which was the staple food of the Incas, is also rich in calcium and iron. I find myself getting very hungry for this salad. I have used a boiling method, not unlike cooking pasta, for cooking this grain. Quinoa can also be prepared by simmering as described on page 64.

Salad

 1 cup dry quinoa
 8 cups water
 Pinch of sea salt
 ½ cup carrots, chopped
 ⅓ cup parsley, minced
 ¼ cup sunflower seeds

Dressing

 2-3 cloves garlic, minced
 ¼ cup freshly squeezed lemon juice
 2 tablespoons extra-virgin olive oil
 2 tablespoons tamari or shoyu

Rinse quinoa with warm water and drain through a fine strainer. Place quinoa in 3-quart pan and dry-roast on low heat (about 5-8 minutes). Stir grains constantly until they begin to change color and give off a nutty aroma. Bring water to boil in a large pot. Add salt and toasted quinoa to boiling water. Boil for 10-12 minutes. Remove from heat and drain quinoa through a large strainer (in the same way you would prepare pasta).

Prepare dressing and place in a large bowl. Add carrots, seeds, and parsley. Add cooked quinoa and toss well. Serve at room temperature or chilled.

Preparation time: 15-20 minutes
Makes 4 to 6 servings

FOR BABIES 6 MONTHS & OLDER
Reserve some plain cooked quinoa. Puree quinoa with water or breast milk.

Rice Balls Rolled in Sesame Salt

I did a cooking project with elementary children on brown rice and its various uses. To my surprise, they literally licked the bowls when we prepared this simple snack. Rice balls travel well in a lunchbox or backpack and give children the nutritional boost they need to stay on the go.

> ¾ cup brown rice
> ¼ cup sweet brown rice
> 1½ cups water
> Pinch of sea salt
> 1 cup brown sesame seeds
> 1 teaspoon sea salt

To make rice

Boiled rice will not hold together to form balls. It is best to pressure-cook the rice for rice balls. Rinse and drain rice. Place rice, salt and water in the pressure cooker. Close cooker. Place on medium heat and bring up to pressure. When pot is up to pressure, you will hear a gentle, steady hissing sound. Lower heat and time for 35-40 minutes. Remove from heat and allow pressure to come down naturally or by running cold water over the top. Allow rice to cool to room temperature before making rice balls.

To make sesame salt

Rinse seeds and drain through a fine strainer. Put seeds in a skillet (preferably cast iron) on medium heat. Toast seeds, stirring constantly until seeds begin to pop, change color slightly, and give off a toasty aroma. Put toasted seeds and salt in a suribachi (a serrated ceramic mortar) and grind with a pestle or grind seeds and salt together in a blender or food processor. This condiment can be stored in a sealed container and used to flavor many foods (I like it on popcorn).

To make rice balls

Spread about $^1/_3$ cup of the sesame salt on a plate or a shallow baking pan. Moisten hands with water and gather a small handful of cooked rice in your hand. Press your hands around the rice, packing it into small ball about the size of a ping-pong ball. Roll the ball in the sesame salt, covering all sides. Repeat until rice is used up or desired amount is obtained. Rice balls will keep for 5 days in a covered container in the refrigerator.

For added flavor make a tamari-ginger sauce for dipping. Add 1 teaspoon grated ginger to $^1/_4$ cup tamari and $^1/_4$ cup water.

Preparation time: 20 minutes if rice already cooked
Makes 12-15 rice balls. 1 cup sesame salt

FOR BABIES 6 MONTHS & OLDER
Reserve some of the cooked brown rice and blend with water or breast milk to make cereal.

Tempeh Club Sandwiches

Marinated tempeh is very versatile. I especially like this hearty and tasty sandwich with pickles on it. Serve with a simple vegetable soup for an easy-to-prepare meal. To learn more about tempeh or mirin, see "Identifying, Shopping, and Storing Whole Foods" (page 252).

Marinade
>   3 cloves garlic, sliced
>   4-5 slices (1/8-inch thick) of fresh gingerroot
>   1/2 cup water
>   1 tablespoon brown rice vinegar
>   1 tablespoon mirin
>   1/4 cup of tamari or shoyu
>   1 8-ounce package of tempeh
>   1-2 tablespoons high oleic safflower oil
>   8 slices of whole wheat bread

Sandwich fixings
>   lettuce
>   pickle slices
>   sprouts
>   avocado slices
>   tomato slices
>   mustard
>   mayonnaise
>   catsup

To marinate tempeh

In the morning, put all ingredients for marinade in glass container that has a lid that seals. Slice the tempeh block in half. Take each half and cut through the middle to make 4 pieces of tempeh, each slightly smaller than a piece of bread. Put tempeh in the marinade, seal the container, and refrigerate for a minimum of 4 hours.

To make sandwiches

Heat oil in a skillet over medium heat. Remove tempeh pieces from marinade and brown in the skillet for a minute or so on each side. Place on bread with your favorite garnishes.

Preparation time: 5 minutes to make marinade, 5 minutes to make sandwiches
Makes 4 sandwiches

FOR BABIES 6 MONTHS & OLDER
Use ripe avocado. Mash or blend some of the avocado and serve.

Gingered Lentil Sandwich Spread

Gingered lentil sandwich spread tastes scrumptious on whole wheat toast with lettuce, tomato and mayonnaise or wrapped snugly in a whole wheat chappati. Works well as a crackers spread for parties, too.

2 cups cooked lentils
2 tablespoon extra-virgin olive oil
2 teaspoons grated ginger
1 tablespoon whole grain mustard
3 mushrooms, sliced
2 scallions, sliced
½ teaspoon sea salt
¼ cup water

Put cooked lentils and all other ingredients in food processor or blender; blend until smooth. If using a blender, blend ¼ of the mixture, then add the rest a little at a time. Will keep in the refrigerator for several days.

Preparation time: 10 minutes
Makes 2 cups

FOR BABIES 10 MONTHS & OLDER
Reserve plain cooked lentils and puree with a little water. Add cooked brown rice or baked sweet potato to puree for a swell combination.

Hummus

Hummus is a traditional Middle-Eastern dish excellent for vegetarian sand-wiches. The combination of chick-peas and tahini creates a high-protein spread. Tahini is a creamy paste made of crushed, hulled sesame seeds. Serve this delicious spread with warm pita bread and Tabouli (page 102).

> **2 cups cooked chick-peas**
> **5 tablespoons tahini**
> **½ teaspoon sea salt**
> **⅓ cup freshly squeezed lemon juice (juice of 1½-2 lemons)**
> **2-3 cloves garlic**
> **3 tablespoons extra-virgin olive oil**
> **¼ cup cooking liquid from beans or water to desired consistency**

Optional garnishes
> **Chopped parsley**
> **Paprika**

Place cooked chick-peas in food processor or blender with tahini, salt, lemon juice, garlic, and olive oil. Blend until smooth. Add cooking liquid from beans or a little water to get desired consistency. Garnish with chopped parsley or paprika if desired. Stores well refrigerated for at least a week.

Preparation time: 10 minutes
Makes 2¾-3 cups

FOR BABIES 10 MONTHS & OLDER
Reserve some plain cooked chick-peas and mash. Some may enjoy picking up and eating plain cooked chick-peas; be sure they are well-cooked.

VARIATION FOR CHILDREN
Hummus may be too spicy; try reducing lemon juice and garlic by half.

Sage and Rosemary Seitan Sandwiches

*Seitan, also called "wheat meat," is a high-protein food made from wheat gluten. This version of preparing seitan comes from Rachel Albert-Matesz' book, **The Nourishment for Life Cookbook**. Instead of starting with whole wheat flour and removing the starch through kneading and rinsing, Rachel simply starts with gluten flour.*

½ cup wheat gluten flour
½ teaspoon garlic powder
1-2 teaspoons fresh sage, minced
½ teaspoon fresh rosemary, minced
2 tablespoons ground sunflower seeds
1-2 tablespoons tamari
½ cup water

Sandwich Fixings
whole grain bread, mustard, pickle, tomato, lettuce, sprouts...

Mix dry ingredients together in a bowl. Stir in tamari and water and mix well using a spoon, and then your hands. Form into a ball. Oil a small stainless steel bowl. Put dough in bowl and cover bowl with wet cheesecloth secured with a rubber band. Place bowl in a pressure cooker and surround bowl with water to ⅓ the height of the bowl. Bring to full pressure, reduce heat to low and cook 30 minutes. If using a covered pot instead of a pressure-cooker, simmer for 60 minutes. Remove seitan from bowl. Allow to cool before slicing. Place slices on whole grain bread with your favorite fixings.

Preparation time: 40 minutes
Makes 1 cup, enough for 4 sandwiches

FOR BABIES 6 MONTHS & OLDER
This sandwich would be great with a few slices of sautéed summer squash on it. Reserve some of the squash, slice it, steam until soft and puree for baby.

Miso-Tahini and Raspberry Jam Sandwich

Tahini is a creamy paste made of crushed, hulled sesame seeds. Sesame is uniquely resistant to rancidity, perhaps why it has been enjoyed by many cultures for centuries. Miso and tahini mixed together make a wonderful spread with endless variations.

½ cup tahini
1 tablespoon white or mellow miso
Fruit-sweetened raspberry jam
Whole grain bread

Put tahini and miso in small bowl; mix well, adding a little water if necessary. Spread miso-tahini on one piece of bread and raspberry jam on the other. Put it together.

Preparation time: 5-10 minutes
Makes ²/₃ cup of miso/tahini spread or 4-5 sandwiches

FOR BABIES 10 MONTHS & OLDER
Stir a half teaspoon of tahini into baby's warm whole grain cereal for added calories and other nutrients.

VARIATION FOR CHILDREN
Use a heart-shaped cookie cutter and cut out a heart sandwich for a special treat.

Miso Tahini Scallion Spread

Adults may prefer this spread in a more savory version. Skip the jam and add finely chopped scallions to the miso-tahini mixture. Spread on bread or crackers.

Apple Miso
Almond Butter Sandwich

Try this sweet and nutty combo for a new twist on the usual peanut butter and jelly. It's quick to make and I think you'll be surprised at the delicious and satisfying taste.

> $^1/_3$ **cup unsweetened apple butter**
> **1 teaspoon white or mellow miso**
> $^1/_4$ **cup almond butter**
> **Whole grain bread**

Put apple butter in a small bowl and stir miso into it. Spread bread with a light layer of almond butter on one side and apple-miso butter on the other. Put it together.

Preparation time: 5 minutes
Makes 4-5 sandwiches

FOR BABIES 6 MONTHS & OLDER
Stir a half teaspoon of apple butter into baby's whole grain cereal for a new flavor.

FOR BABIES 10 MONTHS & OLDER
Stir a half teaspoon of almond butter into baby's warm whole grain cereal for added calories and additional nutrients.

Tamari-Roasted Nuts

Tamari-roasted nuts make a crunchy addition to salads and grains. I like them on oatmeal. A jar of these nuts makes a welcome Christmas gift as well. Tamari and shoyu are naturally brewed soy sauces that contain no chemicals, preservatives, sugar, or MSG.

> 1 cup almonds
> 1 cup cashews
> 1-2 tablespoons tamari or shoyu
> ½ teaspoon ground cumin
> ½ teaspoon ground coriander
> Pinch cayenne (optional)

Preheat oven to 300° F. Place nuts and seeds on cookie sheet. Toast in oven until they begin to turn golden and give off a nutty aroma (10-12 minutes). Mix tamari and spices together. Sprinkle over toasted nuts; stir and return to oven to dry out (2-3 minutes). For a more even coating, put tamari in a spray bottle and mist roasted nuts, then stir in spices and dry in oven. Store in a sealed jar.

Preparation time: 15 minutes
Makes 2 cups

FOR BABIES 10 MONTHS & OLDER
Remove a few of the toasted nuts before sprinkling with tamari and spices. Grind to a fine meal and stir tiny amounts into baby's cereal or vegetables for added calories and new flavor.

VARIATION FOR CHILDREN
Omit cumin, coriander and cayenne. Tamari-roast just one kind of nut instead of mixing several.

Carrot Flowers

My friend Theresa Lewis sent me this recipe. She made carrot flowers for her son's pre-school class and they were quite the rage. Children appreciate the magic of turning carrots into flowers. I like to cut carrots this way to give a fun look to salads.

    1 pound carrots (about 4 or 5)
    ¼ cup apple juice or orange juice
    1 cinnamon stick, optional

Wash carrots and trim off ends. Cut into 4-inch lengths. Using a sharp paring knife, make a lengthwise slit into each carrot about ⅛-inch deep. Make another lengthwise slit at an angle to the first. Remove the V-shaped strip from the carrot. Cut out 4 more V-shaped strips at equal intervals around the carrot. Repeat this process on each 4-inch length of carrot.

Now slice the carrot lengths into ¼-inch rounds, creating flower-shaped slices. Bring apple juice and cinnamon stick to boil in a 1-quart saucepan. Add carrot flowers and reduce heat to medium. Steam 10 minutes or until tender.

Preparation time: 25 minutes
Makes 8 servings

FOR BABIES 6 MONTHS & OLDER

Omit cinnamon and use water instead of juice. Steam carrots until soft, mash or puree and serve.

Savory Sandwiches to Go

I asked the people at Essential Foods (a Seattle-based food company) if I could learn the secret of how to wrap their popular sandwiches. They were kind and patient enough to let me spend a morning on the assembly line and learn how.

4 12-by-12-inch pieces of plastic wrap or waxed paper
4 whole wheat chapatis or tortillas
2 cups of filling (your choice of grain, bean, vegetable combinations; see "Suggestions for Sandwich Filling," page 118

1. Place one square of plastic wrap or wax paper flat on your working space. Put the chapati in the center of the square.

2. Pack a ½-cup measure (or a large ice cream scoop) with filling. Put filling in a mound in the center of the chapati (Figure 1).

3. Pull up the lower left and upper right corners of the chapati and overlap (Figure 2). Use a light touch and avoid compressing the filling.

4. Hold this configuration in place with your left hand by putting all your fingers on one side of the mound and your thumb on the other (Figure 3). This way you can wrap without smashing the filling.

5. Begin wrapping the sandwich with the right hand. Take the lower right corner of plastic wrap or wax paper and pull it up over the top of the sandwich, taking the chapati with you (Figure 4). Take the lower left corner of wrap or paper and pull it up over the mound, removing your left hand as you do it (Figure 5). Take the upper left corner of plastic wrap or wax paper and bring it over the top of the mound, taking the chapati with it (Figure 6). With 3 sides wrapped you have a fairly firm package. For a final touch, roll the whole sandwich toward the upper right corner (Figure 7). This seals it. If using wax paper, tack the end down with a piece of tape.

The trick is to work quickly and wrap tightly. You will need to practice a few times. Once you have mastered the technique, you'll want to create and eat one of these handy sandwiches every day. Try one warmed or dipped in a little salsa, or both.

Wrapped in plastic this sandwich will keep for a week refrigerated; wrapped in wax paper it should keep for 24 hours.

Preparation time: 15 minutes
Makes 4 sandwiches

FOR BABIES 6 MONTHS & OLDER

Leftover cooked grains like brown rice, quinoa and millet cannot only be used to stuff sandwiches. Puree cooked grains with a little water and warm to make excellent cereal for baby.

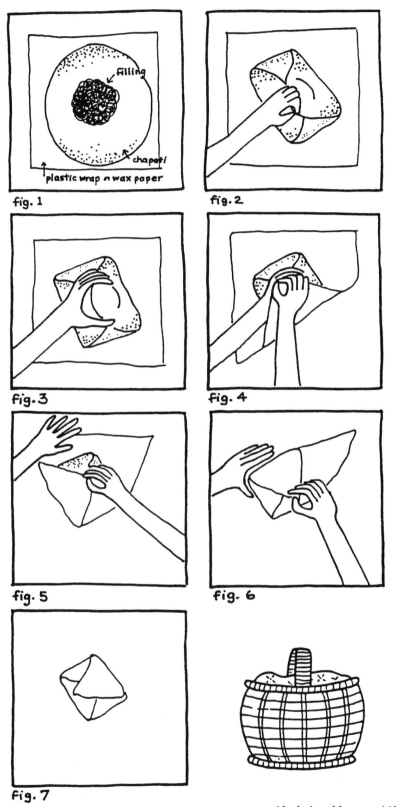

fig. 1

filling

chapati

plastic wrap n wax paper

fig. 2

fig. 3

fig. 4

fig. 5

fig. 6

fig. 7

Suggestions for Sandwich Fillings:

- Tofu Vegetable Breakfast Burritos (page 89)
- Confetti Rice Salad (page 95)
- Santa Fe Black Bean Salad (page 96)
- Dilled Kidney Beans and Rice (page 97)
- Hiziki Pate (page 100)
- Tabouli (page 102) with cooked chick-peas
- Mad Dog Rice Salad (page 103)
- Quick Lemon & Garlic Quinoa Salad (page 105)
- Gingered Lentil Sandwich Spread (page 109)
- Hummus (page 110) with sprouts and tomato
- Indian Rice and Lentils (page 144)
- Sloppeh Joes (page 151)
- Black beans (page 156) and brown rice with scallions, cilantro, and grated cheese
- Grilled Vegetables (page 188)

Grain and Bean Roll-ups

Roll-ups are a simple variation on Savory Sandwiches To Go. Use the suggestions on page 118 for fillings or create your own. They are scrumptious topped with a drizzle of Lemon-Tahini Sauce (page 206).

> 4 whole wheat tortillas or chapatis
> 2 cups filling (your choice of grain-bean-vegetable combinations; see "Suggestions for Sandwich Filling," page 118

Optional garnishes
> Sprouts
> Lettuce
> Avocado slices
> Salsa
> Sliced olives

Place tortilla flat on your working surface. Spread the filling in a fat line down the middle. Put whatever garnishes you want on top. Roll it up like a rug.

Preparation time: 5 minutes
Makes 4 roll-ups

FOR BABIES 10 MONTHS & OLDER

Leftover cooked beans not only make great roll-ups, they can be mashed or pureed to make food for baby. Well-cooked whole beans can be used for finger food when your baby has a few teeth to work with.

Packing a Wholesome Lunchbox

Here is a suggestion for caretakers who pack lunch regularly for a child.
Make a lunchbox chart (a sample is printed below). If your child is five or
older, let them help plan and make the chart. Choose one item that is a
"growing food": a whole grain - bean combination or perhaps a hearty sandwich on whole grain bread. You and your child can use the chart to plan
some favorite combinations. Post your chart for easy reference.

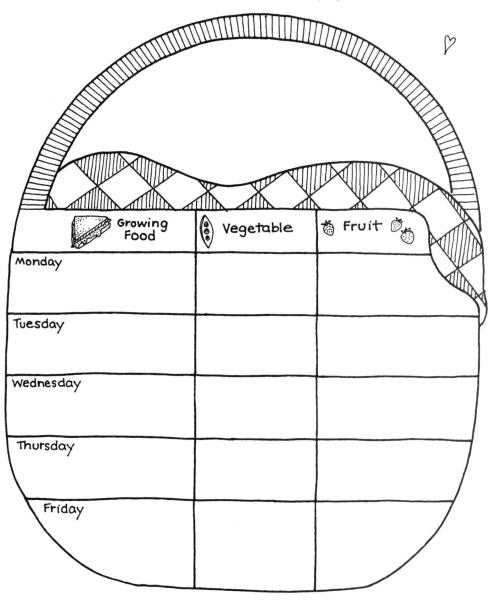

	Growing Food	Vegetable	Fruit
Monday			
Tuesday			
Wednesday			
Thursday			
Friday			

Sample Lunchboxes

Following are a handful of lunchbox combinations I have used:

Growing Food	Vegetable	Fruit
Burrito (whole wheat chappati, mashed pinto beans, salsa, grated cheese)	carrot sticks	orange
Tofu slices sautéed in butter and tamari over brown rice	nori cut in shapes	plum
Karen's Sesame noodles (page 94), mashed sweet potato	celery sticks	red grapes
Rice balls with sesame salt (page 106), lentil soup	steamed green beans	nectarine slices
Whole wheat spaghetti with tomato sauce	corn	apple slices
Apple Miso Almond Butter Sandwich (page 113)	sugar snap peas	melon slices
Sweet Squash Corn Muffins (page 200), kidney beans	blanched bok choy	kiwi slices and raisins
Whole wheat pita bread, Hummus (page 110), Tabouli (page 102)	red radishes	pear
Healthy Home Fries (page 90) with yogurt dip, Tempeh Bacon (page 91)	red pepper slices	dates
Asian Noodle Salad (page 104)	cucumber slices	strawberries
Avocado, cucumber and sprouts sandwich	Roasted Potatoes & Carrots (page 191)	pineapple

On days where you feel like adding something extra, add a fresh flower, a poem, a neat rock or crystal, a jingle bell, a cartoon, a finger puppet or a note from you instead of candy.

Rather than packing juice, tuck in a small container of fruity herbal tea or sparkling water. For an earth-friendly lunchbox, use a bright-colored cloth napkin and silverware instead of wasteful paper and plastic.

Soothing
Soups

Easy Vegetarian Soup Stock

This simple stock is worth the effort for making soups more flavorful and nourishing. This broth is excellent and can be used instead of water to puree food for babies. Kombu is a sea vegetable used here to impart extra nutrients to the broth. For more about kombu, see "Identifying, Shopping, and Storing Whole Foods" (page 255).

2 teaspoons extra-virgin olive oil
1 onion, chopped
1 carrot, cut in large chunks
1 rib of celery, cut in chunks
1 scallion or leek, cut in pieces
Skin of 1 yellow onion
1 3-inch piece of kombu
1 bay leaf
1 teaspoon dried marjoram
1 teaspoon dried thyme
1 quart water
$\frac{1}{2}$ teaspoon sea salt
$\frac{1}{8}$ teaspoon black pepper

Heat oil in a large soup pot. Add onion and sauté until soft. Add vegetables, herbs and water; bring to a boil. Lower heat and simmer 15-20 minutes. Add salt and pepper. Taste and adjust seasoning. Let cool. Strain liquid into an empty quart jar (a rinsed out juice bottle works well). Stores well in the refrigerator while awaiting its debut in your next soup. Should last 3-4 days.

Preparation time: 25 minutes
Makes 1 quart of soup stock

FOR BABIES 6 MONTHS & OLDER
Reserve some of the stock prior to adding salt and use to puree food for extra nourishment.

VARIATION FOR CHILDREN
Make a gentle and nourishing broth by stirring a teaspoon of light miso into a cup of this stock.

Cynthia's Hearty Vegetable-Miso Soup

Wakame is a green, leafy sea vegetable high in calcium and other minerals. Sea vegetables like wakame are purchased dried in packages and reconstituted in water. This hearty soup is excellent when a family member is fatigued. Served with whole grain bread and salad, it is a regular meal in our home.

> 5-inch piece of wakame
> 6 cups water
> 1 potato, diced
> 1 carrot, chopped
> 1 cup chopped greens (watercress, kale, collards, or bok choy)
> 4 tablespoons light or mellow unpasteurized miso
> 1/4-1/2 pound firm tofu, cut in small cubes

Garnish
> 2 scallions, thinly sliced

Place wakame in a small bowl of cold water and soak for 5 minutes. Put water, potato and carrot in a 3-quart pot; bring to boil. Remove wakame from water and chop into small pieces, removing the spine. Add chopped wakame to soup. Lower heat, cover pot and let soup simmer 15-20 minutes, until vegetables are tender. Near the end of cooking time, add chopped greens and tofu cubes and let them simmer 2 or 3 minutes. Ladle about 1/4 cup of broth from the soup into each soup bowl. Dissolve 1 tablespoon of miso into the broth in each bowl. Add more broth with plenty of vegetables to each bowl and stir gently. Garnish each bowl with scallions.

Preparation: 25 minutes
Makes 4 servings

FOR BABIES 6 MONTHS & OLDER
Remove boiled potatoes or carrots from soup after it simmers and mash with fork. Baby will benefit from the nutritious broth made by the seaweed.

FOR BABIES 10 MONTHS & OLDER
Those that can handle soft things to chew can enjoy some pieces of cooked vegetables and tofu cubes from the soup.

Cream of Asparagus Soup with Dill

It is easy to make a creamy soup without the cream. Rolled oats add extra whole grain nutrition and help make the creamy texture. Serve this soup with Quick Lemon & Garlic Quinoa Salad (page 105) and Black-Eyed Peas with Cilantro and Arame (page 157) for a beautiful grain-bean-2-vegetable meal.

> 2 teaspoons extra-virgin olive oil
> 1 onion, chopped
> 1 bunch asparagus, washed and trimmed
> 5 cups stock or water
> ½ cup rolled oats
> ½ teaspoon sea salt
> Freshly squeezed lemon juice

Garnish
> Fresh dill (or dried)

Heat oil in pot. Add onion and sauté until soft. Cut asparagus into small pieces. Add to onion and sauté a few more minutes. Add stock, oatmeal and salt. Bring to boil. Simmer 15 minutes. Transfer to a blender and puree. Reheat if necessary. Add some fresh lemon juice to taste and serve garnished with dill. This soup can also be served cold in warm weather.

Preparation time: 25 minutes
Makes 6 servings

FOR BABIES 10 MONTHS & OLDER
Use some of the rolled oats to make your baby a bowl of warm oatmeal. See page 62 for directions.

Red Lentil Soup with East Indian Spices

(Masoor Dal)

Red lentils are a small, flat, orange-colored legume. They are different than the normal gray-green lentil in flavor and appearance. A lovely Indian vegetarian restaurant in Seattle called Silence-Heart-Nest serves this very flavorful and satisfying soup called Masoor Dal.

2 teaspoons ghee or butter
1 onion, chopped
1-2 tablespoons minced garlic
1 teaspoon turmeric
1 teaspoon cumin powder
1/8 teaspoon cayenne
1 cup chopped tomatoes
1 cup dried red lentils
4 cups water
1 teaspoon sea salt
1 teaspoon each cumin and mustard seeds
1/2 teaspoon ghee or butter
1/4 cup chopped cilantro

Heat butter or ghee in a large pot. Sauté onions and garlic in ghee until brown. Add spices and stir for 2-3 minutes. Add tomatoes and cook until they break down. Wash and drain lentils. Add lentils and water to pot. Let simmer for 45 minutes, stirring often. Stir in salt. Heat 1/2 teaspoon ghee in a small skillet and fry seeds until they pop. Stir fried seeds and cilantro into finished soup.

Preparation time: 1 hour
Makes 4 servings

FOR BABIES 10 MONTHS & OLDER
Reserve 1/4 cup red lentils and simmer in a separate small pan with 1 cup water to make a simpler soup for baby.

Rosemary Red Soup

This soup is a gorgeous red color with a deep, satisfying taste to match. Because of the combination of legumes and vegetables, all you need is some whole-grain bread and salad to make this into a beautifully balanced meal. Try it with Sweet Squash Corn Muffins (page 200) and Dark Greens Salad (page 177).

> 3 medium carrots
> 2 beets
> 1 tablespoon extra-virgin olive oil
> 1 large onion, diced
> 2 tablesoons fresh rosemary or 2 teaspoons dried
> 1 tablespoon fresh oregano or 1 teaspoon dried
> 1 cup dried red lentils
> 2 bay leaves
> 6 cups water or stock
> 2-3 tablespoons light miso

Scrub and chop carrots and beets. Heat oil in a soup pot; add onion and sauté until soft. Add carrots and beets; sauté a few minutes more. Finely chop rosemary and oregano leaves, if using fresh herbs. Wash and drain lentils. Add herbs, lentils, bay leaves, and water or stock to onion mix; bring to a boil. Lower heat and simmer 40 minutes. Remove bay leaves. Puree soup in blender or processor. Dissolve miso in ½ cup water and add to soup. Gently reheat before serving.

Preparation time: 50 minutes
Makes 6-8 servings

FOR BABIES 6 MONTHS & OLDER
Steam a few extra carrot slices and puree with water.

FOR BABIES 10 MONTHS & OLDER
Reserve some pureed soup before adding the miso and serve.

VARIATION FOR CHILDREN
Make a face in the bowl with crackers!

Split Pea Soup with Fresh Peas and Potatoes

My daughter's second grade class had a hot lunch program where parents took turns bringing hot soup and bread to school for the children's lunch. This soup, created by Lee Carrillo, was one of their favorites.

2 teaspoons extra-virgin olive oil
1 onion, chopped
1 stalk celery, chopped
1 carrot, chopped
2 small red potatoes, cubed
1 teaspoon cumin
Black pepper, 1-2 turns of grinder
1 cup green split peas
4 cups water or vegetable stock
1 large bay leaf
½ cup fresh peas (frozen if fresh unavailable)
1 teaspoon sea salt
1 tablespoon fresh dill or 1 teaspoon dried

Heat oil in a pressure cooker or soup pot. Add onions and sauté until they begin to soften. Add celery, carrot, potatoes, cumin, and pepper. Sauté 5-7 more minutes. Add split peas, water, and bay leaf. If pressure-cooking: bring up to pressure, lower heat and cook 40 minutes. If using a soup pot: bring to a boil, lower heat, and simmer for 1½ hours. Add fresh peas, salt, and fresh dill; stir. Continue cooking a few minutes until peas are tender. Soup is ready to serve.

Preparation time: 50 minutes (pressure-cooked), 1 hour 45 minutes (soup pot)
Makes 4 servings

FOR BABIES 6 MONTHS & OLDER
Reserve some fresh peas. Steam them until tender. Puree and serve.

FOR BABIES 10 MONTHS & OLDER
Reserve some soup prior to adding salt. Puree in blender and serve.

Golden Mushroom-Basil Soup

The following three creamy soups are versions of Jeff Basom's sensuous non-dairy soups served at the Bastyr University cafeteria. Jeff's inventive use of vegetables and a touch of cashew butter creates a taste everyone loves. Serve this soup with Dilled Brown Rice and Kidney Beans (page 97) and Garlic Sautéed Greens (page 176) for a well-balanced meal.

1 teaspoon extra-virgin olive oil
4 cups chopped onions (about 2 large or 3 medium onions)
½ teaspoon sea salt
2 cups diced potatoes (about 2 medium potatoes)
½ cup chopped celery (about 2 ribs)
1 large carrot, diced
3½-4 cups water
2 tablespoons cashew butter
2 tablespoons tamari or shoyu
2 teaspoons extra-virgin olive oil
¾ pound mushrooms, sliced
½ cup fresh basil leaves, finely chopped
Sea salt and fresh ground pepper

Heat oil in a 3-quart pot. Add onion and salt. Cover the pot and simmer on low heat, stirring occasionally, until onions cook down to a nice mush (15-20 minutes). Add potatoes, celery, carrot and water to the onion mush; cover and simmer until potatoes are soft (15-20 minutes). Put soup mixture into blender with cashew butter and tamari; blend until smooth. Run the soup through a strainer to remove celery strings. Return soup to pot.

Heat oil in a small skillet. Add mushrooms and sauté until soft. Finely chop basil. Stir sautéed mushrooms and chopped basil into finished soup. Add salt and pepper to taste and serve.

Preparation time: 45 minutes
Makes 6 servings

FOR BABIES 6 MONTHS & OLDER
Remove some of the cooked potato or carrot from the soup and puree.

FOR BABIES 10 MONTHS & OLDER
Blend soup without adding tamari, sautéed mushrooms and basil and reserve a portion for baby.

Creamy Broccoli Soup

A smooth way to enjoy the goodness of broccoli. Serve this soup with Tempeh Club Sandwiches (page 108). A simple feast for a hungry family.

1 or 2 large stems of broccoli with flowerettes
1 teaspoon extra-virgin olive oil
4 cups chopped onions (2 large or 3 medium onions)
½ teaspoon sea salt
1 teaspoon coriander
2 cups diced potatoes (2 medium potatoes)
½ cup chopped celery (2 ribs)
3½-4 cups water
2 tablespoons cashew butter
Sea salt and fresh ground pepper

Cut off the broccoli flowerettes, cut into bite-size pieces and reserve. Peel the broccoli stems and dice into small pieces. Heat oil in a 3-quart pot. Add onions, salt and coriander. Cover the pot and simmer on low heat, stirring occasionally, until onions cook down to a nice mush (15-20 minutes). Add broccoli stem pieces, potatoes, celery, and water to the onion mush; cover and simmer until potatoes are soft (15-20 minutes). Put soup mixture into blender with cashew butter and blend until smooth. Run the soup through a strainer to remove celery strings.

Bring a pan of water to boil. Drop in the broccoli flowerettes and let them cook about 30 seconds. Stir blanched flowerettes into finished soup. Add salt and pepper to taste and serve.

Preparation time: 45 minutes
Makes 6 servings

FOR BABIES 6 MONTHS & OLDER
Reserve some blanched broccoli flowerettes and puree with a few slices of ripe avocado.

FOR BABIES 10 MONTHS & OLDER
Reserve a portion of pureed soup for baby before adding blanched flowerettes.

Thick Potato Cauliflower and Dulse Soup

Dulse is a dark red sea vegetable extremely high in iron (14 milligrams per ¼ cup) and other minerals. The dried leaves can be soaked for five minutes and added to soups or salads. Iron-rich dulse marries well with the simple flavors of potatoes and cauliflower.

1 teaspoon extra-virgin olive oil
4 cups chopped onions (about 2 large or 3 medium onions)
½ teaspoon sea salt
3 cups diced potatoes (about 2 medium potatoes)
½ cup chopped celery (about 2 ribs)
1 large carrot, diced
3 cups of bite-sized cauliflower pieces
3½-4 cups water
2 tablespoons cashew butter
2 tablespoons tamari or shoyu
⅓ cup dry dulse
Sea salt and fresh ground pepper

Heat oil in a 3-quart pot. Add onion and salt. Cover the pot and simmer on low heat, stirring occasionally until onions cook down to a nice mush (15-20 minutes). Add 2 cups of the potatoes, celery, carrot, 1 cup of the cauliflower pieces, and water to the onion mush, cover and simmer until potatoes and cauliflower are soft (15-20 minutes). Put soup mixture into blender with cashew butter and tamari and blend until smooth. Run the soup through a strainer to remove celery strings.

Prepare remaining 1 cup of potatoes and 2 cups of cauliflower. Place the potatoes and cauliflower pieces in a pot of boiling water and cook until tender (10-12 minutes). Prepare dulse by washing in cold water and gently tearing into bite-sized pieces. Drain the cooked potato and cauliflower. Stir cooked vegetables and dulse into the finished soup. Season with fresh ground pepper and serve.

Preparation time: 45 minutes
Makes 6 servings

FOR BABIES 6 MONTHS & OLDER
Steam some extra cauliflower pieces until very soft (20 minutes). Puree with a pinch of dulse and serve.

Nina's Famous Spring Beet Soup

Do you ever get the urge to clean in the spring? Here is a delicious, cleansing soup for your body, invented by my friend, Nina. It's bursting with nutrients and flavor. The fresher the beets, the better. Serve with Szechwan Tempeh (page 164) over quinoa (page 64) for a beautiful and satisfying meal.

> 1 teaspoon extra-virgin olive oil
> 1 medium onion, cut in thin crescents
> 1 clove garlic, minced
> $1/8$ teaspoon sea salt
> 3-4 cups water
> 1 bunch spring beets, cut into large matchsticks (save the beet greens)
> 1 carrot, cut into large matchsticks
> $1/4$ head green cabbage, shredded
> 2 tablespoons freshly squeezed lemon juice
> 1 tablespoon tamari or shoyu

Garnish
> 1 tablespoon fresh dill or 1 teaspoon dried dill

Heat oil in soup pot. Add onions, garlic, and salt; sauté until soft. Add water, beets, carrot, and cabbage and bring to a boil. Lower heat and simmer, covered for 10-15 minutes, until vegetables are tender. Meanwhile, wash beet greens, remove tough stems and cut greens into short, thin strips. Add beet greens, lemon juice, and tamari to soup; simmer another 3-5 minutes. Serve at once, garnished with dill.

Preparation time: 30 minutes
Makes 4 servings

FOR BABIES 10 MONTHS & OLDER
Remove some cooked beet and carrot pieces from the soup and puree, or serve whole as finger foods. Go easy on beets for babies (only a teaspoon or less at a time) as they have a strong cleansing effect on the bowels.

Chipotle Navy Bean Soup

Chipotle chiles are smoked, dried jalapeno peppers that richly enhance humble beans. The smoky flavor is similar to that of cooking beans with ham. Lima beans or pinto beans work equally well. Try this with Luscious Beet Salad (page 180) and Quinoa Garlic Herb Bread (page 199) for a flavorful, well-balanced meal.

> 1½ cups dried navy beans, soaked
> 2 teaspoons extra-virgin olive oil
> 1 onion, chopped
> 2 chipotle chiles, soaked 10-15 minutes in cold water
> 4 cups water or vegetable stock
> 1-2 teaspoons sea salt
> 1 teaspoon brown rice vinegar
> Freshly ground pepper

Drain soaking water off beans. Heat oil in soup pot or pressure cooker. Add onion and sauté until soft. Add drained beans, chiles and water. Bring to a simmer or close pressure cooker and bring up to pressure. Cook for 1 hour in soup pot or 45 minutes in pressure cooker, until beans are creamy. Remove chili pods. For added creaminess, puree part of the soup in the blender, then add back to the pot and mix in. Stir in salt, vinegar, and pepper; serve.

Preparation time: for boiling, 65 minutes; for pressure-cooking, 50 minutes
Makes 6 servings

FOR BABIES 6 MONTHS & OLDER
Chipotle chilies make this soup a bit too spicy for babies. This soup is wonderful served with Quick Lemon & Garlic Quinoa Salad (page 105). Remove some of the plain quinoa before dressing the salad, puree and serve as cereal to baby.

French Lentil and Potato Stew

This simple, hearty stew is my favorite standby for a one-dish meal. Economical in time spent in the kitchen as well as food dollars. The tiny French lentils are wonderful, but if you can't find them, substitute regular brown lentils. Ghee, or clarified butter, gives the buttery taste, but can hold a higher temperature than butter without burning.

1-2 teaspoons ghee or butter
1 onion, chopped
1 teaspoon cumin
1 teaspoon coriander
1 teaspoon freshly grated gingerroot
¼ teaspoon cayenne
¼ teaspoon cinnamon
1 teaspoon turmeric
⅛ teaspoon black pepper
¼ teaspoon allspice
2 red potatoes, cut in cubes
1 parsnip, sliced
1 stalk celery, diced
1 carrot, chopped
1 cup French lentils
4 cups water
1 teaspoon sea salt

Garnish
plain yogurt

Melt ghee or butter in a large soup pot on medium heat. Add onion and sauté until soft. Add all spices and sauté a few more minutes. You can substitute gingerroot and spices with 1 tablespoon of Homemade Curry Paste (page 214) if you like. Add potatoes, parsnip, celery, carrot, lentils, and water. Bring soup to a boil. Reduce heat and simmer, covered, for 50-60 minutes (if using a pressure cooker, bring up to pressure and cook 40 minutes). Stir in salt. Serve stew garnished with a dollop of yogurt.

Preparation time: 1 hour and 10 minutes
Makes 6 servings

FOR BABIES 10 MONTHS & OLDER
Remove some of the cooked potatoes and carrots from the soup, puree and serve.

Recycled Bean Soups

A great way to transform leftover beans! These soups make a nice, quick, well-balanced meal served with Confetti Rice Salad (page 95), Tabouli (page 102) or any other grain-vegetable dish.

White Beans and Fresh Herbs

    2 teaspoons ghee or extra-virgin olive oil
    1 onion, chopped
    1 clove garlic, minced
    1 carrot, chopped
    1 rib celery, chopped
    ¼ cup chopped fresh basil
    1½ cups cooked white beans
    1½ cups water or vegetarian soup stock
    2 tablespoons chopped parsley
    1 tablespoon tamari or shoyu (if beans were not
       already salted)
    1 teaspoon brown rice vinegar

Heat oil in 4-quart soup pot. Add onion and garlic; sauté until soft. Add carrot and celery; sauté a few more minutes. Add beans and water; stir together. You can puree all of the soup in a blender or processor for a smooth soup or puree part of it for a chunkier cream soup. Return pureed part to pot. Stir in fresh herbs. Season with tamari and vinegar; reheat before serving.

Preparation time: 10 minutes
Makes 4 servings

FOR BABIES 6 MONTHS & OLDER
Make Sweet Squash Corn Muffins (page 200) to go with this soup. Reserve some of the pureed squash that goes in the muffin batter for baby.

FOR BABIES 10 MONTHS & OLDER
Puree some of the plain cooked beans with a little water or soup stock. Serve with steamed carrot slices.

Dark Beans and Sensuous Spices

2 teaspoons ghee or extra-virgin olive oil

1 onion, chopped

1 clove garlic, minced

1 carrot, chopped

1 rib celery, chopped

1 teaspoon cumin

1 teaspoon oregano

1 teaspoon coriander

1½ cups cooked red or black beans

1½ cups water or vegetarian soup stock

¼ cup chopped cilantro

1 tablespoon tamari or shoyu

1 teaspoon brown rice vinegar

Heat oil in a 4 quart soup pot. Add onion and garlic; sauté until soft. Add dry spices and sauté briefly. Add carrot and celery; sauté a few more minutes. Add beans and water; stir together. You can puree all of the soup in a blender or processor for a smooth soup or puree part of it for a chunkier cream soup. Return pureed part to pot. Stir in cilantro. Season with tamari and vinegar and reheat before serving.

Preparation time: 10 minutes
Makes 4 servings

FOR BABIES 10 MONTHS & OLDER
Puree some of the plain cooked beans with a little water or soup stock.

Substantial
Suppers

Pan-Fried Tofu and Greens with Almond Ginger Drizzle

(Bathing Rama)

The traditional way to make Bathing Rama is to serve tofu on a bed of cooked spinach, covered with a spicy peanut sauce. To update this classic nutritionally, I have used collards instead of spinach and a sauce made from almond butter. This is a superb one-dish meal when served over udon noodles or other grains.

Marinade
> 3 cloves garlic, sliced
> 4-5 slices ($^1/_8$-inch thick) of fresh gingerroot
> 1 cup water
> 1 tablespoon brown rice vinegar
> 1 tablespoon toasted sesame oil
> $^1/_3$ cup tamari or shoyu
> 1 pound firm tofu
> 1-2 tablespoons toasted sesame oil
> 1-2 large bunches collard greens
> 8 ounces udon noodles

Sauce
> $^1/_4$ cup creamy almond butter
> 2 teaspoons maple syrup
> 2 tablespoons tamari or shoyu
> 1 tablespoon brown rice vinegar
> 1 teaspoon grated gingerroot
> 1-2 teaspoons hot pepper oil
> $^1/_3$ cup water

In the morning, combine all ingredients for marinade. Cut tofu into ½" slabs, then cut slabs into triangles. Put marinade and tofu in a glass storage container with a tight-fitting lid and refrigerate 4-8 hours.

Heat oil in a skillet. Place marinated tofu pieces in oil and brown on both sides. Set aside and prepare greens. Pull the leaves away from the stem. Wash greens carefully. An easy way to do this is to fill your sink with cold water and submerge the greens. Bring 2 quarts of water and ½ teaspoon of sea salt to boil. Submerge greens. Boil for 7-10 minutes. Pour cooked greens into a colander in the sink. Let cool. Squeeze out excess water with your hands. Chop into bite-sized pieces. Set aside.

Bring a large pot of water to boil and cook udon noodles according to package directions. While noodles are cooking, prepare sauce. Put all ingredients in a small pan on low heat. Using a whisk, mix ingredients until smooth and warm. Add extra water for desired consistency. Serve noodles with cooked greens and browned tofu on top. Drizzle sauce over all.

Preparation time: 4-8 hours to marinate; 30 minutes to make dish
Makes 4 servings, 1 cup of sauce

FOR BABIES 10 MONTHS & OLDER
Reserve some unmarinated tofu, cut up into cubes, and serve with bite-size pieces of cooked noodles.

VARIATION FOR CHILDREN
Separate foods. Serve plain noodles, fried tofu, small pile of greens, and a little bowl of the sauce for dipping.

Three Sisters Stew

My colleague, Jackie Williams, shared this incredible stew with me. Native Americans grew corn and planted the beans at the base. The corn stalks served as bean poles. The ground space between the stalks was used to grow squash. The three sisters (corn, beans, and squash) lived harmoniously.

> 1 cup dried Christmas lima beans (*kidney, pinto, black, or Swedish brown beans can be substituted*), soaked
> 3 cups water
> 2 cloves garlic
> 2 tablespoons fresh or 2 teaspoons dry oregano
> 1 teaspoon cumin seeds
> ½ teaspoon cinnamon
> 1 tablespoon extra-virgin olive oil or ghee
> 1 medium onion, chopped
> 1½ teaspoons sea salt
> 2-3 cloves garlic, minced
> 2-3 cups winter squash, cut in chunks (peel if not organic)
> 1 14-ounce can chopped tomatoes
> 1 tablespoon chili powder
> 1½ cups fresh or frozen corn

Optional garnish
> 8-10 tablespoons grated cheese

Drain soaking water off beans. Place beans, water, and garlic in a pot; bring to boil. Cover and simmer until beans are tender (50-60 minutes) or pressure-cook with 2 cups water (45 minutes).

In a large pot, quickly dry toast oregano, cumin seeds, and cinnamon for about 30 seconds. Add oil, onion, salt, and minced garlic; sauté until onion is soft (5 minutes). Add squash, tomatoes, and chili powder and cook until squash is soft (about 20 minutes). Add a little water if mixture is dry.

Add cooked beans and corn to squash mixture; simmer until corn is tender. Adjust seasoning to your taste. Serve hot with grated cheese garnish if desired.

Preparation time: 1 hour and 10 minutes
Makes 6-8 servings

FOR BABIES 6 MONTHS & OLDER
Reserve some peeled squash cubes, steam well and puree.

FOR BABIES 10 MONTHS & OLDER
Reserve some cooked Christmas limas before adding to stew and puree with steamed squash cubes. Serve beans in small amounts to babies.

Indian Rice and Lentils with Caramelized Onions

(Mojadra)

Mojadra is an economical and flavorful dish. Cook the rice and lentils in the morning; just 10 minutes' evening preparation and you have a fast homemade meal. Serve this dish with Mustard Green Salad (page 182) and baked garnet yams for a colorful, well-balanced meal.

1 cup short grain brown rice
1 cup dried brown or green lentils
1 bay leaf
4 cups water
1 tablespoon extra-virgin olive oil or ghee
2 large onions, sliced in thin rounds
½ teaspoon sea salt
2 cloves garlic, minced
1½ teaspoons coriander
1 teaspoon cumin
⅛ teaspoon cayenne

Topping
½ cup plain yogurt with 1 teaspoon fresh dill mixed in

Rinse and drain rice and lentils. Place in a 3-quart pot with bay leaf and water. Bring to a boil. Lower heat and simmer 45-50 minutes.

Meanwhile, put oil in hot skillet. Add onions and a pinch of salt and sauté. When onions begin to soften, add garlic and spices; cover and cook until onions are golden and have begun to caramelize. When rice and lentils are finished, remove from heat and take out bay leaf. Serve rice and lentils topped with onions and a dab of yogurt with dill.

Preparation time: 50 minutes
Makes 6 servings

FOR BABIES 10 MONTHS & OLDER
Puree some of the lentil-rice mixture before adding onions and spices.

Red Bean and Quinoa Chili

I often serve this vegetarian chili to guests and they love it. By pre-cooking the kidney beans, you will have a one-dish meal in 30 minutes. A vegetable dish or salad is all you need to make a nutritionally complete meal.

1 cup dried kidney beans, soaked
1 teaspoon cumin
3 cups water

2 teaspoons extra-virgin olive oil
1 medium onion, chopped
2 teaspoons sea salt
1 large green pepper, chopped
2 cloves garlic, minced
1-2 teaspoons cumin
1 teaspoon dried oregano
$^1/_8$ teaspoon cinnamon
$^1/_8$ teaspoon cayenne
$^2/_3$ cup quinoa, rinsed in warm water and drained
1 cup fresh or frozen corn
1-2 cups organic tomato sauce
1 cup water

Optional garnish
A few tablespoons of grated cheese

Drain soaking water off beans. Place beans in a large pot with cumin and water; bring to boil. Simmer over low heat, covered, until tender (50-60 minutes) or pressure-cook using 2 cups water (45 minutes).

Heat oil in skillet on medium heat. Add onion, salt, garlic, pepper, and spices; sauté for 5-10 minutes. Add rinsed quinoa and stir in. Add corn, tomato sauce, and water to onion/quinoa mixture. Simmer together 20 minutes. Add cooked beans to other ingredients; simmer another 10 minutes. Top each bowl with a sprinkle of grated cheese if desired.

Preparation time: 1¼ hours, 30 minutes if beans pre-cooked
Makes 6-8 servings

FOR BABIES 10 MONTHS & OLDER
Serve plain cooked, mashed beans, pureed with extra cooked corn and water.

Deep-Fried Millet Croquettes

Properly done, deep-frying is actually low in calories. Cooking with oil at the correct temperature is the key. Also, do not use salt in foods you intend to deep-fry. Serve Millet Croquettes with Dark Beans and Sensuous Spices Soup (page 137) and Lightly Cooked Cabbage Salad (page 179).

    1 cup millet
    2½ cups water
    1 carrot
    2 scallions
    1 quart or more high-oleic safflower oil (the pan you use to deep-fry should be ⅔ full)

Gravy
    1 cup water
    1-2 tablespoons kudzu
    1 teaspoon grated gingerroot
    3 tablespoons shoyu or tamari

Garnish
    Lemon wedges

To prepare millet

Rinse and drain millet 2 or 3 times. Put millet and water in a pot and bring to a boil. Reduce heat to low, cover and let simmer 25-30 minutes, until all water is absorbed. Remove from heat.

To make croquettes

Grate carrot and chop scallions. Make sure pieces of both are very small. Add chopped vegetables to cooked and cooled millet. Mix in well. With moist hands, form mixture into croquettes about the size of a golf ball, packing tightly.

Heat oil in a deep, stainless steel pot to 375°. Use a deep-fry thermometer to make sure the temperature is correct. Too high will burn the outside and leave the inside raw. Too low will result in soggy croquettes. When temperature is correct there will be dancing ripples on the bottom of the pan. Cut a piece of brown paper bag and place it where you can drain the fried croquettes.

Lower 3 or 4 croquettes (depending on the size of your pan) into oil with tongs or chopsticks. Croquettes should drop to the bottom, then quickly rise to the top. When croquettes are golden on the outside, remove with a slotted spoon and place on brown paper to drain.

To make gravy

Dissolve kudzu in water. Put in a small pan. Add grated gingerroot. Bring mixture to boil, stirring constantly. When mixture becomes clear and thick (5 minutes), turn heat off. Stir in shoyu. Serve immediately over the croquettes as gravy becomes jelly-like if allowed to sit and cool. Garnish each plate with a lemon wedge. A squeeze of lemon is tasty on the croquettes.

Preparation time: 45 minutes
Makes 8-10 croquettes, 1 cup gravy

FOR BABIES 6 MONTHS & OLDER
Reserve some cooked millet and puree with water or breast milk and serve.

FOR BABIES 10 MONTHS & OLDER
Serve some cooked millet and puree with an extra carrot that has been sliced and steamed.

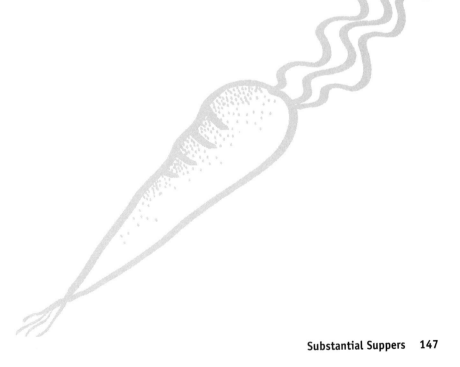

Polenta Pizza

A fun, healthful way to enjoy pizza without white flour and mounds of fatty cheese.

    2 teaspoon extra-virgin olive oil
    1 onion, chopped
    1-2 cloves garlic, minced
    1 tablespoon fresh or 1 teaspoon dried oregano
    1 tablespoon fresh or 1 teaspoon dried basil
    ½ of a medium zucchini
    ½ of an eggplant
    1 patty-pan squash
    ½ of a green pepper
    1½ cups chunky tomato sauce
    3 cups boiling water
    1 teaspoon sea salt
    1 teaspoon extra-virgin olive oil or butter
    1 cup polenta
    1-2 tablespoons parmesan cheese

Optional garnish
    8 tablespoons grated jack cheese

Preheat oven to 350° F. Heat oil in a skillet. Sauté onion until soft. Add garlic and herbs; sauté a few minutes more. Cut zucchini, eggplant, squash and pepper into ½-inch cubes. Put vegetables, onion mixture, and tomato sauce into a lightly oiled 8-by-8-inch pan. Cover and bake for 1 hour.

While the vegetables bake, prepare the polenta. Bring water to rapid boil. Add salt and oil. Slowly add polenta, stirring continuously with a whisk. Lower heat and continue stirring in a clockwise motion with a wooden spoon for 10-15 minutes until mixture can hold the spoon upright on its own. Lightly oil a 10-inch pie plate or 8-by-8 pan. Pour polenta into pan and smooth the top. Sprinkle parmesan on top and bake for 30 minutes.

Remove both dishes from oven. Spoon tomato vegetable mixture on top of the baked polenta. Cut into slices and serve with grated cheese on top if desired.

Preparation time: 1 hour
Makes 8 slices

FOR BABIES 6 MONTHS & OLDER
Reserve some of the zucchini, steam it and puree.
VARIATION FOR CHILDREN
Some may prefer a slice of the plain baked polenta.

Peasant Kasha, Potatoes, and Mushrooms

Kasha is the name for toasted buckwheat groats. Kasha and potatoes combine here for a rib-sticking meal. Serve this dish with Creamy Broccoli Soup (page 131) and consider Almond Ginger Drizzle (page 208) for topping the kasha.

> 2 teaspoons toasted sesame oil
> 1 small onion, chopped
> 2 cloves garlic, minced
> ½ teaspoon sea salt
> 2 cups boiling water
> 2 medium red potatoes or 1 large baking potato
> 3-4 mushrooms, sliced
> 1 cup kasha
> Freshly ground pepper

Heat the oil in a 2-quart pot. Add onions, garlic and salt; sauté until the onion is soft. Put water on to boil. Scrub potatoes well and cut into ½-inch cubes. Add potatoes and mushrooms to onions; sauté 1-2 minutes. Add kasha to mixture and stir. Pour in boiling water. Turn heat to low. Cover pot and simmer 15 minutes. Fluff up and serve garnished with pepper.

Preparation time: 25-30 minutes
Makes 6 servings

FOR BABIES 10 MONTHS & OLDER
Remove a baby-size portion, mash potato bits with a fork, slice mushrooms into tiny pieces and serve.

Kasha Salad
Turn leftover kasha and potatoes into a salad for lunch. Add fresh chopped vegetables, such as parsley, cabbage, red pepper, scallions, and a tablespoon of your favorite vinaigrette.

Sloppeh Joes

Can you tell I was raised in the '50s and '60s? The vegetarian version of the familiar classic was styled from one of my mother's recipes. Serve with corn on the cob and Creamy Cole Slaw (page 184).

    2 teaspoons extra-virgin olive oil
    1 onion, chopped
    1 green pepper, chopped
    1 clove garlic, minced
    ¼ teaspoon sea salt
    1 8-ounce package tempeh
    ⅔ cup fruit-sweetened, organic catsup
    2 teaspoons whole grain mustard
    1 tablespoon brown rice vinegar
    ½ teaspoon ground cloves
    4 whole grain hamburger buns

Optional garnishes:
    Lettuce
    Pickles
    Sprouts

Heat oil in a 10-inch skillet. Add onion, pepper, garlic and salt; sauté until soft. Crumble tempeh with fork or by hand; add to onion mixture. Let the tempeh brown. Mix ketchup, mustard, vinegar, and cloves together in a small bowl. Add to tempeh mixture, mixing well. Warm buns in oven if desired. Spoon tempeh mixture onto buns and serve with your favorite garnish.

Preparation time: 20 minutes
Makes 4 servings

FOR BABIES 6 MONTHS & OLDER
Try some steamed zucchini with Sloppeh Joes. Reserve some of the zucchini and puree for baby.

FOR BABIES 10 MONTHS & OLDER
Serve a warmed bun with a little apple butter.

Mexican Bean
and Corn Casserole

Pinto beans and coarsely ground corn (polenta) make this dish delicious and nutritious vegetarian fare. This recipe has been very popular in my classes on beans.

  1 cup dried pinto beans, soaked
  1 garlic clove
  1 teaspoon cumin seed
  3 cups water

  1 teaspoon extra-virgin olive oil
  1 onion, chopped
  ½ teaspoon sea salt
  1 clove garlic, minced
  ½ red or green pepper, chopped
  1 cup chopped zucchini or shredded green cabbage
  2 teaspoons ground cumin
  1 teaspoon oregano
  ½ cup organic tomato sauce
  ¼ cup water
  3 cups water
  1 teaspoon sea salt
  1 tablespoon extra-virgin-olive oil or butter
  1 cup polenta
  1 tablespoon parmesan cheese

Drain soaking water off the beans. Place beans in a large pot with garlic, cumin seeds, and 3 cups water. Bring to boil, then simmer over low heat, covered, until tender (50-60 minutes) or pressure-cook in 2 cups of water (45 minutes).

Heat oil in a large skillet. Add onion, salt, and garlic; sauté until soft. Add pepper, zucchini, cumin, and oregano; sauté 5 more minutes. Add cooked beans to the vegetables with tomato sauce and ¼ cup water. Check taste and add salt if necessary.

In a separate pot, bring 3 cups water to boil. Add salt and oil. Slowly add polenta, stirring continuously with a whisk. Lower heat and continue stirring in a clockwise motion with a wooden spoon for 10-15 minutes until mixture can hold the spoon upright on its own. Preheat oven to 350° F. In a lightly oiled casserole dish, spread the bean and vegetable mixture across the bottom. Spread the polenta on top. Sprinkle top with parmesan cheese. Bake, covered, for 25 minutes at 350° F; remove cover and bake 5 minutes more at 400° F.

Preparation time: 60 minutes for beans, 40 minutes for casserole
Makes 8 servings

FOR BABIES 6 MONTHS & OLDER
Reserve some of the zucchini; steam it and puree.
VARIATION FOR CHILDREN
Serve the bean-vegetable part of the casserole in a bowl and cut some strips of polenta to use as dippers.

Curried Lentils and Cauliflower

My friend, Joy Taylor, made this dish for me many years ago. I jotted down the recipe and adapted it over time. Try serving it over brown basmati rice, which is prepared the same as boiled brown rice (page 58).

  1 cup dried lentils
  1 bay leaf
  2 cups water

  2 teaspoon extra-virgin olive oil
  1 onion, chopped
  1 clove garlic, minced
  1 teaspoon sea salt
  1 teaspoon ground coriander
  1 teaspoon ground cumin
  1 teaspoon turmeric
  ¼ teaspoon cinnamon
  1 small head cauliflower, cut in small flowerettes
  ½-1 cup tomato sauce
  1 teaspoon freshly grated gingerroot
  ¾-1 cup water

Optional garnishes
  ½ cup roasted cashews
  ½ cup plain yogurt

Wash and drain lentils. Place in pot with bay leaf and water; bring to boil. Lower heat, cover and let simmer 25-30 minutes, until lentils are soft.

Heat oil in a large pot. Add onion, garlic, and salt; sauté until onion is soft. Add coriander, cumin, turmeric, and cinnamon. Add cauliflower, tomato sauce, gingerroot, and water; stir well. (You may substitute 2 tablespoons of Curry Paste, page 214, for the spices and gingerroot.) Cover and let simmer until cauliflower is tender (10-15 minutes).

Stir cooked lentils into cauliflower-tomato mixture, discarding the bay leaf. Serve over whole grains and garnish with roasted cashews or plain yogurt if desired.

Preparation time: 30-35 minutes
Makes 4 servings

FOR BABIES 10 MONTHS & OLDER
Set aside some of the plain cooked lentils and puree them, or steam extra cauliflower and puree it with some water.

VARIATION FOR CHILDREN
Some may prefer plain lentils served with plain cooked rice and a few roasted cashews on the side.

Black Bean Tostados

We often set out black beans, brown rice, salsa, guacamole, and other favorite toppings and let guests create their own tostados or burritos or whatever. It's a crowd pleaser. Make extra beans and recycle them into soup, spreads, dips or casseroles later in the week.

1 teaspoon extra-virgin olive oil
1 onion, chopped
2-4 cloves garlic, minced
1 teaspoon cumin seeds
2 cups dried black beans, soaked
4-6 cups water
1 teaspoon sea salt
¼ cup chopped cilantro leaves
½ cup chopped tomatoes
12-14 flat corn tortillas

Optional garnishes
avocado slices or guacamole
black olives
grated cow, goat or soy cheese
leaf lettuce, thinly sliced
plain yogurt
salsa
sprouts

Heat oil in a large pot. Sauté onion, garlic, and cumin in oil until onions are soft. Drain soaking water off beans. Add beans and 6 cups water to onions and spices; bring to boil. Turn down to simmer and cook, covered, until beans are tender (50-55 minutes), or pressure-cook beans in 4 cups water (45 minutes). Stir salt, cilantro and tomatoes into cooked beans.

Bake or heat tortillas (read the instructions on the package). Serve tortillas, beans and garnishes in separate bowls. Let each diner create their own tostado.

Preparation time: 1-2 hours, 20 minutes if beans precooked
Makes 6-7 cups of beans or 12-14 tostados

FOR BABIES 10 MONTHS & OLDER
Reserve some cooked black beans before adding tomatoes and cilantro, mash well and serve. Serve beans in very small amounts to babies.

Black-Eyed Peas and Arame with Cilantro

Arame is a sea vegetable that has been finely shredded, cooked, and then naturally sun dried. When reconstituted, it looks like small, black threads. Its milder flavor makes it a useful introductory sea vegetable. This dish, created by my talented friend Minx Boren, delights the tastebuds with its unique combination of flavors. Goes well with Sweet Squash Corn Muffins, page 200, and Susan's Succulent Supper Salad, page 186.

> 2 cups dried black-eyed peas
> 4 cups water
> 1 cup arame, soaked in cold water
> 2 tablespoons tamari or shoyu
> 2 tablespoons brown rice syrup or maple syrup
> ½ tablespoon grated gingerroot
> 1 teaspoon brown rice vinegar

Garnish
> ¼-⅓ cup chopped cilantro

Put peas and water in a pot; bring to boil. Lower heat and simmer until tender (30-35 minutes). Add arame, tamari, syrup, and gingerroot. Gently stir and simmer mixture 10 more minutes. Add vinegar just before serving and garnish with cilantro.

Preparation time: 45-50 minutes
Makes 6-8 servings

FOR BABIES 10 MONTHS & OLDER
Remove some black-eyed peas when tender and puree with a little water.

Nut Burgers

This delicious burger recipe will give you opportunity to pile up a bun with mustard, pickle, tomato or whatever and chow down without bothering a single cow. The nut and grain combination makes a complete protein; all you need is a vegetable soup or salad to round out the meal.

¾ cup sunflower seeds
¾ cup walnuts
1 teaspoon cumin
1 teaspoon oregano
⅛ teaspoon cayenne
2 cloves garlic, finely chopped
1 cup cooked brown rice
1 small carrot (or ½ of a large one), grated finely
2 tablespoons tomato sauce
1-2 teaspoons cold-pressed oil
4 whole grain hamburger buns

Grind nuts and seeds to a fine meal in a small grinder or food processor. Pour into a bowl and add cumin, oregano, cayenne, and garlic; mix well. Fold in cooked brown rice. Add tomato sauce a little at a time until you get a stiff, but workable texture. Form mixture into patties with moist hands. Refrigerate patties for a few hours if possible. Lightly coat a skillet with oil and brown patties on both sides. Serve on whole grain buns with your favorite fixin's.

Preparation time: 15-20 minutes (without refrigeration time)
Makes 4 burgers

FOR BABIES 6 MONTHS & OLDER
Puree extra cooked brown rice with a little breast milk or water.

Tempeh and Red Pepper Stroganoff

Tempeh, originally an Indonesian food, is made from soybeans. This high-protein food can be baked, boiled, fried or steamed. This mouth-watering tempeh recipe is quick to make and is a beautifully balanced meal served over quinoa, whole wheat couscous or udon noodles next to a salad of wild greens.

1 tablespoon extra-virgin olive oil
1 large onion, chopped
1-2 cloves garlic, minced
½ teaspoon oregano
½ teaspoon thyme
1 large carrot, matchsticked
1 red pepper, cut into thin strips
1 8-ounce package tempeh, cut into ¼" strips
3 tablespoons whole wheat pastry flour
¼ cup mirin
3 tablespoons tamari or shoyu
1½ cups soy milk or water
Freshly ground black pepper

Garnish
½ cup chopped parsley

Heat oil in a large skillet. Add onion, garlic, and herbs; sauté until onions soften. Add carrots, then pepper, then tempeh letting each cook a few minutes before adding the next. When tempeh starts to become golden, add flour; stir it in, coating the ingredients well. In a separate bowl, mix mirin, tamari, and soy milk together. Add slowly, stirring as you go to make a nice gravy. Season with black pepper. Simmer on low heat for 10-15 minutes or place in a casserole and bake at 300° F. for ½ hour for deeper flavors. Serve over your favorite whole grains or noodles garnished with parsley.

Preparation time: 35 minutes
Makes 4 servings

FOR BABIES 6 MONTHS & OLDER
Puree some of the cooked carrot pieces or serve this dish over cooked quinoa. Blend some of the cooked quinoa with water or breast milk and serve as cereal.

Bok Choy and Buckwheat Noodles in Seasoned Broth

(Yaki-Soba)

This traditional Japanese dish makes a quick, healthy family meal. Soba is a hearty noodle made from buckwheat and wheat flour that can be found in natural food stores and Asian markets. Bok choy is a beautiful vegetable that has big dark green leaves with a thick white stem. If you can't find it at your regular grocery store, try an Asian market - it's worth the trip!

1 package soba noodles
2 teaspoons toasted sesame oil
1 onion, cut in thin half moons
2-3 cloves garlic, minced
1 carrot, cut into matchsticks
5 shiitake mushrooms, cut into bite-size pieces
2 cups chopped bok choy
4 cups water
$^1/_3$ cup tamari or shoyu
½ lb. firm tofu, cut into ½" cubes
1 tablespoon freshly grated gingerroot
2 scallions, cut into thin slices

Prepare soba noodles according to package directions. Drain and set aside.

Heat oil in a 4-quart soup pot. Add onion and garlic; sauté over medium heat until onion begins to soften. Add carrot and mushroom pieces; sauté a few minutes more. Add bok choy, water, tamari, tofu, and gingerroot. Bring heat up until mixture begins to simmer. Cover and let simmer for 10 minutes.

Serve this dish by placing a handful of noodles in each serving dish. Ladle broth and vegetables over the noodles. Garnish with scallions.

Preparation time: 30 minutes
Makes 4 servings

FOR BABIES 6 MONTHS & OLDER
Reserve some carrots and bok choy. Steam until tender, puree with some of the broth and serve.

FOR BABIES 10 MONTHS & OLDER
Serve plain slices of tofu and/or cooked soba noodles cut into small pieces.

VARIATION FOR CHILDREN
Serve plain noodles on a plate with a bowl of vegetable broth.

Tofu-Kale-Mustard-Dill Supper Pie

*This recipe is an adaptation of the wonderful tofu quiche found in Annemarie Colbin's book, **The Natural Gourmet**. This version utilizes super nutritious kale and carrots. Kale is a big-leafed, dark green plant, rich in Vitamin A, Vitamin C, and calcium. Umeboshi vinegar, made from umeboshi plums, gives a sour-salty zip to the filling. This dish is a perfect combination of grains, beans, and vegetables. Serve with a salad of wild greens for a well-balanced meal.*

Crust

> 2 cups whole wheat pastry flour
> $1/3$ cup cold-pressed vegetable oil
> $1/3$ cup water
> $1/4$ teaspoon sea salt

Filling

> 2 teaspoons extra-virgin olive oil
> 1 onion, chopped
> Pinch of sea salt
> 2 carrots, thinly sliced into half moons
> 1 bunch kale leaves, stems cut away
> Pinch of sea salt
> 1 pound firm tofu
> 1 tablespoon umeboshi vinegar
> 1 tablespoon extra-virgin olive oil
> 1 tablespoon mustard
> 2 teaspoons tamari or shoyu
> $1/2$ teaspoon dried dill or $1\frac{1}{2}$ teaspoon fresh dill

To make crust

Preheat oven to 350° F. Put flour in a bowl. In a separate bowl, whisk water, oil, and salt together. Slowly pour liquid into flour, blending with a fork. Gather dough into a ball; it should be moist and pliable. Roll out into a crust on a floured surface or a piece of wax paper. Transfer to an 8- or 9-inch pie pan. Trim edges. Prebake for 10 minutes in the oven.

To make filling

Heat oil in a large skillet. Add onion, salt, and carrots; sauté until onion is soft. Wash kale leaves and remove stems. Stack several kale leaves on top of one another and roll up. Cut into very thin slices. Repeat until all kale is cut. Add to onion mixture and sauté until kale begins to wilt but retains its rich green color. Set aside. Blend the tofu, vinegar, oil, mustard, tamari, and dill in a blender or food processor until smooth. If using firm tofu, you may need to add a little water.

To assemble pie

Put the onion-carrot-kale mixture in the bottom of the prebaked crust. Pour the tofu mixture over the top, covering the vegetables. Bake 30 minutes until the top of the pie begins to turn beige at the edges. Cut and serve.

Preparation time: 55 minutes
Makes 8 slices

FOR BABIES 6 MONTHS & OLDER
Steam some extra carrot slices and puree.

FOR BABIES 10 MONTHS & OLDER
Reserve some cubes of tofu and serve with carrot puree.

Szechwan Tempeh

Tempeh can be stored in the refrigerator for a week or it can be stored in the freezer for 6 months. Allow an hour or two for frozen tempeh to thaw before using. The sweet and salty qualities of Szechwan Tempeh are nicely balanced by serving it atop some basmati brown rice or quinoa. Try Spinach Salad (page 185) and Baked Winter Squash (page 194) as accompaniments.

> ¼ cup cold-pressed, high oleic safflower oil
> 1 8-ounce package tempeh, cut into ¼" strips
> 2 tablespoons white miso
> ¼-⅓ cup water
> 2 tablespoons tamari or shoyu
> 2 tablespoons mirin
> 2 tablespoons balsamic vinegar
> 2 tablespoons brown rice syrup
> 2 teaspoons toasted sesame oil or hot pepper oil

Garnish
> 1 scallion, thinly sliced

Heat 2 tablespoons of safflower oil in a 10-inch skillet. Place half of the tempeh strips in the skillet and let them quick-fry, turning them so that both sides brown. Remove fried tempeh onto a paper towel and repeat the process with the other half of the tempeh strips. In a small bowl, mix miso and water together with a whisk until miso is dissolved. Add tamari, mirin, vinegar, syrup, and sesame oil to miso and whisk again. Lower heat on skillet. Place fried tempeh back in the skillet and pour sauce over the top. Sauce will begin to thicken. Remove from heat, garnish with sliced scallion and serve immediately.

Preparation time: 15 minutes
Makes 3 servings

FOR BABIES 6 MONTHS & OLDER
Serve this dish over cooked long-grain brown rice. Reserve some of the cooked grain and puree with water or breast milk to make cereal for baby.

VARIATION FOR CHILDREN
Reserve some of the crispy fried tempeh before adding the sauce and serve with a sprinkle of tamari.

Seitan and Shiitake Mushrooms in Cashew Mirin Sauce

Here's another use of Rachel Albert-Matesz' easy and delicious seitan, this time in a sensuous sauce. The sage and rosemary in the seitan give it a very savory flavor which makes it usable in many dishes where you might use beef or sausage. This dish is lovely served with mashed potatoes and lightly steamed broccoli.

1 cup Sage and Rosemary Seitan (page 111)
2 teaspoons extra-virgin olive oil
1 onion, sliced in half moons
10-12 shiitake mushrooms, sliced

Sauce
¼ cup cashew butter
1 tablespoon mirin
2 tablespoon tamari
½ cup water

Prepare seitan according to directions on page 111. While seitan is cooling, heat oil in skillet. Sauté onions until soft. Add mushrooms and sauté 5 more minutes. Slice seitan into strips and add to skillet. Turn heat to low. Place all ingredients for sauce together and whisk until smooth. Pour sauce over onions, mushrooms and seitan. Stir gently until sauce begins to thicken. Serve immediately.

Preparation time: 40 minutes to make seitan, 20 minutes for the dish
Makes 4 servings

FOR BABIES 6 MONTHS & OLDER
This dish is wonderful served over plain cooked quinoa or brown rice. Reserve some cooked grain and puree with breast milk or water and serve as cereal.

FOR BABIES 10 MONTHS & OLDER
Stir a half teaspoon of cashew butter into baby's warm whole grain cereal for added calories and other nutrients.

VARIATION FOR CHILDREN
Children may prefer slices of plain seitan and sautéed mushrooms with the sauce on the side for dipping.

Tempeh Tacos

One of my students at Bastyr University, Jeff Johnson, presented this dish as part of his final project and I thought they were not only very tasty but so easy-to-make! I served them to my family and got raves. Jeff, of course, got an A.

> 1 pound tempeh (2 8-ounce packages)
> 2 tablespoons extra-virgin olive oil
> 3 tablespoons tamari
> ¼ cup lime juice
> 1 tablespoon Mexican seasoning
> 1 onion, chopped
> ¼ cup chopped cilantro
> 12 taco shells

Optional taco fixings
> shredded lettuce
> sprouts
> salsa
> feta cheese
> avocado slices

Crumble, chop, or grate tempeh into small pieces and place in a mixing bowl. Combine 1 tablespoon of the olive oil, tamari, lime juice, and chili powder in small bowl and pour this marinade over the tempeh. Let stand 10 to 30 minutes. The longer time allows more absorption of the flavor.

Heat the other tablespoon of oil in a large skillet. Add onion and sauté until soft. Add marinated tempeh and keep mixture moving in the pan until tempeh turns golden brown. Add chopped cilantro just prior to serving. Warm taco shells according to directions on package. Fill shells with tempeh mixture and your favorite fixings.

Preparation time: 30 minutes to marinate, 15 minutes to make tacos
Makes 6-8 servings

FOR BABIES 6 MONTHS & OLDER
Serve tacos with ripe avocado slices and reserve some of the avocado for baby. Puree or mash well and serve.

Dr. Bruce's Awesome Grilled Salmon

Dr. Bruce Gardner, a family practitioner, prepared this mouthwatering delicacy for us one summer and I have never forgotten it. The ginger-lime marinade makes this dish awesome. To put meat, poultry, or fish into a healthy perspective, serve it in 3-4 ounce portions accompanied by whole grains and vegetables.

> **2-3 pounds salmon filet**

Marinade
> $^2/_3$ **cup tamari or shoyu**
> **2 teaspoon toasted sesame oil**
> **2 tablespoons grated ginger**
> **Juice of 1 large lime**
> **4 cloves garlic, minced**
> **4 scallions, finely chopped**

Garnish
> **2 red peppers, cut in big slices**

To marinate salmon

Put tamari, oils, gingerroot, lime juice, garlic, and scallions in a small mixing bowl; whisk together. Place fish in a shallow pan and pour marinade over the top. Marinate one hour in the refrigerator.

To grill salmon

When the coals in your grill are just becoming white, remove fish from pan and place fish on the grill, skin side down. Brush the top with part of the marinade and grill the fish for about 5 minutes. The rule of thumb for cooking fish is 10 minutes of cooking time per inch of thickness. Turn the fish over. Remove the skin, it should come off easily. Brush the top with marinade again and grill for 4-7 minutes more, until the fish is tender at the thickest part. Flip it over and serve grilled side up. Roast chunks of red pepper on grill while cooking fish and serve as a garnish with the fish.

Preparation time: 1 hour for marinating, 10-15 minutes for grilling
Makes 8 to 10 4-ounce servings

FOR BABIES 6 MONTHS & OLDER
This grilled salmon is delightful served with Lemon Basil Potato Salad (page 98). Reserve some of the boiled potatoes and mash with water or breast milk.

Thea's Greek Shrimp Stew

We serve this rich, scrumptious stew to company for a special treat. The recipe is really fast and easy-to-make. Serve it with warm whole grain bread and Susan's Succulent Supper Salad (page 186) for a simple feast.

1 tablespoon extra-virgin olive oil
2 onions, chopped
½ teaspoon sea salt
4 cloves garlic, minced
3 cups organic chopped or diced tomatoes
1 cup organic tomato sauce
2 teaspoons prepared whole-grain mustard
3 tablespoons fresh dill (1 tablespoon dried)
1 teaspoon brown rice syrup or honey
1 pound cooked shrimp
¼ pound feta cheese, crumbled
1 cup chopped parsley

In a large soup pot, heat oil, then add onions, salt, and garlic. Sauté until soft. Add tomatoes, tomato sauce, mustard, dill, and syrup; simmer 20 minutes. Five minutes before serving, add shrimp, feta and parsley. Stir well and serve.

Preparation time: 30 minutes
Makes 6 servings

FOR BABIES 6 MONTHS & OLDER
This stew is wonderful served with a warm whole grain bread like the Rice Bread on page 198. Take part of the leftover cooked brown rice used for making the bread and puree it with water to make cereal for baby.

Rainbow Trout Poached in Herbs

When I was growing up, my family went to Southern Colorado in the summer. My dad fished the Conejoes River and caught fresh rainbow trout. This fish has long been a favorite of mine. I like this recipe because the family shares the WHOLE fish together.

> 2 teaspoons extra-virgin olive oil
> 1 onion chopped
> 2 quarts water
> 1 cup white wine
> 2 bay leaves
> 4-5 sprigs fresh thyme
> 4-5 sprigs fresh parsley
> 1 whole, fresh rainbow trout
> ½ lemon
> 2-3 feet of cheesecloth

Heat oil in an 8-quart pot. Add onion and sauté until soft. Add water, wine and herbs. Bring mixture to a gentle simmer and let it cook 10-12 minutes. While poaching liquid is simmering, prepare fish. Gently rinse the whole fish. Cut lemon into thin slices. Place lemon slices in body of fish then wrap the whole fish in cheesecloth leaving long ends of cloth at the head and tail. Lower the fish into the poaching water leaving the two long ends of the cheesecloth draped over the edge of the pan. Let fish cook in simmering poaching liquid for 10 minutes. Lift fish out by the dry ends of the cheesecloth. Remove fish from cheesecloth. Open down the middle and remove head, spine and tail. Gently lift out the meat of the fish and serve immediately.

Preparation time: 20-25 minutes
Makes 3-4 small servings

FOR BABIES 6 MONTHS & OLDER
This dish is lovely served with long grain brown rice. Reserve some of the cooked rice and puree with water to make cereal for baby.

FOR BABIES 10 MONTHS & OLDER
If your baby has some incisors and molars, it might be time to introduce fish. This fish is very tender and mild-tasting. Be extremely careful about removing all tiny bones before serving to baby.

Baked Chicken with Mushrooms and Rosemary

Occasionally, I will bake this tasty chicken dish and use it as a side dish with a large amount of brown rice, steamed vegetables and salad. Mushrooms are heavenly when you bake them whole.

> 8-10 whole mushrooms
> ½ cup white wine, stock or water
> 2 tablespoons tamari or shoyu
> ¾-1 pound chicken breasts (from organically fed, free-range chickens)
> 1 three-inch sprig of fresh rosemary

Preheat oven to 350° F. Wipe mushrooms clean with a damp towel or rag. Put wine and tamari in an 8-inch baking dish. Place chicken breasts and cleaned mushrooms in the dish. Remove leaves from rosemary sprig, chop them and sprinkle on top of the chicken. Cover the dish and bake for one hour. Remove cover and broil for a minute or two before serving, if desired.

Preparation time: 65-70 minutes
Makes 4 small servings

FOR BABIES 6 MONTHS & OLDER

Serve dish with basmati brown rice. Reserve a portion of cooked rice, puree with a little water and serve as cereal to baby. You can use a little of the juice from the chicken and mushrooms to puree rice.

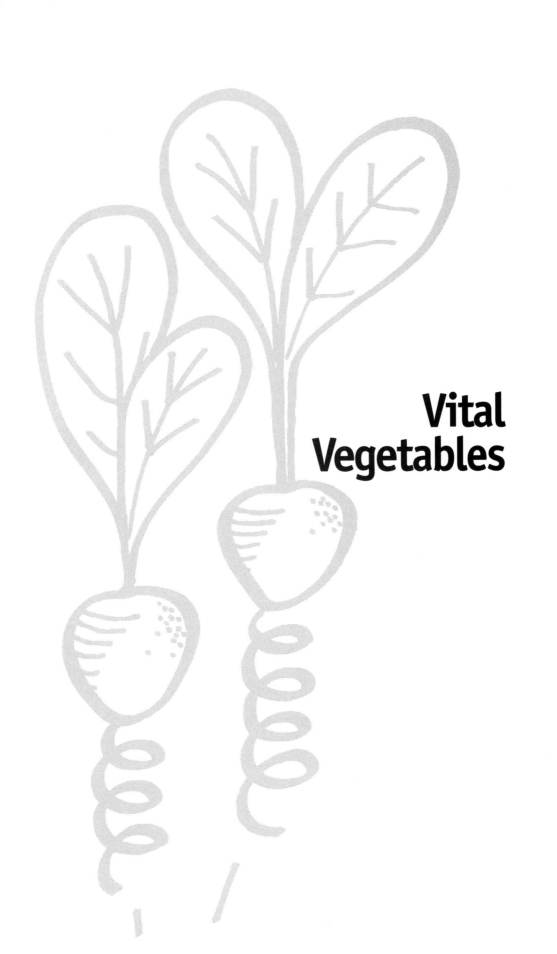

Vital
Vegetables

Quick-Boiled Greens

Vitamin A, vitamin C, folic acid, calcium, iron, and even protein are a part of most dark leafy greens. These powerful vegetables should be a daily part of the diet, especially for nursing mothers. Cooked greens can be used in a variety of interesting dishes — soups, salads, casseroles, and more.

Choose 8 cups of
>   **Beet greens**
>   **Bok choy**
>   **Broccoli**
>   **Chinese cabbage (napa)**
>   **Collard greens**
>   **Dandelion greens**
>   **Endive**
>   **Escarole**
>   **Kale**
>   **Mustard greens**
>   **Swiss chard**
>   **Turnip greens**
>   **Watercress**

Optional Garnishes
>   **Lemon wedges**
>   **Brown rice vinegar or umeboshi plum vinegar**

For greens with tough stems, such as collards, kale or chard, cut the leaves away from the stem before washing. Wash greens carefully. An easy way to do this is to fill your sink with cold water and submerge the greens. If the water has sediment, drain the sink and repeat.

Bring 2 quarts of water to boil. Submerge greens. Boil tender young greens (such as watercress or escarole) for about 30 seconds. Tougher leaves (such as mature collards or kale) need to be cooked for 5-10 minutes. Timing is everything. If you remove the greens too soon they will be bitter. If you let them cook too long they will lose nutrients and have a flat taste. Remove a piece and test every minute or so. You are looking for a slightly wilted leaf that still has a bright green color and (most important) a succulent, sweet flavor. Pour cooked greens into a colander in the sink. Let cool. Squeeze out excess water with your hands. Chop into bite-sized pieces. Serve with a few drops of lemon juice or vinegar. Reserve cooking water for watering your plants.

Preparation time: 10 minutes
Makes 2 cups, 4 servings

FOR BABIES 10 MONTHS & OLDER

Take a teaspoon or two of plain cooked greens and puree with whatever grains or vegetables baby is eating tonight.

Leftover cooked greens? Use them in:

Cynthia's Hearty Vegetable-Miso Soup (page 125)
Add to Creamy Broccoli Soup Base (page 131)
Pan Fried Tofu and Greens (page 140)
Bok Choy and Buckwheat Noodles (page 160)
Tofu-Kale-Carrot-Mustard-Dill Supper Pie (page 162)
Sesame Greens (page 174)
Greens in Cashew Curry Sauce (page 175)
Garlic Sautéed Greens (page 176)
Dark Greens Salad (page 177)
Use in sandwiches instead of lettuce

Sesame Greens

Sesame greens make a tasty and impressive side dish for any meal. Try these greens with Szechwan Tempeh (page 164) and quinoa or as a side dish with Dr. Bruce's Awesome Grilled Salmon (page 167).

> 2 cups Quick-boiled Greens (page 172)
> 1 teaspoon brown rice syrup
> 1-2 teaspoons brown rice vinegar
> 1 teaspoon toasted sesame oil
> 1 teaspoon hot pepper oil
> 2 tablespoons toasted sesame seeds (page 106)

Prepare greens. Mix syrup, vinegar, and oils together. Pour dressing over greens; add seeds and toss well. Serve warm or cold or at room temperature.

Preparation time: 15 minutes
Makes 2 cups, 4 servings

FOR BABIES 10 MONTHS & OLDER
Take a teaspoon or two of plain cooked greens and puree it with whatever grains or vegetables baby is eating tonight.

Greens in Cashew Curry Sauce

Greens in Cashew Curry Sauce is a mouthwatering treat served over cooked rice or quinoa. For texture, top with a few whole, roasted cashews. Some people are unaware that cashews have the lowest fat content of all nuts. Serve this dish over grain with Rosemary Red Soup (page 128) for a very colorful grain, bean, two vegetables combination.

> 2 cups Quick-boiled Greens (page 172)
> ¼ cup cashew butter
> 1 tablespoon Homemade Curry Paste (page 214)
> 1 tablespoon tamari or shoyu
> ¾ cup water

Prepare greens. Combine cashew butter, curry paste, tamari, and water in the blender and blend until creamy. Combine greens and blended sauce in a pan. Gently heat before serving.

Preparation time: 15 minutes
Makes 4 servings

FOR BABIES 10 MONTHS & OLDER
Stir a half teaspoon of cashew butter into baby's warm whole grain cereal for added calories and other nutrients.

Garlic Sautéed Greens

Consider this recipe as part of a New Year's Day meal designed to bring good luck and fortune. Black-eyed peas for the silver, a dab of pumpkin for the gold, and a helping of collard greens for the greenbacks. Complete the meal with a generous slice of cornbread.

8 cups chopped raw greens
1 tablespoon extra virgin olive oil or ghee
1 tablespoon minced garlic

Garnish
½-1 teaspoon brown rice vinegar
½ teaspoon tamari

For greens with tough stems, cut the leaves away from the stem before washing. Wash greens carefully. An easy way to do this is to fill your sink with cold water and submerge the greens. If the water has a lot of sediment, drain the sink and repeat.

Heat oil in a 10-inch skillet. Add garlic and sauté a minute or so. Add greens and keep them moving in the skillet. Turn frequently so that all the greens reach the heat. When all greens have turned bright green and begun to wilt, remove from heat. Sprinkle vinegar and tamari over the top. Toss gently and serve.

Preparation time: 15 minutes
Makes 2 cups, 4 servings

FOR BABIES 10 MONTHS & OLDER
Serve these greens with Black-eyed Peas (page 157); reserve some unseasoned peas for baby, mash well or puree and serve.

Dark Greens Salad with Creamy Ginger-Garlic Dressing

This is a delicious way to add dark greens to your diet — just plop them into your favorite salad. The dressing is not only good on salads; it makes an excellent sauce for cooked grains.

Salad

       2 cups Quick-Boiled Greens (page 172)

       ½ head red leaf lettuce

       1 bunch watercress, tough stems removed

       ½ cucumber, thinly sliced

Dressing

       ½ pound tofu

       1 teaspoon grated ginger root

       2 cloves garlic, minced

       2 tablespoons extra-virgin olive oil

       2 tablespoons freshly squeezed lime juice

       2 teaspoons tamari or shoyu

       ⅓-½ cup water, to desired consistency

Prepare Quick-Boiled Greens and set aside in the refrigerator. Wash lettuces and watercress by placing leaves in a sink full of cold water. Drain and repeat. Spin or pat dry. Tear greens into bite-size pieces. Place lettuce and watercress in a large salad bowl. Add Quick-Boiled Greens and cucumber and toss together. Set aside.

Place all ingredients for dressing in a blender. Blend until smooth. Serve salad with about 2 tablespoons of dressing on top of each serving. Leftover dressing will keep in the refrigerator for about a week.

Preparation time: 15 minutes
Makes 4 servings, over 1 cup dressing

FOR BABIES 10 MONTHS & OLDER

Reserve some of the tofu. Cut up into cubes and steam. Serve in cubes or mashed.

Romaine Radicchio Salad with Lemon-Olive Oil Dressing

The simplest lemon and olive oil dressing can turn flavorful, fresh greens into an elegant salad. Radicchio is a sturdy, burgundy-colored lettuce. If unavailable, substitute 1-2 cups red cabbage.

Salad
> ½ head romaine lettuce
> 1 small head radicchio
> 3 thin rounds of red onion
> ½ cup alfalfa sprouts
> 2 tablespoons crumbled feta cheese (optional)

Dressing
> Juice of ½ lemon
> 2 tablespoons extra-virgin olive oil
> 1 teaspoon tamari or shoyu
> 1 clove garlic, peeled and split in half
> ¼ teaspoon fresh ground black pepper

In the bottom of a salad bowl, whisk together the lemon juice, oil, and tamari with a fork. Add the garlic clove and pepper; let rest. Wash and dry romaine and raddiccio salad greens by placing leaves in a sink full of cold water. Drain and repeat. Spin or pat dry. Tear lettuce and radicchio into bite-size pieces. Place greens and raddichio in salad bowl on top of dressing. Add sprouts, onion rounds, and feta cheese on top. Before serving, remove garlic clove. Toss salad and dressing together and serve.

Preparation time: 10 minutes
Makes 6 servings

FOR BABIES 10 MONTHS & OLDER
Reserve a tablespoon of alfalfa sprouts and blend in with baby's cereal or vegetables. If your baby has teeth, try chopping sprouts fine and serving raw.

Lightly Cooked Cabbage Salad with Sweet Asian Dressing

A colorful winter salad that rounds out any meal. The dressing is also excellent on noodles! For directions on how to toast sesame seeds, see Rice Balls with Sesame Salt, page 106.

Salad
- ½ large head green cabbage, shredded (8-10 cups)
- 1 carrot, cut into matchsticks
- ½ of a red pepper, cut into small strips
- ¼ cup toasted sesame seeds

Dressing
- 1 teaspoon grated gingerroot
- 1 clove garlic, minced
- 2 tablespoons brown rice vinegar
- 2 tablespoons mirin
- 2 tablespoons toasted sesame oil
- 2 tablespoons tamari or shoyu
- 1 tablespoon hot pepper oil
- 1 tablespoon maple syrup

Bring a large pot of water to boil. Cut up cabbage, carrot, and pepper and keep in separate piles. Drop shredded cabbage into boiling water and cook for 30-45 seconds. Add carrot and pepper to cabbage; cook 15 seconds more. Pour cooked vegetables into a colander and rinse with cold water to stop cooking. Let drain.

Place all dressing ingredients into a small bowl; whisk together and set aside. Gently squeeze the water out of the cooked vegetables and put into a salad bowl. Add sesame seeds and dressing. Toss gently and serve immediately.

Preparation time: 15 minutes
Makes 8 servings

FOR BABIES 6 MONTHS & OLDER
Steam an extra carrot and puree.

FOR BABIES 10 MONTHS & OLDER
If your baby has some teeth, reserve some plain cooked cabbage and carrot pieces and serve as finger food.

Luscious Beet Salad
with Toasted Pumpkin Seeds

This recipe was inspired by Jeff Basom and his friend Tara. I love it because it uses the WHOLE beet. Adds beautiful color and a bounty of vitamins to a simple rice and fish meal. If beet greens are unavailable use watercress, collard greens, raw spinach or arugula leaves.

Salad
>   4 large beets
>   ¼ cup pumpkin seeds, toasted
>   1 bunch beet greens
>   2 scallions, finely chopped
>   ¼ lb. feta cheese (optional)

Dressing
>   3 tablespoons extra-virgin olive oil
>   2 tablespoons balsamic vinegar
>   ¾ teaspoon Dijon mustard
>   ¼ teaspoon freshly ground pepper
>   1 tablespoon finely chopped fresh basil

Wash beets and remove tops. Place beets in a large pot filled with water and bring to a boil. Lower heat and simmer until beets are tender (about an hour). Set aside to cool.

Toast pumpkin seeds by placing seeds in a dry skillet over medium heat. Move the skillet back and forth over the heat with one hand; stir the seeds using a wooden spoon with the other hand. This will toast the seeds evenly and prevent burning. When seeds begin to pop and give off a nutty aroma they are ready. Remove seeds from skillet and set aside.

To prepare beet greens, bring a large pot of water to boil. Wash beet greens by submerging the bunch in a sink full of cold water. Shake off water and chop the bunch into bite-size pieces. Drop greens into boiling water and let it cook for about 30 seconds, just enough to make the stems tender. Place greens in a colander and run cold water over them to halt cooking.

Place all dressing ingredients in a jar and shake well. Peel beets and cut into small cubes. Squeeze excess water out of the cooked beet greens. Put cubed beets, beet greens, pumpkin seeds, and scallions in a salad bowl. Pour dressing over salad and toss gently. Crumble feta cheese on top. Serve at room temperature or chilled.

Preparation time: 1 hour to cook beets, 15-20 minutes to assemble salad
Makes 6 servings

FOR BABIES 10 MONTHS & OLDER
Reserve a teaspoon of the toasted pumpkin seeds, grind them to a fine powder and stir into baby's cereal or pureed vegetables for extra calories and other nutrients.

VARIATION FOR CHILDREN
Cook the beets in apple juice instead of water and serve plain, cut-up cooked beets.

Mustard Green Salad with Tofu-Dill Dressing

The sharp taste of calcium-rich mustard greens works well with an easy-going tofu dressing. Buy mizuna mustard greens if possible; they are the tenderest. You can use less water in making the dressing and create a creamy sauce for pasta or grains. Tempeh and Red Pepper Stroganoff (page 159) over quinoa served with this salad makes a fresh, well-balanced meal.

Salad
> ½ bunch mustard greens
> ½ head green leaf lettuce
> ½ bunch red radishes, sliced
> 1 handful alfalfa sprouts

Dressing
> ½ pound tofu
> 2 tablespoons brown rice vinegar
> 1 tablespoon fresh dill or 1 teaspoon dried dill
> ½ cup water

Wash mustard greens and lettuce by placing leaves in a sink full of cold water. Drain and repeat. Spin or pat dry. Tear greens into bite-sized pieces and place in a large salad bowl with radishes and sprouts on top. Set aside. Place all ingredients for the dressing in blender and blend until smooth and creamy. Dress salad before serving with about ¾ cup of the dressing; toss well. The leftover dressing will keep in the refrigerator for about a week.

Preparation time: 10 minutes
Makes 6 servings, 1½ cups dressing

FOR BABIES 10 MONTHS & OLDER
Reserve some of the tofu. Cut into cubes. Steam and serve cubes or mash.

Watercress Salad
with Ginger Dressing

This salad is quick, light, and nutritious. Watercress is rich in minerals and is usually free of pesticides as it grows easily and abundantly. The ginger dressing is a favorite of mine from Silence-Heart-Nest, a Seattle restaurant.

Salad
>1 bunch watercress, tough stems removed
>½ head red leaf lettuce
>1 cucumber, thinly sliced

Dressing
>2 tablespoons chopped ginger
>2 teaspoons chopped celery
>½ teaspoon maple syrup
>6 tablespoons extra-virgin olive oil
>3 tablespoons toasted sesame seeds
>⅛ teaspoon white pepper
>⅛ teaspoon celery seed
>½ teaspoon catsup
>3 tablespoons soy sauce
>3 tablespoons brown rice vinegar
>3 tablespoons water

Wash watercress and lettuce by placing leaves in a sink full of cold water. Drain and repeat. Spin or pat dry. Tear greens into bite-sized pieces and place in a large salad bowl. Add cucumber and set aside.

Place ginger, celery, maple syrup, oil, seeds, pepper, celery seed, and catsup in the blender and blend. Add soy sauce, vinegar and water; blend again until creamy. Before serving, toss salad with ¼-⅓ cup of the dressing. The remainder of the dressing will keep in the refrigerator for at least a week.

Preparation time: 10 minutes
Makes 6 servings, ¾ cup dressing

FOR BABIES 6 MONTHS & OLDER
This salad is a lovely accompaniment to Deep Fried Millet Croquettes (page 146) and millet is a wonderful beginner grain for babies. Reserve some of the plain cooked millet before deep-frying, puree with water or breast milk and serve as cereal.

Creamy Cole Slaw

This has the familiar look and taste of traditional cole slaw, but with about half the mayonnaise, therefore half the fat. Serve it with corn on the cob and Sloppeh Joes (page 151) for a new twist on traditional fare.

Salad
> 3 cups green cabbage, shredded (about ¼ head)
> 1 carrot, grated
> 1 scallion, chopped finely
> 1 cup red cabbage, shredded

Dressing
> 3 tablespoons mayonnaise
> 2 tablespoons freshly squeezed lemon juice
> 1 teaspoon brown rice syrup
> 1 teaspoon tamari or shoyu
> Freshly ground pepper

Combine cabbages, carrot, and scallion in a bowl. Toss together and set aside. Combine dressing ingredients in a small bowl and blend with a whisk or a fork until mixed well. Pour dressing over vegetables and toss again.

Preparation time: 5-10 minutes
Makes 6 servings

FOR BABIES 6 MONTHS & OLDER
This recipe goes well with Dilled Brown Rice and Kidney Beans (page 97) to make a simple summer meal. Reserve some of the plain cooked rice before adding the beans and dressing and puree it with a pinch of grated carrot reserved from the slaw.

VARIATION FOR CHILDREN
Serve separate little piles of the grated or shredded vegetables before adding dressing.

Spinach Salad
with Balsamic Vinaigrette

This hearty salad served with whole grain bread and a spread such as Gingered Lentil Sandwich Spread, page 109, makes a nice summer meal. Leftover vinaigrette works well on grain or bean salads for lunchboxes.

Salad
> 1-2 bunches spinach, washed well, dried, stems removed
> ¼ cup walnuts, roasted and chopped
> ½ small red onion, sliced in thin rounds

Dressing
> 3 tablespoons extra-virgin olive oil
> 2 tablespoons balsamic vinegar
> ¾ teaspoon Dijon mustard
> ¼ teaspoon fresh ground pepper

Wash spinach by placing leaves in a sink full of cold water. Drain and repeat. Spin or pat dry. Tear spinach into bite-sized pieces. Place in a large salad bowl. Toast walnuts on a cookie sheet in the oven at 350° F. for 10-12 minutes. Add cooled walnuts and red onion to spinach. Place all dressing ingredients in a jar and shake well. Dress salad just before serving. Leftover dressing will keep in the refrigerator for at least a week.

Preparation: 10 minutes
Makes 6 servings, ⅓ cup dressing

FOR BABIES 6 MONTH & OLDER
This salad makes a completely satisfying meal served with a thick soup or stew. Serve it with Three Sisters Stew (page 142). Remove some of the cooked squash from the stew, puree and serve to baby.

Susan's Succulent Supper Salad

My friend Susan Wilson made up this feast of a salad that gets raves in my classes. Served with soup, bread, and a spread, you have a most satisfying meal. I've used romaine, spinach, and arugula, but any combination of wild greens and salad greens works fine.

Salad

    ½ head romaine lettuce

    1 bunch spinach

    ½ bunch arugula or rocket

    1 cup chopped red cabbage

    1 tart apple, cut in bite-sized pieces

    1 ripe avocado, cut in bite-sized pieces

    ¼ cup raisins

    ¼ cup toasted pumpkin seeds

    3 scallions, finely sliced

    1 or 2 fresh tomatoes, cut in wedges

    1 cup alfalfa sprouts

    ⅔ cup cooked chickpeas

Dressing

    ¼ cup extra-virgin olive oil

    3 tablespoons balsamic vinegar

    2 teaspoons Dijon mustard

    2 teaspoons maple or brown rice syrup

    1 cloves garlic, minced

    ⅛ teaspoon paprika

    ¼ teaspoon tamari or shoyu

Wash lettuces and greens by placing leaves in a sink full of cold water. Drain and repeat. Spin or pat dry. Tear greens into bite-sized pieces and place in a large salad bowl. Add all other salad ingredients. Set aside.

Put all ingredients for dressing in a small bowl or jar and whisk together or shake vigorously. Dress salad just before serving and toss
well.

Preparation time: 20 minutes
Makes 8 servings; 4 servings if used as a main course

FOR BABIES 6 MONTHS & OLDER
Reserve a slice or two of avocado, mash or blend and serve.

FOR BABIES 10 MONTHS & OLDER
Steam a few apple slices and serve with a tablespoon of raisins.

VARIATION FOR CHILDREN
Serve separate piles of raisins, apples, pumpkin seeds, sprouts, avocado.

Grilled Vegetable Salad with Sweet Poppyseed Dressing

Vegetarians take heart! Summer grilling is for you, too! Grilled vegetables are delicious whether served over rice, in a pocket pita or in this incredible salad. Thanks to Susan Wilson for the inspiration.

Salad

1 eggplant, cut in ½-inch rounds
1 red pepper, cut in large wedges
1 onion, cut in large wedges
1 summer squash, cut in long, fat strips
1 zucchini, cut in long, fat strips
10 big mushrooms
Extra-virgin olive oil
8 cups salad greens
1-2 ounces feta cheese, crumbled

Dressing

4 tablespoons extra-virgin olive oil
3 tablespoons brown rice vinegar
2 tablespoons brown rice syrup
1 tablespoon Dijon mustard
2 teaspoons poppyseeds
1 tablespoon fresh dill or 1 teaspoon dried dill

Light the coals in your grill (a small hibachi works fine). While coals are heating, prepare vegetables for grilling. Wash and cut them and brush both sides of each vegetable piece with a light coat of oil. When coals are white-hot, place vegetable pieces on grill and cook a few minutes on each side, until the vegetables just start to brown. Set aside grilled vegetables.

Wash salad greens by placing leaves in a sink full of cold water. Drain and repeat. Spin or pat dry. Tear greens into bite-sized pieces and place in a large salad bowl. Cut grilled vegetables into bite-sized pieces and add them to salad greens. Crumble feta on top. Whisk all ingredients for dressing together or shake up in a small jar.

Dress and toss salad before serving. Save any leftover grilled vegetables to make sandwiches the next day.

Preparation time: 30 minutes
Makes 8 servings, ²/₃ cup dressing

FOR BABIES 6 MONTHS & OLDER
Reserve some slices of zucchini and summer squash. Steam until soft and puree or mash for baby.

VARIATION FOR CHILDREN
You may want to make a shishkebob with the vegetables and serve with a dip (Lemon Tahini Sauce, page 206, or Tofu Dill Dressing, page 182, work well).

Dulse Salad
with Lemon Tahini Dressing

If you're looking for added iron in your diet, search no more. Dulse, a dark red sea vegetable, contains 11 grams of iron per ¼ cup. To find out more about dulse or tahini, see "Identifying, Shopping, and Storing Whole Foods" (page 252). Serve this salad to your favorite pregnant or nursing mom with nutrient-rich Quick Lemon & Garlic Quinoa Salad (page 105) and pinto beans.

Salad

  1 cup dry dulse
  1 red onion, sliced in very thin rounds
  1-2 stalks celery, cut in bite-sized pieces
  1 tablespoon brown rice vinegar
  Pinch of sea salt
  4 red leaf lettuce leaves

Dressing

  ¼ cup tahini
  2 tablespoons extra-virgin olive oil
  1 clove garlic
  Juice of 1 lemon
  ½ teaspoon tamari or shoyu
  ⅓ cup water

Soak the dulse in cold water. Meanwhile cut the other vegetables for the salad. Clean the soaked dulse well, removing any small pebbles. Pat dulse dry. Combine dulse, red onion, and celery with vinegar and salt; refrigerate for an hour or so. Combine all dressing ingredients in the blender and blend until smooth. Serve the salad on a lettuce leaf with 1 tablespoon of dressing on top. Leftover dressing will keep in the refrigerator for a week.

Preparation time: 15 minutes, 1 hour to marinate
Makes 4 servings, ¾ cup dressing

FOR BABIES 6 MONTHS & OLDER
Toast dulse in a 250° oven for 12-15 minutes. Crumble toasted dulse into flakes and store in a sealed jar. Sprinkle flakes into baby's cereal or other foods to make them iron-fortified.

Roasted Potatoes & Carrots with Cumin and Cinnamon

Children love these succulent, roasted vegetables. The time involved is just slow baking in the oven, not you in the kitchen. Serve this dish with Nut Burgers (page 158) or Sloppeh Joes (page 151) for a healthy version of burgers and spuds.

> 6 red potatoes, quartered
> 2-3 carrots, sliced at an angle into chunks
> 3 tablespoons extra-virgin olive oil
> 2 teaspoons cumin
> 1/4 teaspoon cayenne
> 1/8 teaspoon cinnamon

Preheat oven to 350° F. Scrub potatoes and carrots. Remove any eyes from the potatoes. Cut up vegetables and place in an 8-by-8-inch baking dish. Mix oil and spices together in a small bowl and drizzle over top of the vegetables. Mix vegetables with a wooden spoon so they are evenly coated. Cover pan and bake 45 minutes. Remove cover and bake for another 15 minutes.

Preparation time: 1 hour and 10 minutes
Makes 4 servings

FOR BABIES 6 MONTHS & OLDER
Remove a little potato and carrot before adding oil and spices and bake in a separate dish. Blend baked vegetables with a little water.

Rosemary and Garlic Roasted Potatoes
Substitute 2 cloves fresh garlic and 1-2 tablespoons fresh rosemary chopped fine for the cumin, cayenne, and cinnamon.

Potato Gratin

*This recipe was inspired by one in a book called **Gourmet Under Way** by The Resource Institute in Seattle. Traditional potatoes au gratin are loaded with milk and cheese; this lighter version is equally satisfying.*

4 - 6 red potatoes, sliced ¼-inch thin
2 teaspoons extra-virgin olive oil
1 red pepper, sliced thin
1 large onion, sliced thin
2 cloves garlic, minced
2 tablespoons parmesan cheese (optional)
fresh ground black pepper

Place sliced potatoes in a steamer basket and steam 10 minutes until edges are limp. Heat oil in skillet. Add peppers, onions, and garlic; sauté a few minutes. Preheat oven to 350° F. Layer steamed potatoes and vegetables in a casserole. Cover and bake 30-40 minutes. Uncover the casserole and top with parmesan and black pepper. Turn oven up to 400° F. and bake until the top is brown, approximately 10 minutes.

Preparation: 50 minutes
Makes 4 to 6 servings

FOR BABIES 6 MONTHS & OLDER
Put some of the steamed potatoes in a separate baking dish and bake 30-40 minutes as well. Remove and puree with water or breast milk.

Identifying Winter Squashes and Sweet Potatoes

Just about everyone loves the taste of sweet vegetables. I returned home to Kansas one Thanksgiving and prepared baked winter squash and sweet potatoes mashed together for the family gathering. Several relatives praised me for the offering and asked for the recipe. I repeated many times that it was simply baked buttercup squash and sweet potatoes. My grandmother was sure I was wrong. She insisted that there must be brown sugar, pineapples, marshmallows, or all three in the dish.

The autumn harvest brings pumpkins and a wide variety of winter squashes, each with its own unique and unbelievably sweet flavor. These vegetables not only score high on taste, but are rich in vitamin A, vitamin C, fiber, and trace minerals. Here is a description of some of the varieties to shop for:

Acorn squash
Shaped like a large acorn with prominent ridges, comes in dark green, yellow or orange; sweet, light flesh.

Buttercup squash
Shaped like a pumpkin but smaller, green or gold skin; meat is dark orange, moist and creamy.

Butternut squash
Gourd-shaped with a neck and a bulbous base, buff-colored skin; flesh is orange and firm.

Delicata squash
A small, oblong shape, yellow skin with green stripes; particularly sweet, golden-colored flesh.

Golden turbans
Like a double-decker pumpkin, distinctive turban shape, comes in hues of green, gold, orange and red; mild, pleasant flavor.

Hubbard squash
Large, smooth-skinned squash with a gray-green color, classic flavor.

Kabocha squash
Pumpkin-shaped and dark green with gray-brown nubs on the outside; dark orange flesh inside.

Spaghetti squash
A large, oval-shaped squash with yellow skin; insides become long thin golden strands when cooked.

Sugar pie pumpkins
Small, dark orange pumpkins; perfect for pie-making.

Sweet potatoes and yams
Beige or brown skins and are shaped like a potato with pointed ends. The meat is gold or dark orange.

Baked Winter Squash

Wonderful served with black beans, brown rice and collard greens — a beautiful balance of colors and nutrients. See page 193 for a description of the many varieties of winter squash to choose from. Clean the seeds and roast in oven on a cookie sheet for 15 minutes at 250° F. A delicious snack; uses the whole food.

1 winter squash

Preheat oven to 350° F. Small squashes can be washed and baked whole. Larger squashes can be cut in half. Be sure to use a strong, sharp knife. Scoop out the pith and seeds. Lay squash flat on a lightly oiled baking dish. Bake until tender. Test by inserting a fork; it should slide in easily and feel soft. Small squashes, such as delicata, will only take 35-45 minutes to bake, while a squash weighing 3 pounds may take up to 90 minutes.

Preparation time: Depends on size of squash, see directions
2½ pounds of winter squash makes 2-3 cups of cooked squash or 4 servings

FOR BABIES 6 MONTHS & OLDER
Puree baked squash with a little breast milk or water.

Leftover baked winter squash? Use it for:
Baby food
Sweet Squash Corn Muffins (page 200)
Pumpkin Pecan Muffins (page 202)
Halloween Cookies (page 223)
Yummy Yam Frosting (page 243)
Add to hot cooked breakfast cereal
Freezes well for later use

Fresh Breads
and Muffins

Homemade Whole Grain Bread

Jeff Basom, the chef at Bastyr University, shares his unique way of making bread. Jeff's bread is economical and nutritious and children love the soft, light texture. Using leftover grains or cereal as a starter dough is a beautiful example of the transformative quality of whole foods.

Starter Dough

　　2 cups cooked whole grains
　　2 cups water
　　¼ cup cold-pressed vegetable oil
　　1 tablespoon sea salt
　　1 tablespoon dry yeast
　　1 cup whole wheat flour (more or less)

Blend grains and water in a blender or food processor until creamy; pour into a large mixing bowl. Mix in oil, salt, and yeast. Add enough flour to make the mixture look like thick cooked cereal. Cover the bowl with plastic wrap or a damp towel and leave for 12-24 hours at room temperature. Once the dough is fermented, it can be refrigerated for up to a week before using to make bread.

To make the bread

　　¼ cup sweetener (such as barley malt or maple syrup)
　　2 cups whole wheat flour
　　3-4 cups unbleached white flour or whole wheat flour

After the 12-24 hours, add sweetener to starter dough and stir. Add whole wheat flour, stirring it in. As you add the white flour, the mixture will be too difficult to stir. Knead it by hand in the bowl and continue to add white flour. When dough is less sticky, transfer it to a floured surface and knead 10-15 minutes or until dough is soft and springy, but not too sticky. Wash and dry mixing bowl and oil it. Place dough in bowl, cover and let rise in a warm place 1½-2 hours.

To make loaves

Lightly oil 2 loaf pans. Divide dough in half. Punch down and loaf the dough in the following way (children love to help with this part):

• Flatten half of the dough into a square on your working surface. Press all of the air out of the dough by vigorously slapping the dough with the palms of both hands.

• Fold the flattened dough into a triangle and press it down again.

- Fold 2 corners into the center and press again.
- Fold the top point into the body of the dough and press it down again.
- Pick up the dough with both hands and begin rolling it into itself. This stretches the outside of the dough and creates a tight roll with no air pockets. Seal the seam by flattening it with the heel of your hand.
- Shape the dough into a nice loaf and place in the pan seam side down. Repeat punching down and shaping with the other half of dough.

To bake the bread

1 teaspoon water
1 teaspoon barley malt or maple syrup
1 teaspoon cold-pressed vegetable oil
¼ teaspoon sea salt

Mix water, syrup, oil, and salt in a small cup or bowl and coat the top of each loaf with this mixture. Cover and let rise in pans for 45-60 minutes until the loaves have doubled in size. Test the bread for readiness. If you press the dough and it wants to stay in, but still has a little spring, it's ready to bake. Preheat oven to 350° F. Bake 45-50 minutes. Bread will come out of pans after 5 minutes of cooling. Let it cool 30 minutes before slicing (if you can wait!).

Preparation time: Each step of actual work takes 5-15 minutes, over a period of 2 days. The fermenting, rising and baking take time.
Makes 2 loaves

Whole-Grain Bread Variations

Here are four delicious versions of Jeff's bread. Follow general directions for Homemade Whole Grain Bread with these more specific ingredients.

Rice Bread

Starter Dough
> 2 cups cooked brown rice
> 2 cups water
> ¼ cup cold-pressed vegetable oil
> 1 tablespoon sea salt
> 1 tablespoon dry yeast
> 1 cup whole wheat flour (more or less)

To make the bread
> Starter Dough
> ¼ cup barley malt
> 2 cups whole wheat flour
> 3-4 cups unbleached flour or whole wheat flour

Orange Millet Raisin Bread

Starter Dough
> 2 cups cooked millet
> 1 cup water
> 1 cup orange juice
> ¼ cup cold-pressed vegetable oil
> 1 tablespoon sea salt
> 1 tablespoon yeast
> 1 cup whole wheat flour (more or less)

To make the bread
> Starter Dough
> ¼ cup barley malt or maple syrup
> 2 cups raisins
> 1 teaspoon cinnamon
> 2 cups whole wheat flour
> 3-4 cups unbleached white flour or whole wheat flour

Quinoa Garlic Herb Bread

Starter Dough
> 2 cups cooked quinoa
> 2 cups water
> ¼ cup extra-virgin olive oil
> 1 tablespoon sea salt
> 1 tablespoon yeast
> 1 cup whole wheat flour (more or less)

To make the bread
> **Starter Dough**
> 6 cloves garlic, minced very fine
> 1 tablespoon chopped fresh basil
> 2 tablespoons chopped fresh parsley
> 2 tablespoons chopped fresh cilantro
> 2 teaspoons chopped fresh rosemary
> 2 cups whole wheat flour
> 3-4 cups unbleached white flour or whole wheat flour

Bean Apple Rye Bread

Starter Dough
> 2 cups cooked beans or 1 cup cooked beans and 1 cup baked
>   winter squash
> 1 cup water
> 1 tablespoon yeast
> 1 tablespoon sea salt
> 1 cup whole wheat flour
> ¼ cup cold-pressed vegetable oil

To make the bread
> **Starter Dough**
> ⅓ cup apple butter
> 2 cups whole wheat flour
> 1 cup rye flour
> 2-3 cups unbleached white flour or whole wheat flour

FOR BABIES 6 MONTHS & OLDER
Reserve part of the cooked brown rice, quinoa, millet, or squash you are using
for the Starter Dough. Put in blender with a little breast milk or water and
puree.

Sweet Squash Corn Muffins

These corn muffins, developed by Nancy Rankin and me, are rich in taste and nutrition. The cooked winter squash imparts vitamin-rich sweetness, and the dulse flakes add iron. Dulse is a dark red sea vegetable that has an unusually high iron content. To learn more about dulse, see "Identifying, Shopping and Storing Whole Foods," page 254. Buttercup, butternut, and delicata squash work well in this recipe.

1½ cups cornmeal
1½ cups whole wheat pastry flour or barley flour
1 tablespoon non-aluminum baking powder
¼ teaspoon sea salt
2 tablespoons dulse flakes
2 cups winter squash or sweet potato puree
⅓ cup cold-pressed vegetable oil
½ cup maple syrup
½ cup water

Topping
¼ cup pumpkin seeds

Preheat oven to 375° F. Lightly oil muffin tins or line with paper muffin cups. Mix cornmeal, flour, baking powder, salt, and dulse flakes together in a large bowl; set aside. In a separate bowl, whisk together squash, oil, syrup, and water, until smooth. Combine wet ingredients with dry mixture and mix with a minimum of strokes. Spoon into muffin cups. Decorate top of each muffin with pumpkin seeds. Bake 20-25 minutes. Top of muffin should crack slightly when done.

Preparation time: 30 minutes
Makes 12 regular muffins

FOR BABIES 6 MONTHS & OLDER
Reserve a portion of the baked winter squash or sweet potato that has been pureed or mashed.

Cranberry Apple Walnut Muffins

A basket of homemade muffins makes a welcome gift or a wonderful addition to a holiday brunch. Buy whole walnuts for this recipe, crack them carefully with a clean cut and use the walnut halves to house tiny presents or make tree decorations.

2 cups whole wheat pastry flour
1 cup cornmeal
1 tablespoon baking powder
1 teaspoon sea salt
1 teaspoon cinnamon
¼ teaspoon ground cloves
1 teaspoon orange zest
2 cups applesauce
¾ cup maple syrup or concentrated fruit sweetener
¼ cup soymilk
⅓ cup cold-pressed canola oil
2 teaspoon vanilla
1 cup cranberries
2 apples, grated
½ cup chopped walnuts

Preheat oven to 375° F. Lightly oil muffin tins or line with paper muffin cups. Put flour, cornmeal, baking powder, salt, cinnamon, cloves, and zest in large mixing bowl, stir and set aside.

Place applesauce, syrup, soymilk, oil, and vanilla extract in blender; blend until smooth. Add cranberries and pulse for a few seconds, just long enough to break up cranberries.

Peel apples. Core and cut apples into thin pieces, about ½" by ¼". Add wet ingredients to dry mixture, fold in apples and walnuts and mix together using a minimum of strokes. Fill muffin cups to top with batter. Bake 25-30 minutes.

Preparation time: 45 minutes
Makes 12 muffins

FOR BABIES 6 MONTHS & OLDER
Use organic applesauce and serve some plain.

Pumpkin Pecan Muffins

Baked sugar pie pumpkin or buttercup squash are delicious in this recipe. These muffins make excellent snacks or breakfast food. They are also a nice accompaniment to Thick Potato Cauliflower and Dulse Soup (page 132) or other savory soups.

> 3 cups whole wheat pastry flour
> 1 tablespoon baking powder
> 1 teaspoon sea salt
> 1 teaspoon cinnamon
> ½ teaspoon cloves
> ½ teaspoon cardamom
> 2 cups pumpkin or winter squash puree
> ½ cup maple syrup
> ½ cup soymilk
> ⅓ cup cold-pressed vegetable oil
> 2 teaspoons vanilla
> ½ cup pecans, chopped

Preheat oven to 375° F. Lightly oil muffin tins or line with paper muffin cups. Mix together flours, baking powder, salt, and spices in large bowl; set aside. Put pumpkin, maple syrup, soymilk, oil, and vanilla in blender; blend until smooth. Add wet ingredients to dry mixture and fold gently, using a minimum of strokes. Gently fold pecans into batter. Fill muffin cups to top with batter. Bake 25-30 minutes.

Preparation time: 45 minutes
Makes 12 muffins

FOR BABIES 6 MONTHS & OLDER
Reserve some of the baked pumpkin or winter squash used in the muffins. Puree with a little breast milk or water.

Banana Blueberry Poppyseed Muffins

Ripe bananas and blueberries marry well with poppy seeds to make a wonderful muffin. Replace whole wheat pastry flour with spelt or kamut flour, and expand your baking expertise to include a variety of whole grain flours. Serve these muffins for breakfasts, snacks or as a side dish to a soup and salad dinner.

2 cups whole wheat pastry flour
1 cup cornmeal
1 tablespoon baking powder
1 teaspoon sea salt
1 teaspoon cinnamon
½ cup poppy seeds
2 cups banana puree (2 ripe bananas plus some water)
½ cup maple syrup or concentrated fruit sweetener
½ cup soymilk
⅓ cup cold-pressed vegetable oil
2 teaspoons vanilla
1 cup fresh blueberries

Preheat oven to 375° F. Lightly oil muffin tins or line with paper muffin cups. Put flours, cornmeal, baking powder, salt, cinnamon, and poppy seeds in large mixing bowl and stir; set aside. Place bananas, syrup, soymilk, oil, and vanilla in blender and blend until smooth. Add wet ingredients to dry mixture and mix together, using a minimum of strokes. Fold in blueberries. Fill muffin cup to top with batter. Bake 25-30 minutes.

Preparation time: 45 minutes
Makes 12 muffins

FOR BABIES 6 MONTHS & OLDER
Mash up some extra ripe banana and serve.

FOR BABIES 10 MONTHS & OLDER
Blend ½ ripe banana with 2 tablespoons blueberries and serve for a naturally sweet treat.

Herb & Garlic Pizza Dough

This recipe was inspired by the unique repertoire of vegetarian chef Jim Watkins. The dough is easy to make, delicious, and can be used for a variety of savory dishes — including pizza!

1 tablespoon yeast
1 cup lukewarm water
1 tablespoon honey
1 tablespoon fresh rosemary
12-15 fresh oregano leaves
1 tablespoon fresh thyme leaves
3-4 cloves garlic
½ teaspoon sea salt
1 tablespoon extra-virgin olive oil
1½ cups whole wheat pastry flour
1 cup unbleached white flour

To make dough

Combine yeast, ½ cup of warm water, and honey in a large mixing bowl. Gently stir, then set aside. Let rest for 10 minutes while yeast comes to life.

Chop rosemary, oregano, thyme, and garlic together until very fine. Add herbs, garlic, salt, oil, and remaining water to yeast mixture. Add flour a little at a time. Mix together with a spoon until it becomes too hard to stir. Then transfer to a floured surface and knead until smooth (10-12 minutes). Add more flour to surface when necessary to keep dough from sticking. Place dough in an oiled bowl. Cover and let rest 30 minutes.

To make pizza

Preheat oven to 350° F. Roll dough out to desired shape. Prebake 10-12 minutes. Remove from oven. Raise oven temperature to 450° F. Cover pizza crust with desired toppings and bake 10-12 minutes.

Preparation time: 30 minutes for dough, 25 minutes to finish pizza
Makes dough for one 15-inch pizza

FOR BABIES 6 MONTHS & OLDER
Use zucchini slices for pizza topping. Reserve some and steam; puree and serve.

Sauces
and Stuff

Lemon Tahini Sauce

This dressing is so versatile it is worth making up a regular batch to have around. I love it as a topping on brown rice, soba noodles, or as a lively salad dressing. Tahini is a creamy paste made of crushed, hulled sesame seeds. Look for it with other nut butters or Mid-Eastern foods.

½ cup tahini
¼ cup extra-virgin olive oil
Juice of 1½ lemons
1 clove garlic
1 teaspoon tamari or shoyu
1/16 teaspoon (just a pinch) cayenne
¾ cup water

Place all ingredients in a blender or processor; blend until smooth. Allow mixture to set for a half hour if possible to allow flavors to meld. Sauce will keep in the refrigerator for 10-14 days.

Preparation: 5 minutes
Makes 1½ cups

FOR BABIES 10 MONTHS & OLDER
Add a little tahini to baby's cereal for extra calories and other nutrients.

Tahini Oat Sauce with Scallions

This creamy simple-to-make sauce is just the thing to serve over whole grains or whole grain noodles. Serve Tahini Oat Sauce over brown rice with cooked greens, roasted sweet potatoes, and kidney beans for a well-balanced grain-bean-vegetable combination.

¼ cup rolled oats
1 cup water
Pinch of sea salt
2 tablespoons tahini
1 tablespoon tamari or shoyu
1 tablespoon water
1 scallion, finely chopped

Put the oats, water, and salt in a small pan; bring to a boil. Lower heat, cover, and simmer 10-12 minutes. Put oat mixture in the blender with tahini, tamari, and water; blend until smooth. Return to small pan, adding chopped scallion. Gently reheat, if necessary, before serving.

Preparation time: 15 minutes
Makes 1 cup

FOR BABIES 6 MONTHS & OLDER
Cook twice the amount of oatmeal and reserve some for baby's meal. Puree with a little water or breast milk if too thick or lumpy.

Almond Ginger Drizzle

A sensuous topping for grains or vegetables. I especially like it served over kasha. You can substitute different nut butters to create slight variations in taste. A ceramic ginger grater is a very useful kitchen gadget to have on hand for recipes that call for freshly grated ginger.

1/4 cup almond butter
2 teaspoons maple syrup
2 tablespoons tamari or shoyu
1 tablespoon brown rice vinegar
1 teaspoon grated gingerroot
1-2 teaspoons hot pepper oil
1/3 cup water

Put all ingredients in a small pan on low heat. Using a whisk, mix ingredients until smooth and warm. Serve immediately over grains, beans or cooked vegetables.

Preparation time: 5 minutes
Makes 1 cup

FOR BABIES 10 MONTHS & OLDER
Stir a half teaspoon of almond butter into baby's warm whole grain cereal for added calories and other nutrients.

VARIATION FOR CHILDREN
Omit hot pepper oil and use as a dipping sauce for raw vegetables.

Creamy Ginger-Garlic Dressing

This lively dressing is delicious served on pasta, rice, kasha, cooked greens, steamed vegetables, and green salads.

½ pound tofu
1 teaspoon grated gingerroot
2 cloves garlic, minced
2 tablespoons extra-virgin olive oil
2 tablespoons lime juice
2 teaspoons tamari or shoyu
¼ cup water

Place all ingredients in the blender; blend until smooth. Will keep in the refrigerator 4-5 days.

Preparation time: 5 minutes
Makes 1 cup

FOR BABIES 10 MONTHS & OLDER
Cut up extra tofu into small cubes. Steam or drop into boiling water for a few seconds. Let cool and serve as finger food.

Mushroom Wine Gravy

Mashed potatoes and gravy — vegetarian style. This gravy is nice served over Sage and Rosemary Seitan (page 111). Arrowroot, which comes from a tropical plant whose tuberous root is dried and ground into a fine white powder, is used in this recipe as a thickener. Whole-foods cooks prefer arrowroot's natural method of preparation over cornstarch, which is bleached and chemically treated during processing.

2 teaspoons butter
¼ pound mushrooms, cleaned and sliced
Pinch of sea salt
1 cup water
1 tablespoon tamari or shoyu
1 tablespoon cashew butter
1 tablespoon arrowroot
2 tablespoons white wine

In a small pan, melt butter. Add mushrooms and salt; sauté until mushrooms are soft. Whisk in water, tamari, cashew butter, arrowroot, and wine. Heat until gravy becomes thick (a few minutes).

Preparation time: 10 minutes
Makes 1½ cups of gravy

FOR BABIES 6 MONTHS & OLDER
Try a new vegetable tonight! Peel, cut, and steam some parsnips (a cream-colored carrot-shaped vegetable with a sweet taste). Puree some with water or breast milk for baby; serve whole as a side dish for the rest of the family.

VARIATION FOR CHILDREN
Reserve some mushrooms and bake whole at 350° F in a covered dish for an hour. They become very succulent and flavorful.

Garlic Ginger Marinade

This marinade will work for tempeh, tofu or fish. The longer the food marinates, the deeper the flavors. Marinate sliced tofu or tempeh overnight. Marinate fish for a few hours before cooking. To find out more about brown rice vinegar or mirin, see "Identifying, Shopping, and Storing Whole Foods" (page 252).

3 cloves garlic, sliced
4-5 slices of fresh gingerroot
1 cup water
1 tablespoon brown rice vinegar
1 tablespoon mirin
¼ cup tamari or shoyu

Combine all ingredients in a bowl or other container. Slice tofu or tempeh into desired size. Add tofu or tempeh to marinade. Seal bowl or container. Refrigerate for 1-3 days.

Preparation time: 5 minutes
Makes 1¹/₃ cups

FOR BABIES 6 MONTHS & OLDER
Serve marinated and pan-fried tempeh over quinoa. Reserve some of the cooked quinoa and puree with a little water or breast milk to make cereal for baby.

Cranberry Apple Relish

*An adaptation of a recipe from **The Natural Foods Cookbook** by Mary Estella (Japan Publications, 1985) that uses apple juice and maple syrup to add sweetness to tart cranberries. Try a little of this relish on Sage and Rosemary Seitan Sandwiches (page 111) or as a side dish at Thanksgiving.*

1½ cups cranberries
1 cup chopped apples
½ cup currants
1 teaspoon orange zest
¼ cup maple syrup
⅛ teaspoon sea salt
1 cup apple juice or water
¼ cup chopped walnuts (optional)

Place cranberries, apples, currants, zest, maple syrup, salt, and juice in a large saucepan. Cover and bring to a boil. Reduce heat, remove cover, and simmer 20-25 minutes until excess liquid has evaporated. Remove from heat. Add walnuts if using. Serve at room temperature. Will keep in a sealed container in the refrigerator 3-4 days.

Preparation time: 30 minutes
Makes 2½ cups

FOR BABIES 10 MONTHS & OLDER
If your baby has teeth, reserve some apple slices, steam until soft, let cool, and serve as finger food.

Ghee

Thought in the East to have many virtues, ghee is noted for taking on and magnifying the properties of food it is combined with, making the food more nutritious. Ghee is sometimes used in my recipes in place of oil, especially in foods that contain Indian spices. Ghee imparts a buttery flavor but can hold a much higher temperature than butter without scorching.

½ pound unsalted butter
1 clean 8-ounce jar with lid

Put butter in a saucepan. Heat butter until it begins to boil, then turn heat to low. White foam (from the milk solids) will accumulate on the top. Use a small strainer and begin gently skimming solids off the top without disturbing the bottom. As you continue this process, the liquid in the bottom of the pan will begin to appear clear and golden. When all the water is boiled out of the butter, the cooking will sound like hissing and the bubbling will stop. Remove from heat and let it cool a few moments. Pour the ghee into the jar. It will solidify as it cools. Store in the refrigerator.

Preparation time: 15 minutes
Makes about 1 cup of ghee

FOR BABIES 6 MONTHS & OLDER

Ghee is a wonderful product to use in place of oil in curry dishes. Use ghee to make Curried Lentils and Cauliflower (page 154) served over basmati brown rice. Reserve a small portion of cooked rice, puree with a little water or breast milk and serve to baby.

Homemade Curry Paste

Jeff Basom created this multiuse flavoring for soups, beans, and all sorts of vegetable dishes. This handy product for busy cooks will keep a month or more in the refrigerator. It also makes a great Christmas gift.

1 pound onions, chopped fine
1 cup extra-virgin olive oil
¼ cup cumin seeds
1 teaspoon fenugreek
1 teaspoon whole cloves
2 teaspoons whole black pepper
2 tablespoons whole mustard seeds
2 teaspoons allspice
1 teaspoon cardamom
4 teaspoons cinnamon
¼ cup turmeric
¼ cup coriander
2 teaspoons cayenne
¼ cup ginger, peeled and chopped fine

Heat oil in a skillet. Add onions and sauté until very soft. While the onions are cooking, grind the cumin, fenugreek, cloves, and pepper to a fine powder. Mix the newly ground spices with whole mustard seeds, allspice, cardamom, cinnamon, tumeric, coriander, and cayenne; set aside. Add gingerroot to onions; let it cook a few minutes. Add the spices to onions and gingerroot; cook 5 more minutes. Store in a sealed jar in the refrigerator where it will keep for several months.

Preparation time: 20-25 minutes
Makes 2 cups

FOR BABIES 10 MONTHS & OLDER

I love to use this paste to make French Lentil and Potato Stew (page 135). Remove some of the cooked potatoes and carrots from the soup, puree and serve.

Wholesome Desserts

How to Use
Alternative Sweeteners

In this chapter I have given readers a wide array of delicious desserts using various alternative sweeteners. I prefer to use the alternative sweeteners in baked goods and desserts because they more closely resemble whole foods and because I believe there are detrimental side effects associated with consuming refined white sugar. Instructions for how to replace natural sweeteners with white sugar are explained under each sweetener listed. See page 218 for "Helpful Hints."

Granulated Natural Sweeteners

Date sugar
Simply ground dehydrated dates. Contains the same nutrient value as dried dates. Substitute cup for cup for white sugar. The taste and appearance is similar to brown sugar, but less sweet. While date sugar works well in baked goods, it does not dissolve well and is not recommended for use as a sweetener in hot beverages. If used to top a baked good, add enough hot water to make a syrup to prevent burning, or sprinkle on top after baking. See hint #4.

Dried cane juice
Juice that has been extracted from the sugar cane and dehydrated. This product is much less refined than white sugar, plus some of the minerals in the cane juice are still present. It resembles brown sugar in appearance and taste, though less sweet. Sucanat is a trade name for organically grown, dehydrated sugar cane juice. Substitute dried cane juice in equal proportions for white or brown sugar. See hint #4.

Thick Liquid Or Syrup-Like Natural Sweeteners

Barley malt
A complex carbohydrate sweetener made from barley that has been soaked, sprouted, and cooked until the starches in the grain are broken down and converted into maltose. Barley malt is dark and thick like molasses and has a malt-like taste. Replace 1 cup white sugar with 1 to 1½ cup barley malt and follow hints #1, 2, & 3.

Brown rice syrup
Made from rice that has been soaked, sprouted, and cooked with a cereal enzyme that breaks the starches into malrose. Rice syrup has a light, delicate flavor and looks similar to honey but is less sweet. Substitute rice syrup one for one for honey, maple syrup or barley malt. To substitute rice syrup for white sugar, use 1 to 1½ cups rice syrup per cup of sugar and adjust liquid to dry ratio according to hint #1. Also see hints #2 & 3.

Concentrated fruit sweetener

A commercially made syrup made from peach, pineapple, pear, and other fruit juices that have been cooked down to a syrup. It imparts a very fruity flavor to dishes it's used in. Concentrated fruit sweetener can be used in a recipe in place of honey, barley malt, rice syrup, or maple syrup in equal measure. Substitute 1 cup concentrated fruit sweetener for 1 cup white sugar and follow hint #1 to adjust liquid to dry ratio.

Frozen fruit juice concentrate

Familiar product found in the freezer section of grocery stores. Thaw juice and use full strength as a thick liquid sweetener to replace white sugar in a recipe. Substitute fruit juice concentrate cup for cup and adjust liquid to dry ratios according to hint #1.

Maple syrup

Made from the boiled sap of sugar maple trees. Forty gallons of sap (from nine trees) makes one gallon of syrup. Maple syrup is available in three grades: A, B, or C. The temperature used and length of time cooked determine the grade. Grade A is best for pancakes and waffles, grade B has better flavor for baking, is less expensive and has a higher mineral content. Replace 1 cup sugar with 1 cup maple syrup and follow instructions under hint #1 for adjusting liquid to dry ratio.

Pureed bananas

Can be substituted for 1 cup sugar in a recipe. Place one cup mashed over-ripe banana in the blender with a few tablespoons of water and blend until smooth. Adjust liquid to dry ratio in recipe according to hint #1. Freezing bananas first and then thawing before using makes an even sweeter puree.

Pureed dates

Can be substituted for 1 cup sugar in a recipe. Pit 1 cup dates and cut into small pieces. Place in blender with ½ to 1 cup hot water and puree to a thick paste. Adjust liquid to dry ratio in recipe according to hint #1.

Sorghum

The concentrated juice of crushed and boiled sorghum stems. The sorghum plant is a relative of millet. Sorghum is thick, light brown syrup with a slight molasses taste. Substitute 1 cup sorghum for 1 cup white sugar and follow hint #1 to adjust liquid to dry ratio.

Helpful Hints

1. When using any liquid concentrated sweetener in place of granulated white sugar, reduce liquid content in the recipe by ¼ cup. If no liquid is called for in the recipe, add 3-5 tablespoons of flour for each ¾ cup of liquid concentrated sweetener. When replacing a liquid sweetener with a dry (e.g., replacing honey with date sugar), increase the liquid content of the recipe by ¼ cup or reduce the flour by 3-5 tablespoons.

2. Due to the presence of a natural starch-splitting enzyme, some malted sweeteners (brown rice syrup or barley malt) may liquefy the consistency of the mixture. This is more likely if eggs are in the recipe. Boiling the malt syrup for 2-3 minutes before using can prevent this. Let it cool slightly before adding to recipe.

3. Heat thick syrups before working with them by setting the jar in hot water for 5-10 minutes. Be sure to oil measuring utensils used with the thick syrups.

4. The dried or granulated natural sweeteners tend to absorb liquid. Check your dough or batter to see if it resembles the texture you are used to and consider adding an extra tablespoon of water or oil if it seems dry. Adding extra moisture is especially important if you are also substituting white flour with whole grain flour in the recipe. Whole grain flours, because of the fiber, also absorb moisture.

Replacing Eggs in Baked Goods

Grind 2 tablespoons of flaxseed; add 6 tablespoons boiling water; let mixture set 15 minutes, then whisk with a fork. This will replace two eggs in any recipe for baked goods.

Replacing White Flour with Whole Grain Flour in Recipes

When replacing white flour with any whole grain flour use ⁷/₈ cup whole grain flour for every 1 cup white flour in the recipe. Whole grain flour contains bran and tends to absorb more liquid than white flour. If you replace white flour with whole grain flour in equal amounts, your dish may come out too dry.

Fruit Sauce

Cooking and pureeing favorite fruits creates wonderful fruit sauces that everyone can enjoy. There's the old favorite applesauce and newer versions such as pear sauce or plum-blueberry sauce. This food is perfect for people of ALL ages!

2 cups of apples, blueberries, cherries, pears or plums
2-4 tablespoons water or juice

Cut fruit into small chunks; place fruit and water in a pot. Bring to a boil, reduce heat to low and simmer, covered, until fruit is tender and the water has been absorbed (about 15 minutes). Puree in the blender or mash with a potato masher.

Preparation time: 20 minutes
Makes about 1 cup fruit sauce

FOR BABIES 6 MONTHS & OLDER
You may want to remove the peels of apples, pears and plums before cooking for a smoother sauce. Fruit sauce is perfect baby food.

VARIATION FOR CHILDREN
Keep skin on fruit if it is organic. Season fruit sauce with cinnamon and nutmeg. Try fruit sauce served on pancakes, whole grain cereals, with granola, or all by itself.

Gingerbread People

Children love making and decorating these tasty little cookie-people. I've used dried cane juice to replace granulated sugar in this recipe. Dried cane juice is a naturally processed sweetener where the juice from organically grown sugar cane is simply extracted and dehydrated. It is similar in flavor to brown sugar.

¼ cup unsalted butter, softened
¼ cup dried cane juice
¼ cup brown rice syrup
¼ cup blackstrap molasses
1 tablespoon freshly grated gingerroot
3 cups whole wheat pastry flour
1 teaspoon baking soda
¼ teaspoon cloves
½ teaspoon cinnamon
½ teaspoon sea salt
¼-½ cup orange juice

Decorations
   raisins
   papaya bits
   peanuts
   dried cranberries

Preheat oven to 350° F. In a large mixing bowl, blend butter and dried cane juice until creamy. Add syrup, molasses, and gingerroot; mix well. In a separate bowl, combine flours, soda, cloves, cinnamon, and salt. Add dry mixture to wet ingredients a little at a time, alternating with orange juice as needed. Work in the last of the flour mixture with your hands. Lightly oil a cookie sheet and roll the dough directly onto it. Cut out figures with a cookie cutter or make up your own shapes. Remove scraps of dough between cutouts to make more cookies. Add decorations before baking. Bake 8 minutes or longer according to thickness of dough.

Preparation time: 15-20 minutes
Makes 8 to 15 cookies, depending upon thickness

Apricot Thumbprint Cookies

These delicious and fun-to-make cookies are perfect with afternoon tea.
Variations in flavor can be made by substituting different nuts and juices as
shown in the Orange Hazelnut adaptation below.

> 2 cups whole wheat pastry flour
> 1 cup almonds (ground into 1½ cup meal)
> 2 teaspoons baking powder
> ¼ teaspoon sea salt
> ⅓ cup cold-pressed vegetable oil or melted, unsalted butter
> ⅓ cup apricot juice (or apple)
> ⅓ cup maple syrup or concentrated fruit sweetener
> 1 teaspoon almond extract
> ½ teaspoon vanilla
> Apricot preserves (fruit-sweetened)

Preheat oven to 350° F. Combine flour, almonds, baking powder, and
salt in a mixing bowl; set aside. In a separate bowl, mix oil, juice,
syrup, extracts together. Add wet ingredients to dry and mix well,
kneading a little. Form dough into balls and flatten to make circles.
Place on lightly oiled cookie sheet. Indent each cookie with your
thumb or your child's thumb and put ½ teaspoon preserves in the
imprint. Bake 15 minutes, until edges turn golden.

Preparation time: 30 minutes
Makes 24 cookies

Orange Hazelnut Thumbprint Cookies

Replace almonds with hazelnuts. Replace apricot juice with orange juice. Add ½
teaspoon orange zest to dry ingredients.

Oatmeal Chocolate Chip Walnut Cookies

These cookies are very easy to make and take very little time. Great for packing in a lunchbox as a special treat.

1½ cups rolled oats
1 cup whole wheat pastry flour
¼ teaspoon sea salt
½ cup maple syrup
⅓ cup cold-pressed vegetable oil or melted, unsalted butter
1 teaspoon vanilla extract
⅓ cup chopped walnuts
⅓ cup malt-sweetened chocolate chips

Preheat oven to 350° F. Combine oats, flour, and salt together in a bowl; set aside. In a separate bowl mix together sweetener, oil, and vanilla. Add wet ingredients to dry mixture and mix well. Stir in nuts and chips. With moist hands form dough into 3" cookies and place on a lightly oiled cookie sheet or one lined with parchment paper. Bake for 15-20 minutes, until golden on edges.

Preparation time: 20 minutes
Makes 1 dozen big 3" cookies

Halloween Cookies

(wheat-free)

The children at the Briar Rose Kindergarten in Seattle happily devoured these Halloween cookies with a swirl of Yummy Yam Frosting (page 243) on top, a healthy harvest treat designed by Rita Carey. Barley flour and spelt flour substitute well for wheat flour in most recipes. You can use dried cane juice or date sugar in this recipe. Date sugar is a naturally produced sweetener that can be used in baked goods. It is simply dried and ground dates, truly a whole foods sweetener!

1 cup barley flour
1 cup spelt flour or kamut flour
½ teaspoon baking soda
1 teaspoon cinnamon
½ teaspoon ginger
¼ teaspoon nutmeg
¼ teaspoon allspice
¾ cup pureed, cooked pumpkin, winter squash,
    or sweet potato
¾ cup dried cane juice or date sugar
½ cup apple butter or plain yogurt
2 tablespoons cold-pressed vegetable oil

Preheat oven to 350° F. Combine flours, soda, cinnamon, ginger, nutmeg, and allspice in a mixing bowl; set aside. In a separate bowl, combine pumpkin, dried cane juice, apple butter, and oil. Add wet ingredients to dry mixture. Lightly oil a cookie sheet and drop by tablespoons onto cookie sheet. Bake 15 minutes.

Preparation time: 25-30 minutes
Makes 2 dozen cookies

Carob Brownies

Carob is an evergreen tree with edible pods. Also known as St. John's Bread, the powder made from the pods is naturally sweet, low in fat, high in calcium, and caffeine-free. I find the dark, fruity taste of carob quite delicious. Try these tasty brownies at your next potluck or school picnic. Cafix, a powder made from grains, figs and other natural ingredients, is stirred into hot water to use as a coffee substitute.

1¾ cup whole wheat pastry or barley flour
1 cup carob powder, sifted
½ teaspoon sea salt
2 eggs, separated
⅔ cup concentrated fruit sweetener or maple syrup
⅓ cup cold-pressed vegetable oil or melted, unsalted butter
1 tablespoon Cafix dissolved in ¼ cup hot water
2 teaspoons vanilla
⅓ cup chopped nuts

Preheat oven to 350° F. In a large mixing bowl, combine flour, carob, salt and nuts; set aside. Separate eggs into two bowls. Beat yolks with a whisk. Add sweetener, oil, Cafix in water, and vanilla to bowl with yolks; mix well. Add wet ingredients to dry mixture and mix well. Beat egg whites until stiff. Fold whites into brownie mixture. Pour into lightly oiled 8-by-8-inch pan. Bake 30-40 minutes.

Preparation time: 50 minutes
Makes 16 brownies

Brown Rice Crispy Treats

The kids at Decatur Elementary did a swell job of making and devouring these quick-to-fix treats during an after-school cooking class I conducted. The recipe is a great example of how to use brown rice syrup, a naturally processed sweetener, made from brown rice that has been soaked, sprouted, and cooked. Rice syrup has a light, delicate flavor. I sometimes substitute ½ teaspoon butterscotch flavoring for the vanilla for a slightly different flavor. This is an adaptation of a recipe from Nancy Rankin.

> 1 teaspoon unrefined sesame oil
> 1 cup brown rice syrup
> 2 tablespoons almond butter or tahini
> 2 teaspoons vanilla extract
> 6 cups dry natural brown rice crispy cereal

Optional additions
> ½ cup peanuts
> ½ cup raisins or currants
> ½ cup unsweetened carob chips
> ½ cup chopped almonds

Put oil in a large pot and heat. Add rice syrup and nut butter. Stir and heat until bubbles form. Turn off heat and add vanilla extract. Add cereal and mix well with a spatula. Stir in optional items and mix lightly. Put mixture into a 9-by-13-inch pan. With slightly wet hands, press mixture flat. Let set to room temperature. Slice and serve. Lasts a week in an airtight container.

Preparation time: 5-8 minutes
Makes 24 squares

Fruitsicles

You can buy Popscicle holders in the summertime at most stores that carry toys or kitchenware. Dream up an endless variety of frozen treats to delight sun-soaked children and adults.

Juicesicles
    1 cup juice (raspberry, grape, cherry, tropical)

Pour in holders and freeze.

Creamy Orange-Vanilla Pops
    ¾ cup orange juice
    ¼ cup vanilla yogurt
    1 teaspoon vanilla

Blend all ingredients in a blender, pour in holders, and freeze.

Banana Raspberry Pops
    1 banana
    ⅓ cup raspberries
    ½ cup water

Blend all ingredients in a blender, pour in holders, and freeze.

Melonsicles
    2 cups of melon chunks (cantaloupe, honeydew, watermelon)
    ¼ cup water

Blend all ingredients in a blender, pour in holders, and freeze. If using watermelon, remove seeds and omit water.

Maltsicles
    8 ounces of malted soy milk

Pour commercially made malted soy milk into Popscicle holders and freeze.

Note how much liquid it will take to fill your Popsicle holders. Each of these recipes makes one cup of liquid, which fills four of the common cylindrical-style holders. Freeze for at least 2 hours. Run warm water on the outside of the holder until the pop pulls out easily. You can also use ice-cube trays to make iced fruit cubes for children to suck.

Preparation time: 5 minutes for making pops, 2 hours for freezing
Makes 4 fruitsicles, depending upon size of holders used

Apricot Kudzu Custard

Kudzu, the dried root of the kudzu plant, looks like broken chalk. It can be dissolved in cool or room-temperature liquid and used as a natural thickener. Kudzu is thought to have an overall calming effect on the body, especially the digestive system. Tahini, a sesame seed paste, is used to give the custard a slightly nutty flavor. This sweetly soothing dessert or snack is easy to prepare. Fit for company with a little granola or a dollop of Nut Cream (page 230) on top.

> 2 tablespoons kudzu
> 2 cups apricot nectar or juice
> 2 teaspoons tahini
> 1 teaspoon vanilla

Dissolve the kudzu in cold or room temperature juice. Put mixture in a small pan over medium heat, stirring constantly. As mixture simmers, it becomes clear and thick. Once this happens, remove from heat. Add tahini and vanilla; mix well. Serve immediately; custard will get rubbery if allowed to cool to room temperature.

Preparation time: 5-10 minutes
Makes 4 servings

FOR BABIES 10 MONTHS & OLDER
Serve a small amount as is.

Raspberry Pudding Gel

This recipe uses the natural jelling agent, agar, to thicken liquid. Agar is a tasteless sea vegetable that looks like small, translucent flakes. Agar thickens at room temperature, unlike gelatin, which must be chilled. By using both agar and kudzu as thickeners you get a much smoother, creamier dessert.

> 1 quart raspberry nectar
> ¹/₃ cup agar flakes
> 1 tablespoon kudzu dissolved in ¼ cup water
> 2 tablespoons concentrated fruit sweetener
> 1 teaspoon vanilla

Garnish
> **Fresh raspberries**

Put juice and agar in a 2-quart saucepan over medium heat; bring a boil. Lower heat and simmer 10 minutes. Add dissolved kudzu in water, stirring mixture constantly until smooth and clear. Remove from heat. Add sweetener and vanilla extract; stir again. Pour into a 9-by-13-inch pan and let gel at room temperature or in the refrigerator for an hour.

Put gelled mixture into blender or food processor and blend for a few seconds until smooth. Pour into individual serving cups. Serve with fresh raspberries on top.

Preparation time: 20 minutes to make, 1 hour to gel
Makes 6-8 servings

Raspberry Cream Parfait
Prepare Raspberry Pudding Gel as above. Also prepare Nut Cream (page 230). Using parfait glasses, layer pudding, fresh raspberries, and cream until you have 6 layers in each glass.

Vanilla Amasake Pudding

Amasake, a traditional Japanese product, is made by fermenting sweet brown rice with into a thick, sweet liquid. It is sold in the refrigerated section of natural foods stores or in aseptic packages on the shelf. Amasake can replace not only sweeteners but also dairy products in natural desserts.

> 1 cup soy milk
> 1 cup amasake
> 2 tablespoons agar flakes
> 1 tablespoon kudzu, dissolved in ¼ cup water
> 2 tablespoons maple syrup or brown rice syrup
> 1-2 tablespoons vanilla

Optional garnishes
> 4 teaspoons fruit-sweetened jam
> Grated nutmeg

Pour soy milk and amasake into a pan. Sprinkle agar over the top. Heat to simmer without stirring. Simmer 10 minutes or until flakes have dissolved. Add kudzu. Stir briskly with a whisk until mixture thickens. Add syrup and stir again. Remove from heat. Stir in vanilla extract. Pour into an 8-by-8-inch pan and let set at room temperature or in the refrigerator for about an hour.

Once set, run the mixture through the blender or food processor for a few seconds to create a creamy pudding texture. Pour into individual serving cups and garnish with a teaspoon of jam or a sprinkle of nutmeg.

Preparation time: 10-15 minutes (plus 1 hour to set)
Makes 4 servings

FOR BABIES 10 MONTHS & OLDER
Try serving a little amasake in a cup.

Butterscotch Amasake Pudding
Use 1 teaspoon butterscotch flavoring in place of vanilla.

Winter Fruit Compote with Nut Cream

Dried fruit has traditionally been used in winter when fresh fruit was un-available. This compote is a tummy-warming treat that's perfect for cold weather. Nut Cream also makes a wonderful topping for cakes and ginger-bread.

Compote:
  ½ cup dried apricots
  ¼ cup pitted prunes
  1 apple, sliced
  1 pear, sliced
  1 cinnamon stick
  ⅛ teaspoon nutmeg
  1 cup apple juice

Nut Cream:
  ½ cup raw, unsalted cashews
  3 tablespoons maple syrup
  2 teaspoons vanilla
  water

Place apricots, prunes, apple, pear, cinnamon, nutmeg, and juice in a medium-sized pan; bring to a boil. Lower the heat and simmer, covered, for 20-30 minutes, until all the fruit is soft. Remove cinnamon stick.

Grind nuts to a fine meal in a blender. Add ground cashews, maple syrup, and vanilla. With blender running, add water a little at a time until you have a thick creamy consistency. Put compote in individual serving bowls and top with Nut Cream.

Preparation time: 35 minutes
Makes 4 servings

FOR BABIES 10 MONTHS & OLDER
Reserve some of the cooked fruit and puree. Serve in very small amounts; a teaspoon with your baby's cereal.

Cherry Banana Jiggle

Gelatin is a product manufactured from animal hooves. The same gelling action can be obtained from agar, a sea vegetable rich in fiber and minerals. To find out more about agar see "Identifying, Shopping, and Storing Whole Foods" (page 252).

> 1 quart cherry juice or cherry cider
> ¼ cup agar flakes
> 1 banana

Pour juice in a medium pan. Sprinkle agar on top; bring to a boil. Lower heat and simmer for 10 minutes or until agar flakes are completely dissolved. Slice banana and put slices at the bottom of a 9-by-13 pan or in 8 individual serving dishes. Remove from heat and pour mixture over bananas. Let set at room temperature about an hour. Chilling in the refrigerator is faster, but may produce a stiff dessert. If chilled in the refrigerator, let dessert set out at room temperature for 10-12 minutes before serving.

Preparation time: 15 minutes to make, 1 hour to gel
Makes 8 servings

FOR BABIES 6 MONTHS & OLDER
Reserve some banana, mash with breast milk or water, and serve.

Pear Plum Crisp

This wonderful autumn dessert uses the fruits of the season and is easy to double for a large gathering. The recipe is easily adapted for apples in winter or peaches and blueberries in summer (see next page).

1 cup rolled oats
½ cup whole wheat pastry flour
½ teaspoon sea salt
¼ cup cold-pressed vegetable oil
¼ cup maple syrup or concentrated fruit sweetener
⅓ cup chopped nuts
2 tablespoons water
2 tablespoons maple syrup or concentrated fruit sweetener
1 teaspoon cinnamon
¼ teaspoon nutmeg
2 teaspoons vanilla extract
5 cups sliced pears and plums (about 3 pears and 5 plums)

Preheat oven to 350° F. Mix oats, flour, and salt together in a bowl. Add oil and sweetener; mix well. Stir in nuts and set aside. In a small bowl combine water, syrup, spices, and vanilla extract; set aside. Slice fruit and place in a lightly oiled pie pan or an 8-by-8-inch baking dish. Pour the liquid mixture over the fruit and toss gently. Spoon the oat-nut mixture evenly on top of the fruit. Cover and bake 45 minutes. Uncover and bake 15 minutes more to crisp the topping.

Preparation time: 1 hour and 20 minutes
Makes 8 servings

FOR BABIES 10 MONTHS & OLDER

Remove some of the baked pear and plum from the bottom of the crisp. Puree and serve.

Apple Crisp

Substitute 5 cups sliced apples for plums and pears. Add 1 teaspoon lemon juice to water, syrup, spices, and vanilla. Bake 1 hour and 15 minutes.

Peach-Blueberry Crisp

Substitute 1 pint blueberries and 3 cups sliced peaches for plums and pears. Sprinkle 1-2 tablespoons tapioca or arrowroot over the fruit before adding liquid mixture and tossing. Bake 50-60 minutes.

Tofu Cheesecake with Hazelnut Crust and Raspberry Topping

This dessert looks like a traditional cheesecake but with half the fat and calories. Tofu comes in various textures such as firm, extra, firm, soft, and silken. Use silken tofu, usually sold in aseptic packages, to get the smoothest texture. The pie is also beautiful without the raspberry topping, garnished only with fresh strawberry and kiwi slices.

Crust

> 1¼ cups rolled oats
> ⅓ cup hazelnuts, ground
> ½ cup whole wheat pastry or barley flour
> ¼ cup cold-pressed vegetable oil
> 2 tablespoons maple syrup
> 1-2 tablespoons water

Filling

> 2 packages of silken tofu (10 ounces)
> ½ teaspoon sea salt
> 2-3 tablespoons freshly squeezed lemon juice
> 6-8 tablespoons maple syrup
> 3 tablespoons tahini
> 2 teaspoons vanilla
> ¼ teaspoon almond extract
> ½ teaspoon rice vinegar
> 1 tablespoon kudzu dissolved in ¼ cup water

Topping

> ½ cup fruit-sweetened raspberry jam
> 2 tablespoons kudzu or arrowroot dissolved in ½ cup water

To make crust

Preheat oven to 350° F. Grind oats and nuts in a food processor or small electric grinder. Blend ground oats and nuts with flour in a mixing bowl. In a separate bowl mix oil and syrup together. Add wet ingredients to dry mixture, adding 1-2 tablespoons of water if necessary. Press mixture into the bottom of a lightly oiled 8-inch springform pan or 9-inch pie pan. Bake for 10-12 minutes. Remove crust from oven and lower oven temperature to 300° F.

To make filling

Place tofu, salt, lemon juice, syrup, tahini, extracts, vinegar, and dissolved kudzu in blender or food processor; blend until smooth. Pour in prebaked pie crust. Bake for 25 minutes. Turn off oven and let pie rest in the oven for 25 minutes. Cool, cover, and refrigerate.

To make topping

Place jam and dissolved kudzu in a pan. Stir with a whisk. Heat, stirring constantly until thick and clear. Let topping cool slightly before pouring on cheesecake. Topping can be added before or after refrigeration.

Preparation time: 1½ hours
Makes 8 servings

FOR BABIES 10 MONTHS & OLDER
Reserve a few cubes of tofu and serve as finger food.

Carrot Cake with Apricot Glaze

This familiar cake looks quite elegant when you decorate the top with fresh raspberries or with a few fresh flowers and date halves. This cake is also delicious frosted with Yummy Yam Frosting (page 243) instead of the Apricot Glaze. I have used concentrated fruit sweetener instead of sugar in the cake. This is a syrup made by concentrating the juices of pears, peaches, and pineapples. It lends a very fruity taste to any dish.

Cake

    1 cup whole wheat pastry flour

    1 cup unbleached white flour

    1 tablespoon non-aluminum baking powder

    $\frac{1}{8}$ teaspoon sea salt

    1 teaspoon cinnamon

    $\frac{1}{4}$ teaspoon nutmeg

    $\frac{1}{2}$ cup concentrated fruit sweetener or maple syrup

    $\frac{1}{2}$ cup cold-pressed vegetable oil

    $\frac{1}{2}$ cup water

    1 cup apple or apricot juice

    2 eggs

    3 large carrots, finely grated

    1 tablespoon grated lemon peel

    $\frac{1}{3}$ cup chopped walnuts

    $\frac{1}{3}$ cup raisins or currants

Glaze

    1 tablespoon kudzu

    1 cup apricot juice or nectar

    1 tablespoon freshly squeezed lemon juice

    1 tablespoon concentrated fruit sweetener

To make cake

Preheat oven to 350° F. Lightly oil a 10-inch tube pan or 2 round 8-inch cake pans. Sift together flours, baking powder, salt and spices in a mixing bowl; set aside. Put sweetener, oil, water, juice, and eggs in a separate bowl; whisk together. Add wet ingredients to dry mixture and mix well. Fold in carrots, lemon peel, nuts, and raisins. Pour batter in pan(s); tap on counter to release air bubbles and bake for 50-60 minutes or until knife inserted in center of cake comes out clean. Remove and let cool.

To make glaze

Dissolve kudzu in juice in a small pan. Heat mixture on medium heat, stirring constantly, until it becomes clear and thick (5 minutes). Remove from heat, add lemon juice and sweetener; stir well. Spread over the top of tube cake or between layers and on top of layer cake.

Preparation time: 1½ hours
Makes 12 servings

FOR BABIES 6 MONTHS & OLDER

Reserve some extra carrot. Slice and place in a small, covered baking dish; bake while the cake is baking. Mash or blend and serve.

Blueberry-Strawberry Tart

A cheerful dessert, this tart gets its beauty and sweet taste from the lovely berries of summertime. Kudzu and arrowroot are both naturally processed thickeners. Kudzu gives the thickened liquid a glossy sheen and is thought to have a soothing effect on the digestive system. Arrowroot is less expensive and can be found at most stores.

1¼ cup rolled oats
¼ cup almonds, ground
¼ cup walnuts, ground
¼ cup whole wheat pastry flour
Pinch of sea salt
¼ cup maple syrup
2 tablespoons cold-pressed vegetable oil
2 tablespoons water
1 cup blueberries
1 cup strawberries or raspberries
1 cup apple or berry juice
2 tablespoons kudzu (or ¼ cup arrowroot)

Preheat oven to 350° F. Combine oats, ground nuts, flour, and salt together in a bowl. Add 2 tablespoons of maple syrup, oil, and water; mix well. Press the mixture into an 8-by-8-inch pan with wet hands. Bake 10-12 minutes. Remove from oven and let cool.

Wash and trim strawberries and cut in half. If using raspberries, rinse and use whole. Mix juice and kudzu together in a small pan until kudzu is dissolved. Add blueberries and 2 tablespoons of maple syrup; heat mixture, on medium heat, stirring constantly until thick and clear, about 5 minutes. Remove from heat; stir in strawberries or raspberries. Pour mixture on top of prebaked oat-nut crust. Allow to cool at room temperature or in the refrigerator before serving.

Preparation time: 25 minutes
Makes 9 servings

FOR BABIES 10 MONTHS & OLDER
Remove some of the blueberry kudzu mixture just before adding strawberries. Puree in blender and serve.

Mary's Buttermilk Chocolate Cake

I learned how to make this incredible cake from my dear friend, Mary Bowman. The recipe uses no eggs, is EASY to make, and turns out a beautiful cake every time. For a dairy-free version substitute 1 cup soymilk with 1 tablespoon lemon juice added for the buttermilk.

2½ cups whole wheat pastry flour
¼ cup organic cocoa powder
½ teaspoon sea salt
1 teaspoon double acting baking powder
1 teaspoon baking soda
1 cup buttermilk
½ cup cold-pressed vegetable oil
1 cup maple syrup
1 tablespoon vanilla

Preheat oven to 375° F. Mix flour, cocoa, salt, baking powder, and baking soda together in a bowl. Combine liquids separately, then stir into flour mixture. Pour into 8-inch cake pans which have been lightly oiled or lined with parchment paper. Bake for 30 minutes.

Preparation time: 45 minutes
Makes two 8-inch layers

Gracie's Yellow Birthday Cake

Cooked millet makes gives this cake its moist texture and yellow color. My friend Ralfee made four layers of this cake for her birthday, using apricot jam between the layers and Carob Butter Icing (page 241) on top — divine! My daughter loves it served on a pool of Strawberry Sauce (page 244) with sliced strawberries on top.

1½ cups unbleached white flour
½ cup whole wheat pastry flour
1 teaspoon non-aluminum baking powder
1 teaspoon baking soda
½ teaspoon sea salt
1½ cups cooked millet (see page 61)
1 cup orange juice
½ cup water
⅓ cup cold-pressed vegetable oil
½ cup maple syrup
2 teaspoons vanilla
2 eggs, separated

Preheat oven to 350° F. Lightly oil and flour two 8-inch cake pans. Sift flour, baking powder, soda, and salt together in a large mixing bowl; set aside. Put millet and juice in blender; blend until smooth. Add water, oil, and syrup to the millet puree in the blender; pulse briefly. Separate eggs, placing egg whites in a separate glass or metal bowl. Add egg yolks to millet puree and pulse again. Add wet ingredients to dry mixture and mix well. Whip egg whites until peaks form, then fold egg whites into millet mixture. Pour into cake pans. Bake 30-40 minutes, until cake begins to pull away from edge of pan. Let cool in pans for 10 minutes before removing. Wait until completely cool before icing.

Preparation time: 50-55 minutes
Makes an 8-inch 2-layer cake or 18 cupcakes

FOR BABIES 6 MONTHS & OLDER

Reserve some extra cooked millet and puree some with water. Warm slightly before serving.

Carob Butter Icing

This sinfully delicious icing is an adaptation of the carob icing found in Marcea Weber's book, **The Sweet Life**, *a trail blazer in creative uses of alternative sweeteners. One and one-half cups icing will ice the top and sides of 2 eight-inch layers of cake or 1 9-by-13-inch cake.*

½ cup maple syrup or brown rice syrup
½ cup carob powder, sifted
¼ cup creamy cashew or almond butter
⅛ teaspoon sea salt
2-3 tablespoons apple or orange juice
2 teaspoons vanilla

Heat the syrup in a small saucepan. Stir in the carob powder and heat, stirring constantly, until mixture begins to simmer. Add nut butter, salt, and juice; stir with a whisk until smooth. Remove from heat and add vanilla extract. Add a bit more juice if too thick so that cake will ice easily. Ice cooled cake immediately.

Preparation time: 10 minutes
Makes 1½ cups icing

Banana Cream Frosting

By using tofu and banana as a base, you can create sweet creamy icings that children love to lick. This icing works well on Banana Blueberry Poppyseed Muffins (page 203) or Pumpkin Pecan Muffins (page 202), too. One cup frosting is plenty for a dozen cookies or muffins.

6 ounces silken tofu
½ of a ripe banana
2 tablespoons concentrated fruit sweetener
2 teaspoons almond or cashew butter
½ teaspoon vanilla
1-2 tablespoons pineapple juice or water

Blend tofu, banana, sweetener, nut butter, and vanilla extract in a blender or food processor. Add enough juice or water to get a smooth consistency. Refrigerate frosting if not using right away. Store leftover goodies topped with this frosting in the refrigerator.

Preparation time: 10 minutes
Makes about 1 cup

FOR BABIES 6 MONTHS & OLDER
Reserve some extra ripe banana. Mash and serve.

Yummy Yam Frosting

This naturally sweet, beautiful golden-orange frosting comes from the creative mind of Rita Carey. Use it to top cookies, cupcakes, quick breads, graham crackers, or gingerbread people. This recipe makes enough to frost 2 dozen cookies or a one-layer cake.

1 cup mashed baked yams
2 ounces or ¼ cup softened cream cheese or soft tofu
2 teaspoons melted unsalted butter
2 tablespoons maple syrup or brown rice syrup
1 teaspoon lemon or orange juice

Place yams, cream cheese, butter, syrup, and juice in a bowl and cream together. Puree this mixture in a blender, food processor or with a hand mixer to a smooth, spreadable consistency.

Preparation time: 5 minutes
Makes ¾-1 cup frosting

FOR BABIES 6 MONTHS & OLDER
Reserve some extra baked yam. Mash well and serve.

Strawberry Sauce

This is a beautiful, simple sauce that can be used to make a lovely presentation. Serve cake on a pool of this or put sauce in a squeeze bottle and squeeze out a design on top of your favorite cake, pudding, or frozen dessert.

1 pint strawberries
1 teaspoon lemon or orange juice
1 tablespoon rice syrup, concentrated fruit sweetener
  or maple syrup

Wash and trim strawberries. Place all but 4-5 strawberries, juice, and sweetener in blender; blend until smooth. Use at once or refrigerate until used. Will keep several days in the refrigerator. Use remaining strawberries for garnish.

Preparation time: 10 minutes
Makes 1 cup

244

Natural Drinks
and Brews

Water

Our bodies require water. You can save both money and calories by quenching your thirst with plain water. Some parents habitually give juice or soda to a thirsty child. Try offering water first, especially if your child drinks juice and then won't eat. It's important to keep the attention at mealtime on eating, not drinking. Save juices, teas, milks, and other drinks for between-meal snacks. For everyday meals, serve water or no drinks. Avoid ice water with food. Cold drinks can halt the body's warm digestive process.

Water from the tap is no longer a reliably clean way to quench thirst. Filtered tap water or bottled spring water is preferred. The Environmental Protection Agency (EPA) reports more than 700 potentially hazardous chemicals that are found in U.S. drinking water as a result of groundwater pollution. Most water filters remove up to 73 percent of known pollutants.

Lemon Water

This is my favorite drink first thing in the morning. It is also nice served with summer meals. I keep a pitcher of lemon water in the fridge during hot weather.

> ½ **lemon, sliced**
> **1 quart water**

Put lemon slices in a pitcher of water. Let set ½ hour or so. Refrigerate or drink at room temperature.

Makes 1 quart

Sparkling Fruit Juice

Instead of giving your child pop or soda, try this more healthful sparkling beverage.

> **2 cups fruit juice**
> **2 cups sparkling water**

Combine ingredients in a pitcher.

Makes 1 quart

Bubbly Fruit Tea

Another delicious way to dilute fruit juice for youngsters.

> 1 cup fruity hibiscus herbal tea
> 1½ cups fruit juice
> 1½ cups sparkling water

Brew and cool tea. Combine with juice and sparkling water; serve cold.

Makes 1 quart

Banana Milk

A fun recipe that children can make themselves.

> 1 ripe banana
> 2 cups soy, nut, or cow's milk
> 2 teaspoons vanilla

Blend all ingredients in a blender and serve.

Makes 2½-3 cups

Nut Milks

Nut milks, a nutritious and versatile group of foods, taste good on cereals or fruit desserts. You can use them to replace cow's milk in any recipe. Nut milks can be kept in the refrigerator for a couple of days, although they may separate and need to be re-blended. Here are ideas for three nut milks; the possibilities are limitless.

Almond Sesame Milk
> ¼ cup almonds
> ¼ cup sesame seeds
> 2 cups water
> 1 tablespoon maple syrup or brown rice syrup

Place nuts in blender with a few tablespoons of the water and blend until you have a paste. Add the rest of the water and sweetener; blend again. For a smoother milk pour the contents of the blender through a fine strainer lined with cheesecloth to remove nut pulp. Pick up the ends of the cheesecloth and squeeze pulp to remove all the milk.

Almond Cashew Milk
> ¼ cup almonds
> ¼ cup cashews
> 2 cups water
> 3 pitted dates

Place nuts in blender with a few tablespoons of the water and blend until you have a paste. Add the rest of the water and dates; blend again. For a smoother milk pour the contents of the blender through a fine strainer lined with cheesecloth to remove nut pulp. Pick up the ends of the cheesecloth and squeeze pulp to remove all the milk.

Nut Butter Milk
> 2 tablespoons almond, sesame or cashew butter
> 2 cups water
> 1 tablespoon brown rice syrup

Place nut or seed butter in the blender with other ingredients. Blend until smooth.

All variations make 2 cups

Cranberry Ginger Cider

The perfect drink to warm visitors on a chilly night. Serve it in glass mugs so folks can enjoy the deep red color. Float an orange slice on top.

2 cups cranberry juice
2 cups apple cider
8 ¼-inch slices fresh gingerroot
½ teaspoon orange zest

Optional garnish
orange slices

Place all ingredients in a pan. Bring heat up and simmer 15 minutes. Remove pieces of gingerroot. Garnish each cup with an orange slice if desired. Serve warm.

Makes 4 cups

Hot Mocha Milk

I was addicted to caffeine many years ago. Whenever I get the urge for a coffee-like drink, I choose this healthful hot beverage. Cafix is a dry powder made from grains, figs, and other natural ingredients which dissolves in hot water.

½ teaspoon Cafix or other grain beverage
½ teaspoon carob powder
½ cup boiling water
½ teaspoon maple syrup or dried cane juice
¹/₃-¹/₂ cup soy or other milk

Put Cafix and carob powder in a cup. Fill cup halfway with boiling water. Stir in sweetener. Fill cup to top with milk.

Makes 1 cup

Yogi Tea

This drink is filled with many warming spices. It is wonderful on cold winter days. Children love the sweet taste. Traditionally this tea is made with black tea. I have omitted it because most of us don't need the caffeine; children certainly do not.

> 4 cups water
> 10 whole cloves
> 12 whole cardamom pods
> 12 whole black peppercorns
> 2 sticks of cinnamon
> 4 slices fresh gingerroot, ¼" thick
> 1 cup soy, cow or goat milk
> Maple syrup or honey to taste

Bring water, spices, and gingeroot to a boil in a pot. Lower heat and simmer 15-20 minutes. Add milk. If using cow or goat milk, bring to a boil again. Turn heat off. Strain into cup and stir in sweetener.

Makes 4 - 5 cups

Ginger Tea

The perfect drink for a winter cold. Ginger warms the body and increases circulation. Ginger tea is also a very soothing drink to give someone with an upset stomach or nausea.

> 2-inches fresh gingerroot
> 2 cups water
> Freshly squeezed lemon juice
> Maple syrup or honey to taste

Slice 1" of the gingerroot very thinly. Place in pan with water and simmer 10-20 minutes. Peel the other piece of gingerroot, grate it, and squeeze the pieces over a bowl, collecting the ginger juice. Set aside. Strain, and pour simmered liquid into cups. Add a squeeze of fresh lemon and a few drops of ginger juice to each cup. Stir in sweetener if desired.

Makes 2 cups

Appendix

Identifying, Shopping, and Storing Whole Foods

Most major cities have many fine natural foods grocery stores where you can purchase whole foods and whole foods products. A surprising number of national supermarket chains now carry grains and beans in bulk, tofu and tempeh, alternative sweeteners, whole grain products and organic produce. Ask your local grocer to stock items you wish to buy regularly. This is how change begins.

Buying foods in bulk whenever possible reduces waste from unnecessary packaging. When buying packaged products, support manufacturers who use recyclable packaging. Unprocessed foods tend to be more fragile because they still contain life. Pay attention to the manufacturers' recommendations for storage written on labels. Always check the expiration date on perishable products before purchasing them.

If you do not live near a natural foods store, consider gathering a few interested friends together and starting a food-buying club. Write or call the companies listed below to find out about their catalogues and mail order services.

- *GOLDMINE NATURAL FOOD CO., 3419 Hancock St., San Diego, CA 92110, 1-800-475-3663*

- *MOUNTAIN ARK TRADING CO., 120 S. East Ave., Fayetteville, AR 72701, 1-800-643-8909*

- *MOUNTAIN PEOPLE WAREHOUSE, 12745 Earhart Ave., Auburn, CA 95602, 1-800-679-8735*

- *WALNUT ACRES, Walnut Acres Rd., Penns Creek, PA 17862, (717) 837-0601*

Agar, a sea vegetable, is a natural jelling agent that can be used in place of animal gelatin. Agar thickens at room temperature, unlike gelatin, which must be chilled. One-quarter cup of agar gels a quart of liquid. Agar is sold in bars and small packages of translucent flakes; flakes are easier to measure. Look for agar in the macrobiotic section of your natural foods store. Store agar in a sealed container in a cool, dark place.

Alternative sweeteners can be purchased to replace refined sugar in recipes. They include pure maple syrup, rice syrup, barley malt, and concentrated fruit sweetener which are discussed separately in this section. Most syrup-like sweeteners should be refrigerated after opening; however check the label for manufacturer's recommendations. Date sugar, Sucanat, Fruitsource, and other granulated naturally processed sweeteners can be stored on the shelf. Dried fruit stored in an airtight container will keep about one year on the shelf. See "How to Use Alternate Sweeteners" (page 216) for more information.

Amaranth is a whole grain that looks like tiny yellow, brown, and black seeds. It was an important food source for the Aztecs. Amaranth has a very good nutritional profile. It is unusually high in lysine — the amino acid most grains are low in. This makes amaranth high in protein (15-18%). It also contains more calcium, Vitamin A, and Vitamin C than most grains, making it a good food for those with elevated needs. Amaranth has a flavor similar to graham crackers without the sweetness. When cooked it has the texture of gelatinous cornmeal mush. Store whole grains in airtight containers where they will keep for 6-9 months.

Amasake, a traditional Japanese product, is made by fermenting sweet brown rice into a thick sweet liquid. To do this a culture called koji is used. Sold in the refrigerated section of natural foods stores or in aseptic packages on the shelf, amasake can replace not only sweeteners but also dairy products in natural desserts.

Arame, a sea vegetable, is finely shredded, cooked, and then naturally sun dried. When reconstituted, it looks like small, black threads. Its milder flavor makes it a useful introductory sea vegetable. Look for it, dried and packaged, in the macrobiotic section of your natural foods store or Asian markets. Store in a sealed container in a cool, dark place where it will keep indefinitely.

Arrowroot powder comes from a tropical plant whose tuberous root is dried and ground into a fine powder. Arrowroot, a natural thickener, can be substituted for cornstarch, in equal measure. Whole-foods cooks prefer arrowroot or kudzu's natural method of preparation over cornstarch, which is bleached and chemically treated during processing. Two tablespoons of arrowroot can substitute for one tablespoon of kudzu. Arrowroot keeps indefinitely in a sealed container on the shelf.

Baking powder, non aluminum is described under "non aluminum baking powder."

Balsamic vinegar is an Italian, red wine vinegar with a lower-than-average acidity. It's sweet, mellow flavor comes from being aged in wood, making it a distinctive addition to dressings and marinades. Vinegars store on the shelf indefinitely.

Barley is a chewy whole grain. One-third of the barley grown is this country is used to make beer and most of the rest is used for animal feed. **Hulled barley** is the whole grain with only the outside hull removed. **Pearled barley** is a refined product, similar to white rice, where the hull, other outside layers and the germ of the grain are removed. Store whole grains in airtight containers where they will keep for 6-9 months.

Barley malt is a complex carbohydrate sweetener made by cooking soaked, sprouted barley until the starches in the grain are broken down and converted into maltose. Barley malt is dark and thick and has a malt-like taste. Sorghum or rice syrup can be substituted for barley malt. Be careful when using barley malt in a recipe that includes eggs. Check the instructions in "How to Use Alternative Sweeteners" (page 216). Refrigerate after opening.

Basmati brown rice is a long, slender grain with a distinctly aromatic flavor. Basmati rice is popular in Indian and Pakistani cultures. It can be stored in an airtight container on the shelf for 6-9 months.

Brown rice syrup, a naturally processed sweetener, is made from soaked and sprouted brown rice that is cooked with an enzyme which breaks the starches into maltose. Rice syrup has a light, delicate flavor. It looks similar to honey but is less sweet. Substitute rice syrup in equal amounts for honey, maple syrup, or barley malt. To enhance pouring, place rice syrup in a pan of hot water before using. Refrigerate after opening.

Brown rice vinegar is a mild, delicate vinegar made from fermented brown rice. It is less acidic than most vinegars; you can substitute apple cider vinegar for brown rice vinegar. Vinegars store on the shelf indefinitely.

Bulgur is par-boiled, dried, and cracked whole wheat. Store whole grains in airtight containers, where they will keep for 6-9 months.

Cafix, a powder made from grains, figs, and other natural ingredients, is stirred into hot water for a coffee substitute. Cafix and similar products, such as Pero or Inka, are interchangeable and can be stored on the shelf. Instant decaffeinated coffee can be substituted for Cafix.

Canola oil is a popular vegetable oil made from the rape plant. Renamed "canola" for obvious marketing purposes, the rapeseed yields an oil that can hold a fairly high temperature making it suitable for frying. See "cold-pressed oils" and "oils" for more information.

Carob is an evergreen tree with edible pods. The pulp of the pods is ground into carob powder or carob flour which is naturally sweet, low in fat, high in calcium, and caffeine-free. **Carob powder** can be stored on the shelf in an airtight container for 6-12 months. Sift before using if lumpy. **Carob chips** come unsweetened and malt-sweetened. Some chips contain dry milk and most contain palm kernel oil, which is high saturated fat levels. Look for carob products made without palm kernel oil, or use sparingly.

Chipotle chilies are smoked, dried jalapeno peppers. Look for them in the ethnic foods section of your grocery store. Store on the shelf in a closed container.

Cold-pressed vegetable oils are oils that have been extracted by mechanical means rather than using heat and solvents. Be aware that many cold-pressed oils are refined, bleached and deodorized after extraction. This has a significant effect on the nutritional value of the oil, but produces an odorless, tasteless product that many cooks prefer in baked goods. Cold-pressed safflower, corn, or canola oil are commonly used to make desserts. All oils should be stored in the refrigerator.

Concentrated fruit sweetener is a commercial syrup made from peach, pineapple, pear, and other fruit juices that have been cooked into a syrup. Look for it in the refrigerated section of natural foods stores or on the shelf with other sweeteners. Concentrated fruit sweetener can be used in a recipe in place of honey, barley malt, rice syrup, or maple syrup in equal measure. This sweetener imparts a very fruity flavor to dishes it's used in. Refrigerate after opening.

Couscous is actually a tiny pasta made from coarsely ground and steamed wheat. It is usually made from refined wheat, though whole wheat couscous is becoming more commonly available. Store whole grains in airtight containers, where they will keep for 6-9 months.

Dairy products can be healthful used in moderate amounts. Some consumers prefer to buy raw milk products, as homogenization and pasteurization alter nutrient composition and digestibility. When buying raw milk products or any dairy products, buy from organic dairies. Support their efforts by purchasing their products. Check the pull date on all dairy products before purchasing and discard after that date.

Date sugar is simply ground dehydrated dates. It contains the same nutrient value as dried dates. Substitute cup for cup for white sugar. The taste is similar to brown sugar, but less sweet. While date sugar works well in baked goods, it does not dissolve well and is not recommended for use as a sweetener in hot beverages. If used to top a baked good, add enough hot water to make a syrup to prevent burning, or sprinkle on top after baking. Store it in a sealed container in a cool, dry place.

Dried cane juice is juice that has been extracted from the sugar cane and then dehydrated. This product is much less refined than white sugar and some of the minerals in the cane juice are still present. It resembles brown sugar in appearance and taste, though less sweet. Sucanat is a trade name for organically grown, dehydrated cane juice. Substitute dried cane juice in equal proportions for white or brown sugar. Store on the shelf.

Dulse is a sea vegetable extremely high in iron (14 milligrams per 1/4 cup) and other minerals. The dark red, dried leaves can be soaked for five minutes and added to soups or salads. Dulse is also sold dried and broken into tiny bits as **dulse flakes** or **granulated dulse**. Sprinkle into most any food for a nutritional boost. Dulse will store indefinitely in an airtight container in a cool, dark place.

Eggs are best stored in their carton in the refrigerator. Keeping them in their carton prevents moisture loss. I recommended using fertile eggs from free-ranging hens. If you wish to avoid eggs in baked goods, substitute flaxseed and water. See "Replacing Eggs in Baked Goods" (page 218) for a description on how to substitute.

Essene bread is a naturally sweet, moist, flourless bread. Sprouted grains are crushed, hand-shaped, and then slowly baked at low temperatures. The Essenes were a sect of Monks living in early Biblical times and this method of bread-making is attributed to them. Sprouted wheat bread comes in several flavors and is found in the refrigerated or frozen food section of most natural foods stores.

Extra-virgin olive oil comes from the first pressing of the olives and is the highest-quality olive oil. I use extra-virgin olive oil for dressings and light sautéing. Purchase oils in small bottles made of dark glass and use them within a few months to avoid spoilage. Most cooks recommend refrigeration for oils. Hold bottle under warm water for a thirty seconds to restore free-flowing qualities.

Fish should be purchased as fresh as possible, stored in the refrigerator, and used within 24 hours. Look for fish that has firm flesh, a high sheen, and no offensive odors. If you are concerned about pollutants in fish, be aware that toxins tend to accumulate in fatty tissues, so choosing less fatty fish is safer. Pregnant women may want to avoid salmon, bluefish, swordfish, and lake whitefish, which tend to house more contaminants. Offshore species such as cod, haddock, flounder, ocean perch, Pacific halibut, and albacore tuna are usually harvested from less polluted waters.

Flaxseeds are seeds from the flax plant. The oil in the seeds is rich in essential fatty acids and flaxseed oil is sold as a nutritional supplement. Flaxseeds can be ground and used as an egg substitute in baked goods. Grind 2 tablespoons of flaxseed, add 6 tablespoons boiling water, let mixture set 15 minutes. Then whisk with a fork. This will replace two eggs in a recipe. Store flaxseeds in a sealed container in a cool, dry place.

Flour. See "spelt," "unbleached white flour," "whole wheat flour," "whole wheat pastry flour." and "whole grain flours." Store all flours in a cold, dry place for one to two months, in the refrigerator for six months, or in the freezer for up to twelve months.

Fruit sweetener is described under "concentrated fruit sweetener."

Ghee is clarified butter used in traditional Indian cooking. The milk proteins in the butter are removed and only the fat remains. Unlike butter, ghee can hold high heat without scorching. For more information and instructions on how to make ghee, see page 213. Refrigerate homemade ghee.

Herbs, the leaves, stems, roots, and flowers of certain temperate climate plants, can be used fresh or dried to add wonderful, distinctive flavors to whole foods. Fresh herbs have more flavor and more nutritional value. Store dried herbs in closed containers made of dark glass, away from heat and light. Dried herbs keep their flavor for about six months. Substitute 1 teaspoon dried herbs for 1 tablespoon fresh herbs. Some herbs have medicinal effects and are not appropriate for pregnant or nursing moms; for instance, sage can reduce the flow of breast milk. Refer to *Wise Woman Herbal for the Childbearing Year* by Susun S. Weed (Ash Tree Publishing, 1983) for more information.

High-oleic safflower oil comes from safflower seeds that have been genetically altered so that the oil is higher in mono-unsaturated fats. This change allows the oil to hold a higher heat than regular safflower oil, making it suitable for deep-frying. Unrefined high-oleic safflower oil will have a deep amber color and a nutty, earthy flavor. Refined safflower oil is pale yellow and, like other refined oils, is bland and tasteless.

Hiziki, of all the sea vegetables, is the richest in calcium. Its thick, black strands have a firm texture and look striking with other colors. As with several other sea vegetables, soak in cold water before using. The strong taste can be moderated by cooking hiziki in apple juice and by combining it with other vegetables. Store hiziki in a sealed container in a cool, dark place where it will keep indefinitely.

Hulled barley. See "barley."

Kamut is a nutritionally superior whole grain that is a relative of the wheat family. Some who are allergic to modern strains of wheat can tolerate kamut. Flour made from kamut is golden-colored and can be substituted for wheat in baked goods. Store it as you would other whole grain flours.

Kasha is roasted buckwheat groats. It is a brown-colored grain with angular edges. Buckwheat is actually the seed of a plant related to rhubarb that originated in Russia. Store whole grains in airtight containers, where they will keep for 6-9 months.

Kombu is a dark green sea vegetable sold in thick strips. It contains glutamic acid, which acts as a tenderizer when added to cooking beans. As with other sea vegetables, kombu is mineral-rich. Store kombu in a sealed container in a cool, dark place where it will keep indefinitely.

Kudzu, from the root of the kudzu plant, looks like broken chalk. The kudzu plant grows wild in the southern states of the U.S., but there is no American company producing and marketing it. Natural food distributors import packaged kudzu from Japan making it very pricey. Kudzu can be dissolved in cool or room-temperature liquid and used as a thickener. The thickened liquid will have a smooth, glossy appearance. In macrobiotic practice, kudzu is recommended for its soothing effect on the digestive system. You can substitute 2 tablespoons of arrowroot for 1 tablespoon of kudzu. Look for kudzu (sometimes spelled "kuzu") in the macrobiotic section of your natural foods store. Kudzu will keep indefinitely stored in a sealed container on the shelf.

Maple syrup is made from the boiled sap of sugar maple trees. About 40 gallons of sap (from nine trees) makes 1 gallon of syrup. Maple syrup is available in three grades: A, B, or C, determined by the temperature used and length of time cooked. The lighter the color, the better the quality (and the more expensive). Store in a cool location to prevent fermentation and crystallization. During hot weather, refrigerate. Freezing maple syrup may damage flavor.

Millet is a small, round, golden grain that continues to be a major food source in Asia, North Africa and India. Store whole grains in airtight containers, where they will keep for 6-9 months.

Mirin, a versatile sweet cooking wine, is made from sweet brown rice and contains no additives. Dry sherry may be substituted for mirin. Store mirin in a closed container in a cool, dry place.

Miso is a salty paste made from cooked and aged soybeans. The soybeans are mixed with various grains and other ingredients to produce different flavors. The longer miso is aged and the darker its color, the stronger and saltier the taste. Miso is traditionally used as a soup base, but can also be used in spreads, dressings, dips, or as a substitute for salt. Unpasteurized miso contains beneficial enzymes and organisms that aid digestion. Refrigerated miso will keep indefinitely.

Mochi is made from sweet brown rice that has been cooked, pounded into a paste, and then compressed into dense bars. Mochi requires cooking. When broken into squares and baked at 400° F. for 10 minutes, it puffs up and gets gooey inside. It can also be grated and melted into foods. Refrigerate opened packages and eat within one week. Extra packages can be stored in the freezer and thawed in about 2 hours.

Molasses, a by-product of sugar refinement, has a strong bittersweet flavor. Only blackstrap molasses has appreciable amounts of iron and calcium. Barley malt or sorghum can be substituted for molasses. Molasses will keep for up to 6 months in a sealed container in a cool place; however refrigeration is safest.

Non aluminum baking powder is recommended for use as a leavening agent in non-yeasted baked goods. Stored in a closed container in a cool, dry place, non aluminum baking powder will keep indefinitely.

Nori, a dried and rolled sea vegetable, resembles dark green or black paper. While nori is most commonly used in making sushi, it can also be eaten directly from the package by lightly toasting and crumbling onto foods. Store in the freezer in a zip-lock bag to preserve freshness.

Nuts and seeds are best bought and stored in their shell, for flavor as well as freshness. Because of their oil content, nuts and seeds are subject to rancidity. Store shelled nuts and seeds in an airtight container in the refrigerator for up to 3 months or the freezer for 12 months.

Oils are described individually under their specific names. Oils should be used sparingly. Extra-virgin olive oil and unrefined sesame oil are the highest quality oils. These are the least processed and least likely to go rancid. Unrefined oils usually have a darker color and retain some of the flavor of their origin. Refined oils are pale, odorless, and tasteless because they have been bleached and deodorized during the refining process. Look for "cold-pressed" on the label of oils, which indicates an oil that has been extracted by mechanical means rather than using heat and solvents. For baked goods, some cooks prefer using a tasteless oil such as cold-pressed safflower or canola oil, although unsalted butter makes a lighter, more digestible baked product. For infrequent light frying, cold-pressed canola, sunflower, or high-oleic safflower oil can hold a high temperature. Store oils in dark glass, in the refrigerator and use within 6 months.

Poultry is recommended for consumption as a side dish or occasional main dish. Three to four ounces daily are ample. Purchase organically raised poultry to feed your family as factory-produced poultry is notorious for being laden with antibiotics, hormones, and other undesirable toxins. Fresh poultry can be kept 1-2 days in the refrigerator, best if used within 24 hours.

Quinoa (keen-wah) was cultivated in Peru for thousands of years. This staple food of the Incas has been rediscovered and is now grown in the United States. Quinoa contains all 8 amino acids, making it a complete protein. It also contains appreciable amounts of calcium and iron. Store whole grains in airtight containers, where they will keep for 6-9 months.

Radicchio is a small, burgundy and white colored head of lettuce leaves. The leaves have a slightly sharp taste.

Ramen is a dry block of quick-cooking pasta. The cooked noodles are curly. Ramen is made from a variety of flours and usually comes packaged with a packet of dry seasonings to be used in cooking. Look for ramen made from whole grain flours.

Rice syrup is described under "Brown Rice Syrup."

Sea salt is sodium chloride from sea water. Commercial table salt contains potassium iodide (iodine), dextrose, sodium bicarbonate, and other additives. The iodine is included for people with no access to seafood or sea vegetables. High-quality sea salt, such as Lima or

Celtic sea salt, contains no additives and many minerals. Salt-related health problems come from consuming processed foods where large amounts of sodium have been added, such as diet soft drinks. Small amounts of high-quality salt are beneficial to our health and vastly improve the flavor of whole grains and legumes.

Sea vegetables are purchased dried and are available in packages or occasionally in bulk. Look for sea vegetables in the macrobiotic section of your natural foods store or in Asian markets. Sea vegetables should be stored in sealed containers in a cool, dark place. Properly stored, they will keep indefinitely. See "arame," "dulse," "hiziki," "kombu," "nori," and "wakame" for information about specific sea vegetables.

Seitan, also called "wheat meat," is a high-protein food (21 grams in ¼ cup) traditionally made by combining wheat flour and water to make a dough and then removing the starch from the dough by alternating rinses of warm and cold water. When the starch is rinsed away, the gluten or protein part of the grain remains. The gluten substance is dense and chewy, not unlike beef. It is also rather bland, but can be seasoned in a salty herbal solution to give the wheat meat flavor. A short-cut version for making seitan is given in this book on page 111. Instead of making a dough, rinsing and seasoning, I begin with a product called wheat gluten flour which is a wheat flour that has had the starch removed.

Shiitake mushrooms have a dark brown cap, a beige underbelly and a tough stem. When cooked they have a delicious savory taste and a chewy texture. It is said that shiitake mushrooms are a natural source of interferon, a protein thought to boost the immune system. The mushrooms are sold fresh, which is best, or they can be purchased dried and packaged. Store fresh mushrooms in a paper bag in the refrigerator.

Shoyu is made from soybeans, wheat, water, and sea salt, but unlike commercial soy sauces, shoyu does not contain sugar, monosodium glutamate, and other additives. Both shoyu and tamari are naturally brewed and aged and used to flavor dishes. Tamari is similar to shoyu but contains little or no wheat. Store shoyu or tamari in a sealed container on the shelf indefinitely.

Soba is a traditional type of Japanese noodle made principally from buckwheat. For more information, see "Selecting Whole Grain Noodles & Pasta" (page 65).

Sorghum is a syruplike sweetener with a rich, dark taste. It is made by concentrating the juice of crushed and boiled sorghum stems. The sorghum plant is a relative of millet. Barley malt can be substituted for sorghum. Refrigerate after opening.

Soy beverage or soy milk, best known by commercial names such as Westsoy and Edensoy, is a high-protein alternative to cow's milk. Manufacturers of soy beverages have succeeded in producing various delicious milks from soybeans. Do not substitute soy milk for infant formula as it does not contain all of the necessary nutrients for growing babies. Soy beverage usually comes in aseptic packages that require refrigeration after opening.

Spelt was a staple grain in Biblical times. Spelt is easier to digest than whole wheat and makes a suitable substitution for wheat in baked goods. It is sold as flour, flakes and in its whole form. Store whole grains in airtight containers, where they will keep for 6-9 months.

Spices are the whole or ground buds, fruits, flowers, barks, or seeds of usually tropical-zoned plants. In traditional Indian cooking, spices are sautéed in butter or ghee to enhance their flavor before added to a dish. To maintain optimum potency, spices should be stored in closed containers made of dark glass away from heat and light and used within six months.

Sucanat. See "dried cane juice" (page 254).

Tahini is a creamy paste made of crushed, hulled sesame seeds. Seeds used for tahini are either raw, toasted, or lightly toasted, each giving the tahini a slightly different flavor. Sesame is uniquely resistant to rancidity, perhaps why it has been enjoyed by many cultures for centuries. Look for it with other nut butters or Mid-Eastern foods. Refrigerate after opening.

Tamari is a naturally brewed soy sauce made from soybeans, water, and sea salt. Tamari and shoyu are interchangeable. Also see "shoyu."

Tempeh, originally an Indonesian food, is made from soybeans that have been cooked and split to remove the hull. A culture is added to the cooked beans, which age for several days before forming into a solid piece which can be cut and sliced. This high-protein food can be baked, boiled, fried, or steamed. Store tempeh in the refrigerator and use within 1 week. Tempeh can also be frozen for up to 6 months; allow 1 hour to thaw.

Toasted sesame oil has a darker appearance and nuttier taste than plain sesame oil and delivers a lot of flavor in small amounts. Store in the refrigerator.

Tofu is soybean curd made from the "milk" of soybeans. Tofu's low calories, relatively high protein, and bland flavor make it a versatile ingredient. A variety of textures are available: firm, soft, and silken. Soft or silken tofu works well for dressings and desserts, while firm tofu holds its shape well for stir-frys and marinated dishes. Tofu can be purchased in bulk and in packages. Be sure to note the expiration date on packages. Cover bulk tofu and packaged tofu that has been opened in fresh water and store in the refrigerator in a sealed container. Change the water daily and use within a week. To freshen tofu, drop in boiling, salted water for a few minutes; remove and use.

Udon noodles are traditional Japanese noodles made from a combination of whole wheat, brown rice, and white flours. See "Selecting Whole Grain Noodles & Pasta" (page 65) for more information.

Umeboshi plum paste is a puree made from pitted umeboshi plums. Plums and paste will keep indefinitely stored in a sealed container on the shelf. A pinch of sea salt in 1 tablespoon of lemon juice can be substituted for 2 teaspoons of paste, although it doesn't produce quite the same flavor.

Umeboshi plum vinegar is the leftover juice from the umeboshi plum-pickling process. The salty-sour taste gives a lift to soups and salad dressings and eliminates the need for salt in a recipe. Stores indefinitely in a sealed container in a cool, dry place.

Umeboshi plums come from Japanese plums that are picked green and pickled in sea salt with shiso leaves. Their unique salty-sour taste adds zip to recipes. One tablespoon of lemon juice with a pinch of sea salt can substitute for 1 plum in a recipe.

Unbleached white flour is flour that has had the bran and germ removed in a refining process. But unlike regular white flour, it has not been bleached. When used in combination with whole grain flours, this flour gives muffins, crusts, and cakes a lighter texture. Store in an airtight container in a cool, dry place for up to a year.

Vegetables and fruits should be purchased frequently and used within a few days to ensure freshness. Fresh produce is best, frozen produce is a distant second. Use your senses when shopping for produce. Fresh fruit should have a fragrant smell and fresh vegetables should look perky, with rich color. Store ripe fruits and vegetables separately in the refrigerator. Tropical fruits and citrus fruits, including tomatoes and avocados, do well at room temperature. Potatoes, onions, garlic and winter squashes prefer an unrefrigerated location, store them in a cool, dark place. Cut the leaves from root vegetables as the flow of sap continues to the leaves at the expense of the root. Most fresh produce benefits from storage in open plastic bags. Wash, dry and reuse your plastic bags to avoid waste.

Wakame is a green, leafy sea vegetable high in calcium and other minerals. A small amount expands when soaked; after soaking, remove the main rib or stem and cut leaves into small pieces. Often used in soups, wakame can also be toasted and ground into a condiment. Store in a sealed container in a cool, dark place indefinitely.

Water from the tap is no longer a reliably clean way to quench thirst. Filtered tap water or bottled spring water is preferred. The Environmental Protection Agency (EPA) reports more than 700 potentially hazardous chemicals that are found in U.S. drinking water as a result of groundwater pollution. Most water filters remove up to 73 percent of known pollutants.

Wheat berries are whole wheat kernels. They can be purchased as soft red winter wheat or hard winter wheat berries. Store all whole grains in airtight containers, where they will keep for 6-9 months. Wheat berries can be placed in a container with soil, covered with a thin layer of soil, and watered regularly to make wheat grass.

Wheat gluten flour is used in this book to make a quick and easy version of seitan or "wheat meat." This flour has had the starch removed from the wheat and only the gluten or protein part of the grain remains. Bob's Red Mill Natural Foods Inc. (5209 SE International Way, Milwaukee, OR 97222) is one company that produces gluten flour.

Whole grain flours, including whole wheat, barley, brown rice, buckwheat, kamut, and spelt flour, should be stored in airtight containers, where they will keep for 2 months at room temperature, 6 months in the refrigerator, and a year in the freezer. The essential oils in grains are released when grains are ground into flour making them more susceptible to spoilage.

Whole grains, such as brown rice, buckwheat, oats, quinoa, and millet can be stored in airtight containers at room temperature. Unground whole grains will keep this way for 6-9 months. Whole grain pastas stored in airtight containers will keep over a year.

Whole wheat flour is ground from hard winter wheat and contains more gluten than whole wheat pastry flour, making it a suitable choice for yeasted breads. See "whole grain flours" for storage information.

Whole wheat pastry flour is ground from soft spring wheat and has less gluten, making it better for whole grain cakes, crusts, and unyeasted breads. See "whole grain flours" for storage information.

Nutritional Analysis of the Recipes

Attaching numbers to food is difficult. Each piece of food that Nature provides is unique. The analysis of broccoli grown in your garden may be different than the analysis of broccoli bought at the supermarket. Laboratories vary, equipment varies, even the most reliable resources differ in their assignment of numbers to food. The numbers on this chart reflect data from the best available resources under these circumstances.

Optional ingredients are not included in the analysis. When a choice of two ingredients or two amounts is given in a recipe, the first choice has been used in the analysis. The * indicates lack of available data for that nutrient.

The following data is to be used as a guide for composing menus to meet your needs. I urge you to let smell, taste, and common sense prevail over milligrams of anything when making your food choices.

Recipe Title
(Data is for 1 serving unless otherwise indicated)

Bustling Breakfasts

Recipe	Page	Calories	Protein (g)	Fat (g)	Cholesterol (mg)	Carbohydrates (g)	Calcium (mg)	Iron (mg)	Sodium (mg)	Vit A (IU)	Vit C (mg)
Whole Grain Baby Cereal *1 adult-size serving*	p. 74	167	3.47	.9	0	35.8	18	.75	539	0	0
Ancient Grain Raisin Cereal	p. 76	200	6.4	3.2	0	37.7	36	4.22	200	4	.3
5-Grain Morning Cereal	p. 77	163	5.46	1.5	0	32.4	12	1.89	112	3	0
Steal-Cut Oats w/ Dates & Cin.	p. 78	175	6.7	2.7	0	32.1	28	2.04	69	5	0
Sunny Millet with Peaches *1 serv w/ 1 T. apple butter*	p. 79	174	4.44	1.7	0	35.9	8	1.26	70	133	3
Orange Hazelnut Muesli *1 serv w/o topping*	p. 80	280	8.17	8.7	0	44.8	55	2.50	5	139	31.6
Nut and Seed Granola *¼ cup*	p. 81	133	3.99	7.9	0	13	18	1.44	12	19	0
Kasha Breakfast Pilaf	p. 82	179	5.43	3.5	0	34.3	24	1.43	75	20	7.1
Jam-filled Mochi *1 serv w/ 1 tsp. Jam*	p. 83	156	3	1.3	0	33	*	*	2	*	0
Essene Bread and Fresh Fruit *1 one-inch slice w/ 1 c. blueberries*	p. 84	248	8	3	0	47	29	2	11	150	19
Warming Miso Soup	p. 85	51	4	2	0	5.2	40	90	522	136	1.3
Goldie's Whole Grain Pancake Mix	p. 86	73	2.21	.5	0	15.8	85	.51	85	15	.1
Banana Buttermilk Pancakes *1 pancake*	p. 87	98	3.37	1.9	22	17.7	84	.57	96	66	1.2
Blueberry Sauce *1/3 cup*	p. 88	70	.25	.2	0	17.3	7	.27	3	25	3.9
Tofu Vegetable Breakfast Burrito	p. 89	291	12.7	8.9	0	41.9	112	4.64	212	408	28.3
Healthy Home Fries	p. 90	151	3.75	.1	0	33.9	10	.57	140	79	22.6
Tempeh Bacon	p. 91	163	9.93	11.6	0	5.4	17	.98	211	28	.2

Recipe Title

(Data is for 1 serving unless otherwise indicated)

Lively Lunchboxes

Recipe Title		Calories	Protein (g)	Fat (g)	Cholesterol (mg)	Carbohydrates (g)	Calcium (mg)	Iron (mg)	Sodium (mg)	Vit A (IU)	Vit C (mg)
Karen's Sesame Noodles	p. 94	318	10.7	9.7	0	45.9	76	3.8	530	8	.9
Confetti Rice Salad	p. 95	294	5.37	18	0	29.9	44	2	53	3154	31.2
Santa Fe Black Bean Salad	p. 96	136	5.69	5.1	0	18.1	36	2	185	770	25.9
Dilled Brown Rice and Kidney Beans	p. 97	297	8.05	11.4	0	42.1	54	2.52	270	5	1.6
Lemon Basil Potato Salad	p. 98	192	3.34	7.2	0	29.3	42	1.03	183	132	24.1
Aunt Cathy's Crunchy Ramen Cole Slaw	p. 99	173	3.42	14.3	0	10.2	31	1.15	53	1861	18.3
Hiziki Pate	p. 100	86	5.65	4.5	0	6.6	105	5.21	490	259	9.6
Tempeh Avocado Sushi Rolls 1 piece	p. 101	49	2.13	1.1	0	7.7	13	.36	177	532	.8
Tabouli	p. 102	205	4.25	10.8	0	24.5	34	1.71	273	332	16
Mad Dog Rice Salad 1 cup	p. 103	277	9.38	9.4	0	40.5	78	2.5	103	3613	11.6
Asian Noodle Salad	p. 104	350	10.9	16.5	0	46.5	61	2..07	794	48	.5
Quick Lemon & Garlic Quinoa Salad	p. 105	300	9.23	14.5	0	35.2	74	5.47	506	2934	13.2
Rice Balls Rolled in Sesame Salt 1 rice ball	p. 106	59	1.86	2.4	0	7.7	10	.49	78	6	0
Tempeh Club Sandwiches 1 plain sandwich	p. 108	285	18	9.5	0	32.7	42	2.74	361	*	.3
Gingered Lentil Sandwich Spread ¼ cup	p. 109	88	4.19	3.9	0	9.9	17	1.14	164	73	0
Hummus ¼ cup	p. 110	124	4.3	7.5	0	10.9	33	1.31	95	6	3.7
Sage and Rosemary Seitan Sandwiches ¼ cup seitan	p. 111	86	11.8	1.8	0	4	21	1.25	398	1	.1
Miso-Tahini and Rasp. Jam Sandwich 1 sandwich	p. 112	341	11.1	15	0	44.4	76	3.18	470	17	1.6
Apple Miso Almond-Butter Sandwich 1 sandwich	p. 113	252	8.11	9.8	0	35	79	2.6	396	15	1.8
Tamari-Roasted Nuts ¼ cup	p. 114	219	7.89	18.3	0	9.5	59	2.9	267	33	.1
Carrot Flowers	p. 115	30	.83	.1	0	7.2	19	.45	21	16876	6.0
Savory Sandwiches To Go 1 sand. w/ black bean and rice filling	p. 116	269	10.2	4.5	0	47.5	41	2.83	28	28	.8

Recipe Title

(Data is for 1 serving unless otherwise indicated)

Soothing Soups

Recipe	Page	Calories	Protein (g)	Fat (g)	Cholesterol (mg)	Carbohydrates (g)	Calcium (mg)	Iron (mg)	Sodium (mg)	Vit A (IU)	Vit C (mg)
Cynthia's Hearty Veg-Miso Soup	p. 125	82	4.39	1.5	0	13.7	49	.99	539	5773	13.8
Cream of Asparagus Soup w/ Dill	p. 126	67	2.68	2.9	0	8.7	21	.65	181	335	14
Red Lentil Soup w/ East Indian Spices	p. 127	119	5.79	3.3	6	17.7	54	2.61	283	841	16.1
Rosemary Red Soup	p. 128	83	3.66	2.5	0	12.4	29	1.13	169	8702	5.9
Split Pea Soup w/ Fresh Peas & Potatoes	p. 129	184	7.55	3	0	33.5	45	1.83	561	5269	18.4
Golden Mushroom-Basil Soup	p. 130	150	4.42	5.1	0	22.5	63	1.68	655	3695	16.2
Creamy Broccoli Soup	p. 131	133	5.48	3.7	0	23.6	126	1.56	206	1953	82.7
Thick Potato Caulifl & Dulse Soup	p. 132	156	6.24	3.6	0	26.4	85	3.7	675	3448	50.3
Nina's Famous Spring Beet Soup	p. 133	94	4.63	1.5	0	18.5	140	2.54	554	8775	45.3
Chipotle Navy Bean Soup	p. 134	209	12.3	2.5	0	35.9	89	4.34	71	1613	*
French Lentil and Potato Stew	p. 135	109	4.4	1.0	2	21.7	33	1.32	375	3418	11.8
White Beans and Fresh Herbs Soup	p. 136	141	7.26	3.0	0	23	102	3.42	279	5306	8.1
Dark Beans and Sensuous Spices Soup	p. 137	137	7.11	3.1	0	22	53	2.15	275	5135	6.3

Substantial Suppers

Recipe	Page	Calories	Protein (g)	Fat (g)	Cholesterol (mg)	Carbohydrates (g)	Calcium (mg)	Iron (mg)	Sodium (mg)	Vit A (IU)	Vit C (mg)
Pan-Fried Tofu and Greens	p. 140	485	23.6	21.8	0	57.3	446	5.11	565	11125	109
Three Sisters Stew	p. 142	175	7.71	3.0	0	31.9	73	2.96	157	3093	19.5
Indian Rice & Lentils *1 serv w/ 1 T. topping*	p. 144	204	6.86	3.7	1	36.4	76	1.79	200	32	4.9
Red Bean and Quinoa Chili	p. 145	241	11.5	3.4	0	43.3	69	5.19	451	418	20.5
Deep-Fried Millet Croquettes *2 croquettes w/ ¼ c. gravy*	p. 146	283	7	8.9	0	43.6	46	2.05	798	5188	4
Polenta Pizza *1 slice*	p. 148	292	10.45	8.5	16	46.0	167	3.18	766	937	23.4
Peasant Kasha, Potatoes, and Mushrooms	p. 150	84	4.6	2.4	0	11.3	18	1.39	96	0	7.2
Sloppeh Joes *1 serv on a bun*	p. 151	317	19.1	8.6	0	43	62	3.22	781	98	33.9
Mexican Bean and Corn Casserole	p. 152	200	8.54	1.3	5	34.8	153	3.22	584	425	16.1
Curried Lentils and Cauliflower	p. 154	119	6.1	2.8	0	18.8	53	2.29	192	170	41.8
Black Bean Tostadas *1 plain bean tostada*	p. 156	190	9.77	2.0	0	35.2	97	3.44	188	102	1.9
Black-Eyed Peas and Arame	p. 157	100	5.34	.4	0	19.9	76	2.02	424	68	*
Nut Burgers *1 plain burger*	p. 158	506	14.8	30.2	0	48.7	152	4.46	336	5203	3.8

Recipe Title

(Data is for 1 serving unless otherwise indicated)

Substantial Suppers (cont.)

		Calories	Protein (g)	Fat (g)	Cholesterol (mg)	Carbohydrates (g)	Calcium (mg)	Iron (mg)	Sodium (mg)	Vit A (IU)	Vit C (mg)
Tempeh and Red Pepper Stoganoff	p. 159	239	15.8	8	0	24.8	82	2.82	802	6176	51.5
Bok Choy and Buckwheat Noodles in Seasoned Broth	p. 160	312	15.5	7	0	52.6	263	3.69	1345	7833	21.1
Tofu-Kale-Mustard-Dill Supper Pie *1 slice*	p. 162	295	9.04	15.2	0	35.1	107	2.8	198	7468	17.5
Szechwan Tempeh	p. 164	401	18.4	27.7	0	20.1	40	1.59	1042	88	.9
Seitan and Shiitake Mushrooms	p. 165	237	16.3	11.3	0	14.2	61	2.59	927	1	3.9
Tempeh Tacos *¼ cup filling*	p. 166	210	17.4	10.3	0	12.3	34	1.53	539	474	6.3
Dr. Bruce's Awesome Grilled Salmon *one 4 oz. serving*	p. 167	188	19.9	10.3	62	2.9	48	1.16	570	945	34.8
Thea's Greek Shrimp Stew	p. 168	226	23.5	7.4	131	15	244	3.22	540	1280	31.7
Rainbow Trout Poached in Herbs *one 4 oz. serving*	p. 169	187	29.2	4.8	80	0	96	3	38	70	0
Baked Chicken w/ Mush. & Rosemary	p. 170	131	15.7	3.9	42	2.7	33	1.19	562	45	.9

Vital Vegetables

		Calories	Protein (g)	Fat (g)	Cholesterol (mg)	Carbohydrates (g)	Calcium (mg)	Iron (mg)	Sodium (mg)	Vit A (IU)	Vit C (mg)
Quick-Boiled Greens (examples)	p. 172										
½ c. cooked kale		21	2.5	.25	0	3.5	103	.9	23	4500	50
½ c. cooked collards		31	3.4	.7	0	4.7	170	.7	18	7410	72
½ c. cooked broccoli		17	2.4	.25	0	4.5	86	.7	13	1940	70
½ c. cooked bok choy		12	1.2	.15	0	2	175	.47	15	2535	13
Sesame Greens *1 serv using kale*	p. 174	67	3.52	4.6	0	5	109	1.22	25	4570	51
Greens in Cashew Curry Sauce *1 serv using collards*	p. 175	150	6.95	9.5	0	11	202	1.89	166	7414	72.6
Garlic Sautéed Greens *1 serv using collards*	p. 176	66	3.52	4.2	0	5.7	181	.78	19	7411	74.3
Dark Greens Salad *1 serv w/ 2 T. dressing*	p. 177	82	6.57	3.6	0	8.7	248	2.02	115	8513	84.3
Romaine Radicchio Salad *1 serv w/ dressing*	p. 178	56	.94	4.8	0	3.2	31	.55	63	541	17.1
Lightly Cooked Cabbage Salad	p. 179	100	2.54	7.4	0	8.2	56	.97	281	2798	41.6
Luscious Beet Salad	p. 180	85	2.5	5.4	0	8.5	80	1.88	159	2606	17.2
Mustard Green Salad *1 serv w/ 2 T. dressing*	p. 182	25	2.52	.9	0	2.7	58	1.06	10	1243	12.9
Watercress Salad *1 serv w/1 T. dressing*	p. 183	70	1.01	7.1	0	2.1	46	154	40	1469	13.7
Creamy Cole Slaw	p. 184	71	1.98	5.6	4	5	31	.44	111	3488	27.1

Recipe Title

(Data is for 1 serving unless otherwise indicated)

Vital Vegetables (cont.)

		Calories	Protein (g)	Fat (g)	Cholesterol (mg)	Carbohydrates (g)	Calcium (mg)	Iron (mg)	Sodium (mg)	Vit A (IU)	Vit C (mg)
Spinach Salad *1 serv w/ 1 T. dressing*	p. 185	112	2.97	10.3	0	4.7	65	1.76	52	3696	16.6
Susan's Succulent Supper Salad	p. 186	218	6.1	14.7	0	19.8	81	3.53	66	3481	29.7
Grilled Vegetable Salad *1 serv w/ 1 T. dressing*	p. 188	142	4.44	9.5	6	13.0	120	2.11	132	3120	35.8
Dulse Salad *1 serv w/ 1 T. dressing*	p. 190	157	8.7	5.3	0	20.5	104	11.6	690	420	12.9
Roasted Potatoes & Carrots	p. 191	333	5.71	11	0	55.1	40	3.64	29	10145	29.7
Potato Gratin	p. 192	161	4.4	2.5	0	31	42	.72	37	717	45.1
Baked Winter Squash *1 cup*	p. 194	130	3.7	.82	0	31	57	1.43	2	8610	27

Fresh Breads & Muffins

		Calories	Protein (g)	Fat (g)	Cholesterol (mg)	Carbohydrates (g)	Calcium (mg)	Iron (mg)	Sodium (mg)	Vit A (IU)	Vit C (mg)
Rice Bread *1 thick slice*	p. 198	197	5.33	3.4	0	36.9	15	1.9	323	0	0
Orange Millet Raisin Bread *1 thick slice*	p. 198	247	6.17	3.6	0	49.2	22	2.29	325	2	.6
Quinoa Garlic Herb Bread *1 thick slice*	p. 199	189	5.65	3.6	0	33.8	20	2.39	323	11	.7
Bean Apple Rye Bread *1 thick slice*	p. 199	190	6.45	3.5	0	34.9	22	2.19	322	6	.5
Sweet Squash Corn Muffins *1 muffin*	p. 200	239	4.62	8.1	0	40	97	2.01	283	1532	4.6
Cranberry Apple Walnut Muffins *1 muffin*	p. 201	321	4.82	10	0	56.6	103	1.52	262	101	3.7
Pumpkin Pecan Muffins *1 muffin*	p. 202	258	4.92	10	0	40.8	106	2.05	265	9013	1.8
Banana Blueberry Poppyseed Muffins *1 muffin*	p. 203	265	5.08	9.8	0	42.5	174	1.8	266	80	3.3
Herb & Garlic Pizza Dough *1/12 of a pie*	p. 204	119	3.13	1.6	0	23.6	11	1.12	90	0	0

Sauces & Stuff

		Calories	Protein (g)	Fat (g)	Cholesterol (mg)	Carbohydrates (g)	Calcium (mg)	Iron (mg)	Sodium (mg)	Vit A (IU)	Vit C (mg)
Lemon Tahini Sauce *2 tablespoons*	p. 206	106	2.12	10	0	3.4	17	.49	33	10	7.8
Tahini Oat Sauce *2 tablespoons*	p. 207	34	1.3	2.1	0	5.4	26	.71	399	68	1.1
Almond Ginger Drizzle *2 tablespoons*	p. 208	66	1.6	5.3	0	3.1	33	.43	264	0	.1
Creamy Ginger Garlic Dressing *2 tablespoons*	p. 209	54	2.25	4.7	0	1.3	30	.58	90	0	1.3

Recipe Title

(Data is for 1 serving unless otherwise indicated)

Sauces & Stuff (cont.)

		Calories	Protein (g)	Fat (g)	Cholesterol (mg)	Carbohydrates (g)	Calcium (mg)	Iron (mg)	Sodium (mg)	Vit A (IU)	Vit C (mg)
Mushroom Wine Gravy ¼ cup	p. 210	41	.92	2.4	3	2.9	11	.37	266	48	.4
Garlic Ginger Marinade ¼ cup	p. 211	20	1.15	0	0	2.5	34	.38	701	0	0
Cranberry Apple Relish ¼ cup	p. 212	137	.39	.1	0	34.6	19	.45	36	14	3.5
Homemade Curry Paste 1 tablespoon	p. 214	82	.68	7.7	0	3.3	26	1.27	2	18	1.9

Wholesome Desserts

		Calories	Protein (g)	Fat (g)	Cholesterol (mg)	Carbohydrates (g)	Calcium (mg)	Iron (mg)	Sodium (mg)	Vit A (IU)	Vit C (mg)
Fruit Sauce 1/3 cup, using plums	p. 219	13	0	.1	0	3.3	1	0	0	75	2.5
Gingerbread People 1 cookie person	p. 220	238	4.36	5.4	12	45	77	3.63	201	226	4.4
Apricot Thumbprint Cookies 1 cookie	p. 221	123	2.47	6.3	0	15.7	40	.63	49	46	0
Oatmeal Chocolate-Chip Cookies 1 cookie	p. 222	204	3.6	10	0	26.7	26	1.03	47	12	0
Halloween Cookies 1 cookie	p. 223	78	1.21	1.4	0	15.7	10	.54	18	145	3.1
Carob Brownies 1 brownie	p. 224	156	3.25	6.6	27	27	40	1.04	79	33	0
Brown Rice Crispy Treats 1 square	p. 225	70	.92	1.3	0	13.9	4	.26	3	0	0
Fruitsicles 1 Juicesicle (using apple juice) 1 Creamy Orange-Van. Pop 1 Banana Rasp. Pop 1 Melonsicle 1 Maltsicle	p. 226	29 33 35 12 80	0 1.06 .3 .25 2.0	0 .3 .3 .1 3.7	0 1 0 0 0	7.3 6.9 7.9 2.8 9.7	4 27 2 4 *	.22 .09 16 .08 .36	2 5 1 3 47	0 100 36 1076 0	.5 23.3 5.1 14.1 3.0
Apricot Kudzu Custard	p. 227	114	1.02	1.4	0	25.6	16	.64	5	1652	1.2
Raspberry Pudding Gel	p. 228	99	.54	1.1	0	21.9	9	1.14	1	11	2.1
Vanilla Amasake Pudding	p. 229	128	4.55	1.1	0	22.9	40	1.32	32	*	*
Winter Fruit Compote 1 serv w/ 1/4 c. nut cream	p. 230	190	2.53	4.7	0	38.5	45	2	6	1352	5.5
Cherry Banana Jiggle	p. 231	71	.17	.1	0	16.6	4	1	1	11	1.3
Pear-Plum Crisp	p. 232	260	4.09	11.6	0	39.4	41	1.3	136	151	6.7
Tofu Cheesecake	p. 234	334	7.12	15.4	0	45	80	2.1	141	9	2.2
Carrot Cake w/ Apricot Glaze	p. 236	274	4.69	12.8	36	37.3	85	1.66	98	5392	2.9
Blueberry-Strawberry Tart	p. 238	170	3.5	8	0	22.7	29	.98	33	33	11.7

Recipe Title

(Data is for 1 serving unless otherwise indicated)

Wholesome Desserts (cont.)

		Calories	Protein (g)	Fat (g)	Cholesterol (mg)	Carbohydrates (g)	Calcium (mg)	Iron (mg)	Sodium (mg)	Vit A (IU)	Vit C (mg)
Mary's Buttermilk Chocolate Cake	p. 239	340	4.9	15.1	1	50.9	103	1.81	252	10	.2
Gracie's Yellow Birthday Cake	p. 240	238	4.43	10.9	36	31.5	81	1.35	136	85	10.3
Carob Butter Icing *2 tablespoons*	p. 241	82	1.18	3.22	0	14.5	31	.57	24	0	0
Banana Cream Frosting *2 tablespoons*	p. 242	42	1.6	1.6	0	5.4	19	.45	1	6	.8
Yummy Yam Frosting *2 tablespoons*	p. 243	62	.8	4.6	14	3.9	14	.19	30	694	1.7
Strawberry Sauce *¼ cup*	p. 244	33	.56	.5	0	7.6	11	.3	1	20	42.6

What to Drink?

		Calories	Protein (g)	Fat (g)	Cholesterol (mg)	Carbohydrates (g)	Calcium (mg)	Iron (mg)	Sodium (mg)	Vit A (IU)	Vit C (mg)
Banana Milk *1 cup*	p. 247	112	9.67	3.0	0	11.7	67	1.33	30	80	3.3
Cranberry Ginger Cider *1 cup*	p. 249	130	0	.1	0	33.5	13	.65	9	5	55
Hot Mocha Milk *1 cup*	p. 249	48	4.8	1.3	0	5	38	.67	43	*	*

The following resources were used to compute the data reflected on the tables above:

1. *Bowes and Church's Food Values of Portions Commonly Used, 15th Edition*, revised by Jean A. T. Pennington, Ph.D., RD (J.B. Lippincott Company, Philadelphia, PA, 1989).

2. Diet Simple Plus for IBM and compatible computers, N-Squared Computing, 3040 Commercial St., Suite 240, Salem, OR 97381.

3. Information gathered from the manufacturers of specific food products.

4. Michael Jacobson's Nutrition Wizard, Public Interest Software, Center for Science in the Public Interest, 1501 Sixteenth St. NW, Washington, DC 20036.

5. Robertson, Laurel, Carol Flinders, and Brian Ruppenthal, *The New Laurel's Kitchen*, Ten Speed Press, Berkeley, CA, 1986.

Bibliography

Ballantine, Rudolph, M.D., *Diet and Nutrition* (Honesdale, PA: The Himalayan International Institute, 1978) pp. 55, 59, 128-130.

Breastfeeding Abstracts, Spring 1987, cited in the Doctor's People (Oct. 1991) p. 3.

Caughlin, Goldie, Nutrition Educator, "What's a Mother to Do?," PCC (Puget Consumers Co-op) *Sound Consumer* (March 1992, No. 228).

Chow, Marilyn P., Durand, Barbara A., Feldman, Marie N., Mills, Marion A., *Handbook of Pediatric Primary Care* (New York, NY: John Wiley & Sons, 1984).

Colbin, Annemarie, *Food and Healing* (New York, New York: Ballantine Books, 1986).

Dorfman, Kelly, "All About Feeding Babies," *Mothering Magazine* (Fall 1987) pp. 33-39.

Ensminger, Audrey H., M.E. Ensminger, James E. Konlande, John R.K. Robson, M.D. *Food and Nutrition Encyclopedia, Vol.2* (Clovis, CA: Pegus Press, 1983) pp. 1460-67.

Firkaly, Susan Tate, *Into the Mouths of Babes* (White Hall, VA: Betterway Publications, 1984).

Gardner, Joy, *Healing Yourself During Pregnancy* (Freedom, CA: The Crossing Press, 1987) pp. 28-37.

Goldsmith, Judith, *Childbirth Wisdom* (Brookline, MA: East West Books, 1990).

Guthrie, Helen, *Introductory Nutrition* (St. Louis, MO: Times Mirror/Mosby College Publishing, 1986).

Haas, Elston, M.D., *Staying Healthy with the Seasons* (Millbrae, Calif., Celestial Arts, 1981), p. 112.

Harnett-Robinson, Dr. Roy, Pediatrician practicing in New York, NY, Interview August 1988.

Infact Newsletter, Fall 1991, p. 2, cited in *Mothering Magazine*, No. 63, (Spring 1992) p. 26.

Kenda, Margaret Elizabeth and Phyllis S. Williams, *The Natural Baby Food Cookbook* (New York, NY: Avon Books, 1982).

"Kiddie Fat," *Nutrition Action Newsletter* (June 1991, Vol.18, No. 5) p. 3.

King, Jonathan, "Is Your Water Safe to Drink?," *Medical Self Care*, November-December 1985, pp. 44-57

La Leche League International, *The Womanly Art of Breastfeeding* (New York, NY: Plume, New American Library, 1981) pp. 288-289.

The Lancet, No. 337, April 1991, pp. 929-933, cited in *Mothering Magazine*, No. 63, (Spring 1992) p. 26.

Leach, Penelope, *Your Baby and Child* (New York, NY: Alfred A Knopf, Inc., 1989).

Liebman, Bonnie, "Baby Formulas: Missing Key Fats?," *Nutrition Action Newsletter*, Vol. 17, No. 8, (October 1990) pp. 8-9.

Mc Dougall, John A., M.D., "The Best Foods for the Expectant Mother," *Vegetarian Times* (January 1985).

McDougall, John A., M.D., *A Challenging Second Opinion* (Piscataway, NJ: New Century Publishing, 1985) pp. 183-184.

McGee, Harold, *On Food and Cooking* (New York, NY: Macmillan Publishing Co., 1984).

Mohrbacher, Nancy and Julie Stock, *The Breastfeeding Answer Book* (Franklin Park, IL: La Leche League International, 1991).

Mohrbacher, Nancy and Judy Torgus, *The New La Leche League Leaders Handbook* (Franklin Park, IL: La Leche International).

Morningstar, Amadea and Urmila Desai, *The Ayurvedic Cookbook* (Santa Fe, NM: Lotus Press, 1990) pp. 260-261.

Oski, Dr. Frank, *Don't Drink Your Milk!* (Syracuse, NY: Mollica Press, Ltd., 1983) pp. 24-27.

Palmer, Gabrielle, *The Politics of Breastfeeding* (London, England: Pandora Press, 1988) pp. 42-48.

Pitchford, Paul. *Healing with Whole Foods* (Berkeley, CA: North Atlantic Books, 1993).

Pearce, Joseph Chilton, *Magical Child Matures* (New York, NY: E.P. Dutton, 1985.

Petrulis, Nina, La Leche Leader, Seattle, WA, Interview January 1992.

Physicians Committee for Responsible Medicine, "The New Four Food Groups," (PO Box 6322, Washington, DC 20015).

Pipes, Peggy, R.D., M.P.H., *Nutrition in Infancy and Childhood* (St. Louis, MO, C.V. Mosby Co., 1981) p. 145.

Pope, Sharon, "Good Nutrition for the Very Young," PCC (Puget Consumers Co-op) *Sound Consumer,* No. 181, April 1988, pp. 1, 3, 6.

Price, Weston, D.D.S., *Nutrition and Physical Degeneration: A Comparison of Primitive and Modern Diets and Their Effects* (Los Angeles, CA: The Academy of Applied Nutrition, 1948).

Pryor, Karen, *Nursing Your Baby* (New York, NY: Pocket Books, 1973) pp. 52-53.

Robbins, John, *A Diet for a New America* (Walpole, NH: Stillpoint Publishing, 1987) pp. 97-121, 189, 266-67, 309-313.

Schardt, David, "The Problem with Protein," *Nutrition Action Healthletter,* June 1993, Vol. 20, No. 5.

Smith, Lendon, Dr., *Feed Your Kids Right* (New York, NY: McGraw-Hill, 1979) p. 36.

Steinman, David, *Diet for a Poisoned Planet, How to Choose Safe Foods for You & Your Family* (New York, NY: Ballantine Books, 1990).

Weed, Susun S., *Wise Woman Herbal for the Childbearing Year* (Woodstock, NY: Ash Tree Publishing, 1986).

Recommended Reading

These are a few of the books that have been inspiring and helpful to me.

Food and health

Ballantine, Rudolph, M.D. *Diet & Nutrition* (Honesdale, PA: Himalayan International Institute, 1978).

Colbin, Annemarie. *Food and Healing* (New York, NY: Ballantine Books, 1986).

Goldbeck, Nikki and David. *The Goldbeck's Guide to Good Food*. New American Library, 1987.

Haas, Elston M., M.D. *Staying Healthy with the Seasons* (Millbrae, CA: Celestial Arts, 1981).

McGee, Harold. *On Food and Cooking* (New York, NY: Macmillan Publishing Co., 1984).

Pitchford, Paul. *Healing with Whole Foods* (Berkeley, CA: North Atlantic Books, 1993).

Price, Weston A., MS, D.D.S., F.A.C.D. *Nutrition and Physical Degeneration* (La Mesa, CA: The Price-Pottenger Foundation, 1945).

Robbins, John. *Diet for a New America* (Walpole, NH: Stillpoint, 1987).

Roehl, Evelyn. *Whole Food Facts* (Rochester, VT: Healing Arts Press, 1996).

Schmid, Ronald F. *Native Nutrition* (Rochester, VT: Healing Arts Press, 1987).

Steinman, David, *Diet for a Poisoned Planet*, *How to Choose Safe Foods for You & Your Family* (New York, NY: Ballantine Books, 1990).

Cooking

Colbin, Annemarie. *The Book of Whole Meals* (New York, NY: Ballantine Books, 1983).

Colbin, Annemarie. *The Natural Gourmet* (New York, NY: Ballantine Books, 1989).

Estella, Mary. *The Natural Foods Cookbook* (Tokyo-New York: Japan Publications, 1985).

Levitt, JoAnn and Linda Smith and Christine Warren. *Kripalu Kitchen* (Summit Station, PA: Kripalu Publications, 1980).

McCarty, Meredith. *FRESH from a Vegetarian Kitchen* (Eureka, CA: Turning Point Publications, 1989).

Robertson, Laurel and Carol Flinders and Brian Ruppenthal. *The New Laurel's Kitchen* (Berkeley, CA: Ten Speed Press, 1986).

Rombauer, Irma S. and Marion Roumbauer Becker. *Joy of Cooking* (New York, NY: Bobbs-Merrill Company, 1975).

Warrington, Janet. *Sweet and Natural Desserts* (Freedom, CA: Crossing Press, 1982).

Weber, Marcea. *Naturally Sweet Desserts* (Garden City Park, NY: Avery

Publishing Group, 1990).

Weber, Marcea. *The Sweet Life* (Tokyo-New York: Japan Publications, 1981).

Breastfeeding, babies and children

Firkaly, Susan Tate. *Into the Mouths of Babes* (Whitehall, VA: Betterway Publications, 1984).

Gardner, Joy. *Healing Yourself During Pregnancy* (Freedom, CA: Crossing Press, 1987).

Goodwin, Mary T. and Gerry Pollen. *Creative Food Experiences for Children* (Washington, DC: Center for Science in the Public Interest [CSPI], 1974).

Kenda, Margaret Elizabeth and Phyllis S. Williams. *The Natural Baby Food Cookbook* (New York, NY: Avon Books, 1972).

Kitzenger, Shelia. *Breastfeeding Your Baby* (New York, NY: Alfred A. Knopf, 1991).

La Leche League International. *The Womanly Art of Breastfeeding* (New York, NY: Plume, New American Library, 1981).

Mason, Diane and Diane Ingersoll. *Breastfeeding and the Working Mother* (St. Martins Press, 1986).

Mendelsohn, Robert S., M.D. *How to Raise a Healthy Child in Spite of Your Doctor* (Chicago, IL: Contemporary Books Inc., 1984).

Mothering Magazine, a quarterly periodical, published by Peggy O'Mara, PO Box 1690, Santa Fe, NM 87504.

Palmer, Gabrielle. *The Politics of Breastfeeding* (Pandora, 1988).

Weed, Susun S. *Wise Woman Herbal for the Childbearing Year* (Woodstock, NY: Ash Tree Publishing, 1986).

Yntema, Sharon. *Vegetarian Baby* (Ithaca, NY: McBooks Press, 1980).

Index

Would you like to order more copies of this book as gifts for a favorite new mom, dad, or friend? Just fill out and mail us this order form.

ORDER FORM

Feeding the Whole Family

Please send me _____ books at $18.00 $ _____

Shipping (see chart) $ _____

WA residents add 8.6% tax $ _____

TOTAL $ _____

Shipping & Handling Rates	
1 book	$4.00
2-4 books	$6.00
5-10 books	$8.00

Name _____

Street _____

City/State/Zip _____

I will be paying by: ☐check   ☐credit card

Please make checks payable to **Moon Smile Press.**

Credit card type: ☐VISA   ☐Mastercard

Card number: _____ Expiration Date:_____

Authorized signature: _____

Allow 2 weeks for delivery
Mail this form (or a photocopy) with your check to:

M O O N   S M I L E   P R E S S

11038 27th Ave. NE
Seattle, WA 98125

phone: 800-561-3039 fax: 206-365-1124

VISIT OUR WEB SITE

You may also order books at **www.feedingfamily.com**